PUBLIC POLICY TOWARD CORPORATE GROWTH

Kennikat Press

National University Publications

Multi-disciplinary Studies in the Law

General Editor

Rudolph J. Gerber
Arizona State University

PUBLIC POLICY TOWARD CORPORATE GROWTH

The ITT Merger Cases

ROBERT M. GOOLRICK

WITH A FOREWORD BY
JOHN V. TUNNEY

National University Publications
KENNIKAT PRESS   //   1978
Port Washington, N. Y.   //   London

Manufactured in the United States of America

Published by
Kennikat Press Corp.
Port Washington, N.Y./London

Library of Congress Cataloging in Publication Data

Goolrick, Robert M.
  Public policy toward corporate growth.

  (Multi-disciplinary studies in the law) (National university publications)
    Bibliography: p.
    Includes index.
    1. International Telephone and Telegraph Corporation. 2. Antitrust law—United States. I. Title.
KF2849.I57G66   343'.73'072   78-1580
ISBN 0-8046-9198-3

CONTENTS

FOREWORD

The Irish poet, William Butler Yeats, wrote:

> "Everything that man esteems
> Endures a moment or a day."

Antitrust policy in the United States has followed the same variable course, moving with the shifting political winds.

For it is political theory that stands at the heart of antitrust policy. The laws prohibiting monopolistic and collusive practices were enacted by politicians serving in Congress and at the policy level are enforced by political appointees of the president in the Department of Justice. Even the federal judges at the trial and appellate levels who are charged with applying the law to the facts are chosen in a political fashion. They are nominated by the president, confirmed by the Senate, and their affiliation with a political party is often a vital factor in the selection process. It is obvious that political values play an important role in determining what type of corporate activity is considered likely to lessen competition or likely to create a monopoly.

No set of circumstances has more clearly reflected the political dimension of antitrust law enforcement than the ITT cases which are the subject of Bob Goolrick's fascinating book. During the period when ITT was the focal point of government antitrust attention, 1969-72, the President of the United States was a friend of big business. Mr. Nixon had raised millions of dollars from corporate executives to finance his winning campaign in 1968. He had no desire to rigorously apply the antitrust laws to corporate activity in a way that would circumscribe the activities of his friends and evoke their animus.

The man who was chosen by John Mitchell to be President Nixon's chief antitrust law enforcement officer, Richard McLaren, came from a corporate law background which would have suggested he had antitrust views similar to the President. McLaren had spent many years defending corporations from alleged violations of the antitrust laws. However, when McLaren got into office, he decided, surprisingly, to break new ground and apply the antitrust laws to prevent certain types of large conglomerate mergers. He thus brought the famous ITT–Canteen, Grinell, and Hartford Fire Insurance Company cases. If he had reflected President Nixon's political philosophy, those cases would never have been filed. When the White House learned the nature of McLaren's antitrust policy, the President said, "Get him out. In one hour." In other words, President Nixon wanted McLaren dismissed and replaced by a person more attentive to the White House's views that business should be left alone and that the chief of the Antitrust Division should not "run around prosecuting people, raising hell with conglomerates, stirring up things at this point."

The political ideology of the President and his administration is not the only factor in the evolution of antitrust policy. The Supreme Court is the final arbiter of what rules are going to be used in the corporate concentration game. Mr. McLaren was sure that although the District Court judges might not accept the theory that "bigness was bad" in conglomerate merger cases, a majority of the Supreme Court justices would. McLaren counted on the fact that the Warren Court in the 1950s and 1960s had consistently ruled with the government in merger cases. The Nixon campaign promise of appointing "strict constructionists" to the Court had not, at the time the ITT cases were filed in 1969, resulted in sufficient Nixon appointments to change the view that mergers challenged by the government would, on appeal, be found illegal.

Most business leaders, scholars, and politicians agreed with McLaren's assessment of the Supreme Court's attitude on antitrust matters in 1969. But the dominant political and economic philosophy of the Court is merely the sum of the views of five of its members. In 1978, with four justices sitting as appointees of President Nixon and one as a nominee of President Ford, the posture of the Court has changed. In the past three years, corporate defendants have won significant merger appeals. [See, for example, *United States v. Marine Bancorporation,* 418 U.S. 602 (1974); *United States v. Connecticut National Bank,* 418 U.S. 656 (1974); and *United States v. General Dynamics Corp.,* 415 U.S. 486 (1974)]

Although idealists may cavil at a governmental structure that produces different statutory interpretations with each change in the composition of the Supreme Court and with each new administration, as a practical matter, the law only means what those who enforce it say it means. When I was in the United States Senate, there always was intense discussion amongst my colleagues when the president nominated a Supreme Court justice as to whether the personal philosophy of the man selected was a criterion for confirmation. Most senators, myself included, would argue that the people of the country had elected the president and, under normal circumstances, he was entitled to choose someone with whom he felt philosophically compatible, to serve on the highest tribunal. For us in the Senate, the inquiry should focus on judicial temperament, scholarship, legal training, ethical standards, etc.

This did not mean that we completely eschewed evaluating the personal values of the person seeking confirmation At the confirmation hearing, many questions were framed in a fashion to reveal the ethical, social, economic, and political thoughts of the prospective justice. If his views were considered too far removed from what most senators considered "mainstream" thinking, his nomination was rejected. Both Judges Haynsworth and Carswell had their dreams of serving on the high court dashed in large part because their ideas on civil rights did not comport with what a majority of Senators deemed minimally acceptable.

The Congress has traditionally been reluctant to legislate with specificity in the antitrust field. This is consistent with the broad standards of prohibition of the Sherman and Clayton Acts which leave it to the federal courts to refine the Congressional mandate. This is not so much an intentional "cop-out" but merely reflects the ignorance of most senators and representatives of the subject matter. "Reciprocity effect," "potential competition," and "aggregate concentration" are phrases that are not well understood on Capitol Hill and there is very little desire to become better informed.

The main reason that Congress has not moved more aggressively into the thicket of antitrust regulation is that the economic issues which are at its center are complex and the merits of the issues are the subject of a fierce debate amongst scholars. There is not a lobby with credible power demanding a Congressional clarification of what should constitute impermissible concentration in various sectors of the economy. Unlike the oil and natural gas pricing issues, where strong lobbies have been aligned both in favor of and against price deregulation for years, no major well-organized special interest group is pushing for definitive legislation on corporate merger policy. Corporations do not want Congress to interfere with their growth policies which they equate with the attainment of greater economic efficiencies and profits, and their views are constantly being communicated to congressmen. In the absence of countervailing pressure forcing the Congress to act, it is easier to do nothing and let the courts untangle the economic confusion.

I can speak with experience when I express the view that Congress is reluctant to legislate in the antitrust field. After sitting through the Kleindienst–ITT hearings in their entirety, I became convinced that ITT had attempted to make use of all its political influence in the Nixon Administration to avoid having the Canteen, Grinell, and Hartford Fire Insurance Company cases heard by the Supreme Court. The pressure applied was successful in that it forced McLaren to settle the cases rather than pursue the litigation through the appellate stage. I believed that the only way such pressure could be avoided in the future was to have a statute requiring the Justice Department to disclose publicly why it agreed to settle a consent decree case instead of going to trial or taking an appeal. The bill I drafted provided that the disclosure had to specify why the settlement was in the public interest. Additionally, I added a provision that the defendant had to publicly disclose all its lobbying contacts with government officials (aside from contacts counsel made in the Justice Department). I remember the relish I took in adding this latter provision because it was directed with a high degree of particularity at the type of activity ITT officials had engaged in.

Despite the fact that the ITT scandal was of major national import, and the Watergate break-in closely followed behind it, giving added impetus to the maxim that "the public's business ought to be conducted in public," it took two years to get the consent decree bill through the Congress. The energy of inertia almost overcame the zeal of the reformers.

It is not beyond the realm of possibility that the Congress will legislate standards for conglomerate mergers and address the thorny issue of the permissible degree of concentration in the economy. It is far more likely, however, that the legislators will continue to avoid taking a position on these matters which they view as arcane and of limited political interest to the voters. If there is to be inaction, it is a sad commentary on our political system. When one observes the way capital is concentrating in fewer and fewer corporations in the United States, and correspondingly fewer executives are making decisions which dramatically affect the economic destiny of the country, it is appalling that the Congress is unwilling to establish more definitive guidelines for capital aggregation. Big may not be bad, but it is not necessarily benign either. National economic policy should not be set by prosecutors and judges. It is the province of elected officials to establish that policy and if they will not, their countrymen are ill-served.

As a final note I would like to say that Bob Goolrick has produced an exceptionally interesting book. By using the ITT cases as a backdrop to a well-informed discussion of the competing antitrust policies struggling for precedence, he has made an adventure story out of what could be a dry, highly specialized, commentary. He writes like a scholarly Agatha Christie as he unfolds the details of the machinations of all parties to the ITT drama. Because he combines a thoughtful description of the essential precepts of antitrust law with a fast moving history of the evolution and final disposal of the ITT merger cases, Mr. Goolrick both informs and captivates his reader.

John V. Tunney

PUBLIC POLICY TOWARD
CORPORATE GROWTH

Robert M. Goolrick is an antitrust lawyer with a strong grounding in economics and a close familiarity with the ITT merger cases. In fifteen years of law practice in Washington he has had extensive experience with mergers and legal controls over corporate growth, and has published a number of articles on legal and business subjects.

John V. Tunney, former United States senator from California, was a member of the Senate Antitrust Subcommittee, and was closely involved in general antitrust matters while in the Senate. He was also a key figure during the ITT-Kliendienst hearings.

INTRODUCTION

In the swirl of events which occupied the nation from 1972 through 1974, the corporate acronym "ITT" became virtually synonymous with "Watergate," "milk prices," "plumbers," and "Dr. Fielding's office" as symbols for the abuse of governmental power. International Telephone & Telegraph Corporation (ITT) gained entry to this notorious list by the 1971 compromise settlement of three antitrust suits brought against it by the Department of Justice in 1969. The compromise became a cause célèbre with the later publication of the "Dita Beard memorandum," which implied that ITT had gained a favorable settlement result in return for a financial pledge for the 1972 Republican Party convention. The series of actions triggered by this disclosure ultimately brought the ITT cases directly into the presidential impeachment process.

The ITT furor, indeed, bore a marked resemblance to Watergate. In both cases there was an attempt by government officials to cover up underlying events to protect the public image of the president. Both cases led to the criminal conviction of a man who had served as attorney general of the United States—John Mitchell in Watergate, Richard Kleindienst in ITT. And the two seemingly unrelated events, ITT and Watergate, shared a causal relationship—but for ITT, there might never have been a Watergate.

In the scope and significance of its underlying issues, ITT perhaps was larger even than Watergate. Both episodes, of course, presented overriding questions of the honest conduct of government in the interests of the public rather than of those holding power. The handling of the ITT cases additionally involved not only huge financial stakes but, more importantly, transcendent questions of national economic policy. The

3

struggle embodied in ITT could have an indelible impression upon the direction of United States antitrust law enforcement for years to come.

Antitrust policy has many elements of generally agreed constancy. The persons charged with conducting our government at any particular time do not materially change those consensual elements, which certainly include disapproval of such garden-variety antitrust violations as collusive price fixing, bid rigging, and allocation of customers. All antitrust officials would agree that the notorious electrical equipment price fixing conspiracies uncovered and prosecuted in the early 1960s should be attacked vigorously.

Other aspects of antitrust policy, however, are controversial and provoke disagreement even among economists and attorneys expert in the area. At this extreme, for example, is the existence of high concentration—or oligopoly—in many United States industries. While oligopoly carries an unsavory connotation in classic economic theory and in the minds of many observers of the current scene, other respected economists would say that, in these times and under present circumstances, high industrial concentration is mandated by economies of scale and efficiencies which further economic progress.

Between these two extremes range a host of antitrust issues of varying degrees of controversy, of which one is corporate growth by merger. Only somewhat less controversial than oligopoly (to which it bears a kinship), this was the underlying subject of ITT, i.e., what should be our national policy toward further growth by large corporations, and how should that policy be determined?

The issue of restricting corporate expansion centers around growth by merger. The converse—growth by internal expansion—meets with little objection; indeed, that method, except in the rare instance where it may beget monopoly power, is generally praised as the apotheosis of the free enterprise system. Moreover, the sudden and significant growth which causes concern is practicable only by merger; the year-to-year increase in corporate financial strength attainable by internal expansion, subject as it is to business fluctuations, is necessarily considerably slower.

As a further refinement, or perhaps more accurately a reflection of reality, the concern over corporate growth in present times focuses upon those mergers whereby large corporations diversify into new lines of business—the diversification merger, or more popularly the "conglomerate" merger. The reason is simply that antitrust enforcement already has severely restricted other avenues of expansion by merger—i.e., the horizontal mergers between competitors and the vertical mergers between suppliers and customers. If a corporation then desires substantial growth by merger, its only practical option is to diversify into new lines of business.

Which is just what ITT did, and which, unexpectedly and paradoxically, brought the Nixon Justice Department down upon it. How and why this happened and what lessons may be drawn for national policy toward corporate expansion are the themes of this book.

Perhaps this study of the substance and process of antitrust policy can also provide a significant glimpse into more general questions concerning the proper functions of the various branches of our government and of the interaction among them in meeting issues of national importance. Former Solicitor General Robert H. Bork has stated:

Antitrust is a microcosm in which ideas battling for dominion in the larger society may be studied in a much smaller scale. You see in antitrust, as elsewhere, the continual debate over the propriety of the legislative decision by Congress versus political choice by courts, the struggle between the ideal of competition and the older guild or mercantilist theory of a protective status for producers, and concern for the general or consumer welfare as opposed to demand of special interest groups.

The ITT merger suits presented those tensions as a paradigm case study.

1

"WE MOVED ON ITT"

In this administration we moved on ITT. We are proud of that record. We moved on it effectively. We required the greatest divestiture in the history of the antitrust law.

Richard M. Nixon, March 24, 1972

That the Nixon administration moved on ITT is beyond cavil. That President Nixon deserved, as he implied, any personal credit for that action is totally unfounded. Nixon's statement, made when ITT had become a cause for criticism of the White House, characteristically sought to hide the turbulence beneath the surface. The ITT story is considerably more complex than the Nixon statement would indicate.

The ITT story begins on February 4, 1969—the date that Richard McLaren, an attorney from Chicago, was sworn in as assistant attorney general of the United States in charge of the Antitrust Division. Looking on at that time were two other men who would play leading roles in the ITT saga, Attorney General John Mitchell and Deputy Attorney General Richard Kleindienst. Neither then knew, however, that in selecting McLaren to oversee the nation's antitrust policies they had chosen a man who would venture to contradict the wishes of the president of the United States.

Richard M. Nixon himself had been sworn into office only two weeks earlier. In Nixon's ascension there were two noteworthy factors—one known, the other perceived only dimly—that gave considerable comfort to the leaders of big business. The known quantity was that Nixon would not enforce an aggressive antitrust policy. Of this there could be no doubt—Nixon, albeit in carefully chosen words, had implied as much. And Nixon's antitrust policy advisory panel had specifically said that the most controversial antitrust issues—high industrial concentration and corporate growth by merger—were no cause for real concern or for enforcement attention. The conglomerate corporations in particular had already basked in the glow of benign antitrust enforcement throughout the 1960s and had felt threatened only by the rumblings of President Lyndon B. Johnson's last attorney general, Ramsey Clark. Now he was gone.

The second, murkier factor was that Nixon himself would be *in control* of government policy. There would be no runaways; Nixon, unlike Johnson, would not have a Ramsey Clark leading his personal crusades. That this was so came not so much from explicit statement of it as from the Nixon style and tone. His campaign organization had been structured in pyramidal fashion, tightly controlled through the person of Nixon's principal assistant, H. R. Haldeman. And Nixon himself had said that what the nation needed was more good solid governing and less undisciplined social theory. The conglomerate corporations, still edgy from the Clark threats, welcomed this personal style of government, given Nixon's view of antitrust policy.

The important, underlying ITT story, then, is the fashion in which these Nixon drives—total command and understated antitrust policy— would come together with the contrary drives of Richard McLaren. For McLaren took a different view of matters. As antitrust chief, chosen presumably for his knowledge and expertise in that subject, he should have a very large if not exclusive say in what was to be the nation's antitrust policy. Furthermore, although it did not become apparent until later, McLaren came to believe that the corporate growth wave of the 1960s posed a grave threat to the future of the United States economic system.

When McLaren emerged publicly as a crusader against conglomerate mergers, the leaders of big business thought they saw Ramsey Clark not only reborn but invigorated. The business leaders mobilized forces to try to counteract McLaren's move. The lead in trying to unseat McLaren was taken by Harold Geneen, president of ITT, naturally enough since ITT was the principal immediate target of McLaren's campaign. Geneen had ample resources to fight back, not only in the courts but also in the halls of government. He found some imposing allies, not the least of them John Ehrlichman, director of the White House Domestic Council and chief adviser to the president on domestic affairs. As if that were not enough, Geneen also got active support from Secretary of Commerce Maurice Stans and Secretary of the Treasury John Connally. Additionally, he had the sympathetic ear of Vice President Spiro Agnew and White House assistants Peter G. Peterson and Charles Colson. Even Solicitor General Erwin Griswold, acting on his own and without any nudging from ITT, disfavored McLaren's cause. Ultimately Geneen's case came to the Oval Office and, contrary to the president's later claim of credit for stopping ITT, Geneen in fact gained the support of Nixon himself.

One might believe McLaren—a virtual neophyte in political power plays—to have been terribly outmanned by this imposing array of men knowledgeable in the workings of government and in the nuances of influencing government policy. On his side, McLaren appeared to stand virtually alone, supported only by the Antitrust Division's career staff (generally considered to be notorious antitrust hard-liners), some liberal economists in academia, and a smattering of senators and congressmen whose influence was offset by their equally prestigious but more conservative colleagues. That McLaren did not cave in ignominiously from the sheer weight of opposing forces is itself remarkable.

McLaren's ability to stand up as he did for as long as he did was due in no small measure to the conspicuous absence from the list of Geneen's allies of Attorney General John Mitchell. Incongruous as it may seem, Geneen did not win Mitchell to his cause; and Mitchell was the key missing link in Geneen's chain of pressure designed ultimately to reach McLaren. Let it be said at the outset that it was not so much that Mitchell was *on* McLaren's side as it was that he was *not* on Geneen's. Nor was Mitchell inclined to succumb to the directives of Ehrlichman, with whom he enjoyed little rapport.

Whether ITT ultimately prevailed in an immediate sense in its campaign to reverse McLaren remains a matter of dispute. The suits against ITT came to resolution by compromise settlement, a settlement which ITT claimed was highly burdensome, others say not. But in a broader sense ITT and the other growth-oriented corporations opposing McLaren's policy did prevail; they obtained a change in the government's policy direction—and this new direction toward corporate growth has continued to the present time.

The complex web of intrigue and maneuvers surrounding the ITT cases was not visible to the public in the 1969-71 period when the events were taking place. That McLaren was embarking upon an expanded attack upon corporate growth was of special note only to that segment of the business, economic, and legal communities which concerns itself with this somewhat esoteric subject. Even that which was reported—the visible portion—turned out to have been but a fragmentary glimpse of the whole story.

This lack of public notice changed abruptly in February, 1972, some five months after the ITT cases had been terminated by the compromise settlement. The impetus for this change was publication of the infamous Dita Beard memorandum. From that time forward discourse on the ITT cases was no longer the sole province of the antitrust specialists. ITT had become front page news and the corporate acronym almost a household word. ITT had bought its settlement, so it was alleged in the wake of the

Dita Beard memorandum, by a sizeable contribution to fund the 1972 Republican National Convention scheduled to be held in San Diego. From that disclosure until the end of the ITT episode—which came only with the resignation of Nixon in August, 1974—ITT was never far from the public eye.

The public concept of the ITT affair, abetted by its reporting in the press, almost uniformly equated it with the allegations fostered by the Dita Beard memorandum. Charges of corruption are not, however, the ITT story with which we are concerned. Our study, rather, explores the genuine conflict of government policy toward corporate growth which Nixon's advisers knew was at the heart of the ITT affair and which, had it been fully understood, might have dispelled the charges of corruption.

To understand the cross currents and the uses of power which embroiled this policy conflict, it is necessary to look back before 1969 at the experience of corporate growth by merger. How do the "growth" corporations grow, and what are their purposes? After that we will examine the context of the ITT cases: the relationship between corporate growth and the federal antitrust laws, and the shaping of that relationship even before the Nixon administration. From there we will turn to the forces which came into play when McLaren, from his own convictions, decided that unrestrained corporate growth must be stopped, in the face of a presidential desire to the contrary.

2

WATCHING THE
CONGLOMERATES

[They were] a varied collection of conglomerateers whose activities were one of the spectator sports of the 1960s.

Ralph L. Nelson
Antitrust Bulletin, 1975

The 1960s indeed saw the blossoming of the conglomerate firm, gathering under a single corporate umbrella products and services of a highly diverse nature. The explosive growth of firms of this kind would be possible only via wholesale mergers and acquisitions. And acquisitions on the scale required were possible only if the corporations could exchange paper—stocks, bonds, debentures, warrants, anything that the financial men could invent. Other conventions were also useful: the ability to defer taxes on the exchange of paper was one; an accounting rule which prevented the dilution of the per-share earnings of the acquiring firm—which in fact under some circumstances gave an accounting boost to those earnings—was another; and, finally, a superheated market for securities was an indispensable aid. Diversification often became eagerly sought as an end in itself, although its practitioners would argue that it was an acceptable method of risk management which, through modern managerial methods and efficiencies, improved competition in stagnating, rigidified industries.

A satisfactory definition of a "conglomerate" corporation is hard to come by. According to the dictionary, a conglomerate is anything composed of heterogeneous materials or elements. The Federal Trade Commission (FTC) economic staff, in the 1940s, began to apply the term, probably for lack of anything more descriptive, to mergers between corporations engaged in dissimilar noncompeting businesses. Later, in the 1960s, the term took on an aura of glamour, and the business world (and the stock markets) basked in it. But, like many descriptive words, the nuance changed over time, and "conglomerate" ultimately attained a pejorative connotation. Now the corporate world prefers the term "diversified."

While the "conglomerate" label theoretically might encompass even small firms conducting two or more discrete businesses, the term has attained a weight of its own. It implies a magnitude, that of a large, multibusiness corporation employing probably thousands of persons and possessing enormous economic power. By some strange twist the category of conglomerates, in the minds of many, also took on a temporal quality. It meant the newly emerging diversifying firms which, with meteoric speed, were gobbling up other companies. The term thus did not include the old-line diversified firms—some much larger than the new conglomerates—which had achieved their present diversification in smaller bites over a longer period of time. Obviously, corporate diversification did not begin in 1960. A large number of long-established firms, not counted among the high-flying conglomerates of the 1960s, had long ago diversified their product lines, to a large extent by acquisitions; Du Pont, General Foods, and Minnesota Mining and Manufacturing were in that category. So were General Electric, IBM, General Motors, and RCA. As the economist George J. Stigler has said, "The full list of merger-created big businesses is most of the list of big businesses." And the FTC's economic staff noted: "Although the recent growth of conglomerate firms . . . represent[s] spectacular examples, diversification is neither a new phenomenon nor one restricted to 'conglomerates.' Firms such as Litton Industries and Textron merely represent extreme examples of what has been happening to many large firms in recent years." But these old-line corporations, according to Congressman Emmanuel Celler, "are not in the normal sense thought of as conglomerate corporations." The FTC staff defined the "conglomerates" as the "relatively new firms" whose "principal characteristic has been rapid growth by means of merger into a variety of unrelated fields." The debate over the conglomerates, therefore, boiled down mainly to the conglomerate merger wave of the 1960s.

Since practically all large mergers during the 1960s were of the conglomerate variety, between corporations in different businesses, the FTC's roster of merging corporations probably furnishes as good a starting point as any for identification of the conglomerates. The list drawn up to cover the 1961–68 period, the heyday of the large conglomerate merger, shows, at the top, twenty-five firms ranked by the magnitude of their acquisition activity. That list, which begins with Gulf & Western Industries, and ends with Georgia-Pacific Corporation, depicts the most active acquiring corporations of the 1960s measured by the dollar amounts of the assets acquired by them. These twenty-five conglomerates accounted, during that period, for 41 percent of all acquired assets. If attention is confined to the most significant category, "large mergers" (which the FTC defines as involving acquired industrial assets of an amount greater than $10 million), then the share of these twenty-five acquisition leaders rises to more than 50 percent.

At the end of 1968 ITT was not yet at the top of the FTC's acquisition list, although its controversial 1969 acquisitions would take it there. But even before the arrival of the Nixon administration ITT, of all the conglomerates which grew up in the 1960s, probably was the acknowledged leader, in terms of its commitment to diversification and the quality of its acquisitions.

By the size and breadth of its expansion by acquisition, and by its systems of management and control, ITT brought the practice of purposeful diversification to its virtual epitome. Formed in 1920 to establish and operate telephone systems in foreign countries (patterned on AT & T's United States system), ITT grew steadily and came to control telephone systems in a number of countries in Europe, Asia, and South America. Like AT & T, ITT soon saw merit in manufacturing telephones and related equipment for its own operating companies and eventually for other customers. (Indeed, in 1925 ITT bought out the foreign operations of AT & T's manufacturing subsidiary Western Electric.) For forty years, while it grew to substantial size, ITT operated mainly outside the United States.

In the late 1950s the ranks of ITT's founders who had guided its fortunes since its inception were thinned by death and retirement. The directors searched for a new chief executive. They selected Harold Geneen, age fifty, who was then executive vice president of Raytheon Manufacturing Company. Geneen was a relative unknown, although his performance in only two years at Raytheon was rated excellent. Geneen was an accountant by training and inclination; he loved organization and happily immersed himself in detail. His career had begun with the "Big Eight" accounting firm of Lybrand Ross Brothers & Montgomery (now Coopers & Lybrand), where he spent eight years before making the move into corporate management. After a stint as chief accountant at American Can Company during the war years, in 1946 Geneen became comptroller of Bell & Howell Company. He left in 1950 to take an equivalent position at Jones & Laughlin Steel Corporation, and in 1956 obtained his first nonaccounting management position at Raytheon.

In addition to his penchant for organization, control, and planning, Geneen had abundant energy and drive. He sought out and dwelled upon new ideas and new directions. When he was hired for the ITT presidency in 1959, its new direction soon became very clear to him. He distrusted ITT's dependence upon overseas business; less than 20 percent of its 1959 earnings came from United States operations. Almost as he came in the door, Geneen saw ITT's Cuban business expropriated. ITT was still profitable, but Geneen felt that its business was unbalanced and subject unduly to the risks and vicissitudes of foreign governments. Thus, after familiarizing himself in depth with ITT's organization and personnel, Geneen's first order of business was an acquisition plan. Before the second half of the 1960s came, he wanted to see over half of ITT's earnings emanating from North America. This goal could hardly be accomplished by internal expansion. ITT's skill and experience lay in telecommunications systems and equipment, but rapid growth in that industry was virtually foreclosed by AT & T's dominant position in the United States. Geneen thought foolhardy any notion that ITT could attempt new entry on a significant scale into other businesses in which ITT had no skill or experience. That route also would require more capital than even ITT could supply. The acquisition route was far superior, in Geneen's view: it offered quick access to new markets; ITT could buy, via acquisition, the technology, skill, management, and personnel needed; and ITT would obtain immediate earnings without the long transition period needed to generate profits after new entry. Thus, to Geneen, a plan for diversification—by acquisitions—seemed both evident and necessary for ITT; he explained, in his habitually cryptic fashion: "We think a philosophy of varied industries can lead to a more efficient corporate vehicle than the traditional pattern and one, moreover, that develops management capabilities and flexibilities that no one industry approach can provide."

Geneen was not unfamiliar with the process of corporate mergers. On the contrary, he was an avid student, finding mergers, from negotiation through implementation, an exciting drama involving a satisfying blend of men and money. At Raytheon he had personally supervised several mergers (but none on the scale which he would later execute). At ITT Geneen assembled a group, headed by Senior Vice President Stanley Luke, which would devote its efforts to refining and implementing his merger plan. In addition, to maximize ITT's acquisition opportunities, Geneen sought an outside expert; he settled on the investment banking firm of Lazard Frères & Company to be ITT's merger adviser. Lazard's responsibility was to search out merger candidates which would fit into Geneen's plans and to assist in consummating the transactions. This role was not unusual; Lazard performed essentially the same function for a number of other corporations. (By 1960 most investment bankers were beginning to develop merger departments as a natural offshoot of their traditional role in arranging financing.) Lazard's senior partner, André Mayer, assigned one of the firm's brightest young men, Felix Rohatyn, then little more than thirty years in age, to have primary responsibility for the ITT account.

Geneen's acquisition plan did not contemplate laying out a lot of cash. He preferred to give "paper" for the businesses to be acquired— common or preferred stock, bonds, debentures, and warrants. Thus, ITT's financial resources would not be depleted—the sellers of the businesses rather would become ITT stockholders or creditors.

Geneen's plan was now set in its broad outlines. He proceeded with its execution. ITT's first United States acquisition under Geneen was small. In 1961 it acquired Jennings Radio Manufacturing Company (a Lazard find), which, while having only $3 million in assets, produced a line of electronics components which supplemented nicely ITT's existing product lines. From this small beginning, under Geneen's leadership, there ensued a dazzling series of acquisitions which would transform ITT. From 1961 to 1968 ITT acquired fifty corporations in the United States. It converted its predominantly foreign operations into predominantly domestic ones, thus, by its own claim, balancing its foreign risks by obtaining a strong domestic base. Sixteen of ITT's acquisitions were "large" ones (of companies having assets over $10 million), and these together accounted for 90 percent of ITT's total of $1.5 billion in acquired assets in this period.

ITT's largest acquisition prior to 1969 was Rayonier, with assets of $292 million, said to be the world's leading producer of chemical cellulose, a form of wood pulp used as a base for production of synthetic materials. Its other large acquisitions included:

Sheraton Corporation of America, with assets of $283 million: an international hotel system (said to be the second largest hotel chain)

Continental Baking Company ($187 million in assets): the nation's largest bread and cake baking company, with 71 bakeries in 60 cities

Thorp Finance Corporation and Aetna Finance Company ($210 million in assets together): consumer finance companies

Avis: the world's second largest car rental system (ITT supplemented the Avis acquisition by acquiring Airport Parking Company of America, one of the nation's largest operators of airport, institutional, and downtown parking lots, and an operator also of taxi and bus airport ground transportation.)

Levitt & Sons: the largest United States developer of planned residential communities

ITT's other acquisitions, while smaller, were nevertheless significant, giving it entry into a number of different products and services. Thus, ITT entered publishing; career training programs; life insurance; semiconductors; silica; electrical transmission and distribution equipment;

heating and air conditioning equipment; pumps and compressors; electrical connectors; automatic controls; vacuum components; and various lesser lines.

In this period from 1961 to 1968, ITT's assets quadrupled, to $4 billion, and it moved from the thirty-fifth largest industrial corporation to the fifteenth position on that list. Thus, going into 1969—the ninth year in ITT's merger plan—Geneen's basic objectives already had been accomplished. ITT was recognized as a full-blown "conglomerate." It had a highly diversified panoply of products and services, and held a strong market position in a number of industries. And most importantly, it had transferred the bulk of its earnings base (60 percent) to North America.

Geneen's acquisition criteria were relatively simple. First, of course, he wanted to acquire United States earnings. He was not interested in "distressed situations"; he wanted "good companies" which were capable, under Geneen's direction, of a minimum 10 percent annual growth rate. Second, since much of ITT's pre–1960 United States business was defense-oriented, Geneen wanted commercial businesses to counterbalance ITT's sales to the government. As a corollary to this objective, Geneen preferred businesses which would bring to ITT a greater degree of public recognition, which he felt was woefully lacking. Hence, Geneen looked primarily for "product lines which will be sold to and identified by the public with the company." (From this thought sprang ITT's practice of tacking its initials in front of the names of companies it acquires, e.g., ITT Continental Baking, ITT Sheraton, etc.)

It was *not* a requirement, announced Geneen, that the acquired business fit with "our general product familiarity and competence," so long as the acquired firm had "an independent stream of management experience and background." If ITT could acquire the specialization needed for day-to-day operation of the business, Geneen was confident that he could supply the necessary top-level management. Hence, Geneen had no fear of taking on unfamiliar (to ITT) product lines. Having re-fashioned the management of ITT's global operations into a pyramidal form, Geneen assured the ITT directors that "these same management disciplines work equally effectively in managing diversified product lines and operations in any single market such as our own domestic U.S. market." Once he had several years of the acquisition program behind him, Geneen boasted that "we have developed the ability through management skills, routines and techniques to set and progressively meet higher competitive standards and achieve them in practically every line and product that we have undertaken."

Finally, Geneen wanted a trouble-free acquisition program, with the absolute minimum of interference. Geneen would shun the takeover fights which brought headlines to many other conglomerates. He sought companies where "there is a 'mutual accord' on improved objectives from the very start." Geneen believed that to attempt to force ITT's attentions upon an unwilling subject was foolhardy. It inevitably resulted in acrimonious charges and countercharges, usually even litigation, attended by considerable unwanted publicity. Even if the hostile takeover attempt were successful, Geneen foresaw problems in integrating an embittered target company into ITT's highly structured corporate system. And, while he once complained mildly of the "pleasant problem of finding enough 'fast-growing' companies to satisfy our requirements," in fact there was no dearth of willing merger partners. Geneen also believed that, given the chance to talk, he could overcome any initial skepticism on the part of the management of a corporation in which he was interested, and could persuade them of the advantages of amalgamation with ITT (which usually included a premium price for the acquired firm's stock and sharply higher managerial compensation for its officers).

During the 1961-68 period ITT's merger program was almost wholly free of bedevilment by the federal antitrust authorities. This too was due, in no small part, to Geneen's planning, guided by antitrust counsel. ITT would avoid the risky types of large mergers within the scope of one of its existing businesses, or one closely related, which would be most likely to call down the wrath of the antitrust enforcers. Only in one instance, albeit an important one—ITT's attempted merger with American Broadcasting Corporation—did antitrust policy rear its head; and in this case (to be discussed in detail later) Geneen abandoned the merger by choice rather than by compulsion.

How long could, or would, ITT's merger splurge continue? Geneen told the ITT directors: "I think we should seek and take all good opportunities as they present themselves up until such time, at least, as we feel that our competence as a management has been stretched too wide in scope and we must of necessity slow down such a program." Given Geneen's high opinion of his own competence, this time might never come. Indeed, although Geneen's original objectives had been substantially achieved by the end of 1968, still ITT's largest—and most controversial—acquisitions were yet to come.

Even with its astounding series of acquisitions, ITT at the end of 1968 ranked only as the third most active acquiring company of the 1960s. The top-ranked company far and away was Gulf & Western Industries, the brainchild of Geneen's rival in conglomeration, Charles Bluhdorn. Gulf & Western acquired $2.9 billion in assets from 1961 to 1968, some 50 percent more than its nearest rival. Bluhdorn started with a chain of automotive parts distributors, not a particularly glamorous business, then expanded by acquisition into production of automotive parts, and followed this initial thrust with a number of large acquisitions unrelated to the automotive business, e.g., New Jersey Zinc Company (zinc and chemicals), Paramount Pictures Corporation (motion pictures and television programs), South Puerto Rico Sugar Company (sugar refining), Consolidated Cigar Corporation (cigars), E. W. Bliss Company (metal work presses), Brown Company (paper), Associates Investment Company (commercial finance), and Providence Washington Insurance Company (life and casualty insurance). Gulf & Western had several unsuccessful sorties after even bigger game, but its celebrated fight to gain control of Armour & Company lost out to General Host Corporation, and its attempt to take over Sinclair Oil Company lost to the competing bid of Atlantic Richfield Corporation. At other times it flirted with Pan American World Airways and Grumman Aircraft, picking up small blocks of stock in each; but unable to gain a position of control, it subsequently decided to sell these shares. While its contested takeover bids usually invoked antitrust charges by the unwilling target, Gulf & Western encountered government antitrust action only in its acquisition of Desilu (a Paramount competitor), which it agreed to divest. (Later, it was to drop a proposed 1969 acquisition of Allis-Chalmers Company because of antitrust objections by the FTC.)

Just slightly ahead of ITT in the merger parade was Ling-Temco-Vought (LTV). In many ways LTV's meteoric rise was the most astounding of all. Unlike ITT, LTV had germinated in the late 1950s from scratch. It was the brainchild and handiwork of an electrician-turned-entrepreneur named James Ling. It has been aptly stated that LTV "came from nowhere" in the 1950s to become the twenty-second largest United States industrial corporation in 1968. In 1958 its assets were $6 million; in 1968 they were $2.6 billion. In the 1961–68 period LTV acquired $2 billion in assets. Ling's major acquisitions included Temco Aircraft Corporation (aircraft), Chance-Vought (aircraft and missiles), Okonite Company (cables), Allied Radio Corporation (consumer electronics), Wilson & Company (meat packing, chemicals and pharmaceuticals, and sporting goods), Greatamerica Corporation (banking and insurance), and Braniff Airways. Only in the Chance-Vought merger had Ling run into an antitrust roadblock, when the Justice Department sued in 1961 claiming this was a horizontal merger between competitors in the aerospace industry. The federal district court, however, disagreed with the government and ruled for Ling because neither firm was among the leaders in the aerospace industry, and the actual competition between them was insignificant. The government gave in at that point and did not appeal.

The list of conglomerates continued, with names such as Tenneco, Teledyne, Litton, FMC Corporation, General Telephone, Textron, Colt Industries, White Consolidated, Rapid-American Corporation, Leasco Data Processing, General American Transportation, and others which gained frequent mention in the financial press. All had the common denominator of substantial acquisitions, of companies sometimes larger even than the acquiring firm, extending into new fields of business.

The scope of the conglomerate merger movement of the 1960s—which the FTC economic staff termed "a veritable avalanche of conglomerate mergers" and which even the *Wall Street Journal* called a "runaway boom in mergers"—was documented in the FTC data. Fifty billion dollars in assets were acquired from 1961 to 1968, which was three times the total assets acquired from 1950 to 1960.* The total of 1968 acquired assets, $15.2 billion, was sixty times greater than the 1950 total of $260 million. Even on a constant dollar basis, it was manifest that the merger wave of the 1960s was indeed a big one. It was equally clear that conglomerate mergers led the way. Counting only "large mergers"—those over $10 million in acquired industrial assets, for which the data is most refined— the 1960s, through 1968, witnessed 551 conglomerate mergers, involving aggregate acquired assets of $29 billion, which accounted for 72 percent of all assets acquired in large mergers. In the peak year 1968 alone there were 150 large conglomerate mergers by which $10.4 billion of assets were acquired. The *New York Times* reported that "about 80 companies that were in *Fortune*'s 1962 listings of the nation's 500 largest industrial companies are now [at the beginning of 1968] part of, or controlled by, other corporations."

From 1948 to 1960 there had been only 14 acquisitions of industrial corporations having assets over $100 million; from 1960 through 1969 there were 103 mergers of that magnitude (of which 24 occurred in 1967 and 30 in 1968). Before 1960 there had been only a single acquisition of a company having assets in excess of $250 million (and that was General Telephone's 1959 conglomerate acquisition of Sylvania Electric). After 1960 and through 1968 there were 23 acquisitions of that giant size.

Why the conglomerates? What were the reasons for the sudden movement toward accelerated corporate growth marked by expansion into

---

*The dollar amount of acquired assets is the standard measure of acquisition activity. It must be obvious, however, that this benchmark is not a reliable indicator of actual business value. For example, whereas Rapid American Corporation paid $200 million for Glen Alden Corporation with its $1.25 billion in assets, Xerox Corporation paid four and one-half times that amount ($910 million) for Scientific Data Systems, which had only $113 million in assets.

unfamiliar territory? Are the conglomerates, as some have contended, a wholly unnatural form of beast, dedicated to the personal aggrandizement of their leaders?

The conglomerates indeed are no more and no less than avid practitioners of corporate diversification. That practice has not been confined to the better known "glamour" companies which caught the eye of the public. Diversification in United States business has been a broader and deeper phenomenon than that. Many hundreds of United States corporations have decided, for one reason or another, to diversify from their original businesses into new products and services.

The reasons for diversification are varied. It may be that the corporation's original business has settled into decline or is threatened by external forces. Under the impetus of technological innovation, changing consumer preferences, and the growth of governmental intervention, many firms have found it desirable to seek new markets as a hedge against possible disruptions to their original businesses. The tobacco companies in the 1960s, in the face of vigorous antismoking drives and the prospect of governmental action, undertook wide-ranging diversification moves. The large dairy companies, presumably foreseeing adverse changes in consumer demand and distribution methods for milk, also have been prime practitioners of diversification. Some of the oil companies, perceiving themselves as facing supply problems and greater government regulation, over the last few years have begun to diversify.

Even if the corporation's original business itself has a bright future, the corporation may have excess capital which it desires to invest. Business firms accumulate capital out of profits not only for renewal or expansion of facilities, but also to guard against future setbacks. Not infrequently the accumulated capital becomes far larger than needed for the original purpose. Of course, this excess could be paid out to shareholders as dividends, but the federal income tax laws furnish an incentive to shareholders to expand the corporation in hopes of obtaining capital gains rather than taking dividends which are taxed at ordinary income rates.

Before 1950 the investment of excess corporate capital probably would be channeled toward the acquisition of competitors, suppliers, or customers. The reason was simple: not only did this provide an investment repository for excess capital, but it well could give the acquiring firm a competitive edge in its market. Mergers between competitors ("horizontal" mergers), unless needed to meld smaller firms into minimum efficient size, are viewed by many economists as a consolidation of market positions designed to achieve the higher profits available in an oligopolistic market. Similarly, "vertical" mergers, between suppliers and customers, again unless necessary to make a small firm competitive, are seen as motivated by a desire to gain a competitive edge over firms having a lesser degree of vertical integration.

As will be discussed in the next chapter, the 1950 amendment to the federal antimerger law (Section 7 of the Clayton Act) virtually foreclosed the investment of excess capital in acquisitions of substantial direct competitors, customers, or suppliers. Even acquisitions of large size in a closely related field would be risky; it was considerably safer to put aside thoughts of a functional fit, except for smaller acquisitions. Hence, firms desiring substantial expansion by acquisition were forced to violate one of the primary rules of business: stick with something you know. While the acquiring firm normally would prefer an acquisition which would enable it to transfer its experience, skills, and knowhow, after 1950 its legal advisers would caution against such acquisitions.

Of course, diversification can come by startup (internal expansion) as well as by acquisition. An outside firm, however, normally will prefer to enter a new market by acquisition if possible. The acquiring firm thereby obtains not only the facilities and personnel needed for the business, but more importantly, the existing market position of the acquired firm. Economists note that an acquisition does not add capacity in the market, and does not require the new entrant to gain market share at the expense of existing firms; therefore, an acquisition is less likely to reduce existing price and profit levels in the market than is entry by internal expansion.

A startup, by contrast, requires not only duplication of physical facilities and the hiring and training of qualified personnel, but also the uncertain risk of customer acceptance. The added capacity and the attempt by the new entrant to attract customers may reduce the industry's price and profit levels. A new entrant usually must withstand a number of loss years before a profitable level of operation will be reached, whereas an acquisition usually will bring an already profitable operation. Thus, if the cost of the acquisition is not unduly in excess of projected startup costs, the acquisition route obviously will appeal to the potential new entrant. If, as sometimes happens, entry by acquisition actually would cost less than a startup, this appeal is magnified.

The interests of the conglomerates—the more aggressive diversifying firms—were not significantly different from those of the many other diversifying firms. Growth to giant size necessarily meant that the conglomerates would have to tread unfamiliar business ground. But, said their critics, the conglomerates were different—they were not simply investing excess capital; indeed, many of them had little or no excess capital. They were merely issuing paper—their own stock or debt instruments—in exchange for the acquired firm. Even on those occasions when cash was paid for the acquisition, it was usually borrowed from a bank. This kind of acquisition activity could have little economic justification, then. Or could it? The conglomerates said yes; diversification was highly desirable for balance and risk-spreading. Combining under a single corporate roof a variety of product lines would smooth out the cyclical patterns in the different lines. What could make more sense, for example, than selling ski equipment in the winter and swimwear in the summer? If the conglomerate could fine-tune a proper mix of goods and services, it could keep its administrative force going full-time, better utilize its production and marketing personnel, protect its shareholders against cyclical downturns, and therefore help stabilize the general economy.

ITT furnished an example of this rationale. Geneen originally started acquiring other companies in the United States to balance ITT's predominantly foreign operations. He was attempting to hedge against political and economic risks in nations which he viewed as less stable than the United States. Even after he had substantially accomplished this goal, by 1969, he continued to look for added stabilization in the domestic areas—e.g., the less cyclical insurance and food service businesses of Hartford Fire Insurance Company and Canteen Corporation to offset other ITT businesses more susceptible to economic fluctuation (hotels, home building, automobile rentals). Geneen's plan seemed to be working. During the 1960s ITT had an unbroken string of quarterly earnings increases, and showed a healthy 12 percent average annual increase in profits.

Some of the defenders of the conglomerates felt called upon to go even further. To offset an outcry of formlessness and lack of purposefulness in the growth of the conglomerates, someone devised the concept of "synergism." A scientific term referring to the cooperative action of two or more agencies (e.g., drugs) working in such a way that the total effect is greater than the sum of the component effects taken independently, synergism was translated into business terminology to claim that the conglomerate would be more efficient in total than would be its component businesses operating on their own. Hence, costs would decrease, which would translate into lower prices to consumers. Synergism was to come about because of centralized management, accounting, and purchasing—a sharing of overhead costs which would eliminate unnecessary duplication and achieve the economies of volume under the oversight of hard-driving overall administration. Thus, according to Geneen, ITT's major asset was its two-thousand-man "central operating management." He said:

We have developed this expert [management] group in order to improve our competitiveness and our efficiencies and to support our operating companies into improved operation in those fields either new or old, that we have entered. It is the *existence* of such a management group that makes possible our entry through acquisition into new fields—and to contribute innovation and new levels of competition to the acquired industries.

Probably some acquired businesses were rendered more efficient by acquisition, and others remained unchanged (or even deteriorated). Many respected economists claim that meaningful efficiencies are obtainable only at the plant level, and that, therefore, any negligible economies achievable by the conglomerates beyond the plant level are not worth the bother of computing. The FTC economic staff, after studying nine conglomerates, including ITT, agreed with that theory, concluding that no substantial economies have been achieved by the conglomerates which could not have been obtained without mergers. The House Antitrust Subcommittee staff in a 1971 report went even further. According to it, "Management difficulties with newly acquired companies showed, if anything, that combination frequently had injurious effects on efficiency, productivity, and corporate values." The subcommittee staff felt that this had been true even of ITT's acquisitions, that the "efficiency and performance" of new subsidiaries deteriorated within the ITT system.

The justifications conjured up by the proponents of the conglomerates probably were more for public consumption than for legal defense. It was a matter of image. The conglomerates did not want to leave the impression that they grew merely to be big: the news must go out that the public would benefit from increased efficiency.

By the end of 1968, then, the conglomerate merger wave was in full swell. Having established the fact of the phenomenon, we now examine whether it was having any impact upon the degree of competition in United States industries of the kind designed to bring into play the federal antitrust laws.

3

THE ANTITRUST PUZZLE

*[In antitrust] it is delusive to treat opinions written
by different judges at different times as pieces of a
jig-saw puzzle which can be, by effort, fitted correctly into a single pattern.*

Judge Charles Wyzanski
in United States v. United Shoe
Machinery Company, 1953

Many corporate executives and their legal advisers would go further
than Judge Wyzanski; they would claim that a consistent pattern in
antitrust policy is apparently a luxury in which the federal government
has never indulged. James Ling, while president of the conglomerate
LTV, complained: "It is impossible for any businessman—or any
attorney—to say with any degree of conviction what national antitrust
policy will be from year-to-year—or even from month-to-month."

Businessmen grounded in planning, predictability, and organization
indeed often have difficulty understanding the free form of antitrust
policy. For good or bad, generality is the hallmark of all of our major
antitrust laws.

The antitrust laws are designed to police the functioning of our private
enterprise economy. The major premise of our system is that entry into
any given business will be unrestrained, and that capital investment decisions accordingly will be made by private citizens impelled by their own
personal profit motivations. The aggregation of these self-interested
decisions, it is held, will turn out also to be in the best interests of our
society as a whole.

A second premise is that the profit-motivated entrepreneurs must act
independently and not in collusion with other entrepreneurs. Private
enterprise grew from popular dissatisfaction in medieval England with
monopolies and closed guild practices. It was felt that concerted action
among entrepreneurs over the long run would result in private monopoly.

The seminal United States antitrust law, the Sherman Act, was enacted in 1890 to formalize and strengthen the common law rules against collusion and monopolies. The latter rules had proved inadequate to deal with burgeoning nationwide business activity (including "trusts" by which competitors pooled their corporate ownerships and thereby accomplished a concert of decision making). The Sherman Act declares unlawful combinations, conspiracies, and agreements in restraint of trade, and monopolization. The Sherman Act as construed by the Supreme Court, however, presented but a minor obstacle to corporate mergers. A merger would not be considered an unreasonable restraint of trade unless it resulted in a virtual monopoly. Consequently, the overwhelming majority of mergers, even between competitors, were unaffected by the Sherman Act.

In the Clayton Act, enacted in 1914, Congress included, in Section 7, a specific provision to control mergers. This effort, however, also turned out to be a virtual nullity because of a loophole of astounding magnitude. The Supreme Court held the statute to apply only when one corporation directly acquired the stock of another. Where stock was not directly acquired, as in a purchase of assets or a statutory merger, the transaction was immune from attack. Hence, the statutory controls were avoided with ease.

Furthermore, it was almost universally believed that the original Section 7 could be applied only to "horizontal" mergers, between competitors. In the 1920s there came to arise concern over "vertical" mergers—between suppliers and their customers—and "conglomerate" mergers (as the FTC staff later denominated them) involving neither competitors nor suppliers-customers. The enforcement agencies were unhappy over these perceived limitations in the statute.

Beginning in the 1920s, the FTC called upon Congress to cure these defects in the original Section 7. Not until the end of World War II, however, did Congress seriously set to work on the matter. The legislators supporting this movement, led by Senator Estes Kefauver and Representative Emmanuel Celler, finally achieved their goal in December 1950.

The 1950 amendment to Section 7 closed the loophole left by the original statute's limitation to stock acquisitions. The language of the section was changed also to apply rather clearly to vertical and conglomerate acquisitions. The amended statute broadly prohibits any corporate acquisition where the resulting effect "may be substantially to lessen compeitition or to tend to create a monopoly in any line of commerce in any section of the country."

The legal historian Roscoe Pound has defined a rule of law as a "legal precept that attaches a definite detailed legal consequence to a definite detailed state of facts." By this standard, Section 7 of the Clayton Act, even as amended, hardly qualifies. But practically speaking, there was no way that Congress could have written a law which could specify all possible economic factors thought to be necessary to distinguish a healthy merger (and it was recognized there were such) from a malefactoral merger. So, the lack of specificity in Section 7 of the Clayton Act means that the courts and enforcement agencies ultimately decide the antimerger policy to be applied in the United States economy. The courts do so by discharging their function of deciding in a specific case whether a merger is lawful, or is unlawful because of its probable effect of substantially lessening competition. Judge Wyzanski has commented: "In the antitrust field the courts have been accorded, by common consent, an authority that they have in no other branch of enacted law."

The role of enforcement agencies in the making of merger policy is less visible but nearly as important. The enforcement agencies obviously make policy by deciding which mergers will be the subject of suits. Perhaps in no other area of law enforcement is prosecutorial discretion so wide or the consequences of its exercise of such overall importance. Former Attorney General Nicholas Katzenbach has noted that under Section 7 of the Clayton Act the Justice Department has "a wide area of discretion between the boundaries of fact and law." Former Federal Trade Commissioner Stephen A. Nye similarly has observed that the antitrust laws "are political laws granting enforcers broad discretion." By withholding suit against a merger involving a particular industry, the enforcement agencies may signal a lack of enforcement interest in that industry; other companies may take this signal to mean that they are free to move ahead with more mergers in that industry. An example is the coal industry; a prosecutorial decision in 1966 not to attack the acquisition of one of the leading coal producers (Consolidation Coal) by a large petroleum firm (Continental Oil) was followed by a series of acquisitions in the coal industry, e.g., Occidental Petroleum Company's acquisition of Island Creek Coal Company, Standard Oil of Ohio's acquisition of Old Ben Coal. That decision, according to some present-day critics, has served to diminish competition in the coal industry and has reduced the development of new coal reserves.

The antitrust spotlight falls mainly upon the assistant attorney general in charge of the Antitrust Division—the most important single antitrust policy making position. The position of antitrust assistant is considered by the antitrust bar to be highly prestigious, and consequently attracts unusually qualified and highly reputed lawyers. One of the reasons for this attraction may be the considerable autonomy which the antitrust assistant historically has enjoyed.

The antimerger policy attitudes of the current Antitrust Division chief naturally are of prime interest to the corporation engaged in or contemplating a merger campaign. Indeed, the policy predilections of the enforcement officials are of as great an import as the merger rules embodied in judicial decisions. As attorney Frederick L. Ballard has commented: "I have always felt that the more important question was, will Justice or the Federal Trade Commission attack my merger. I have always had a feeling that if they attacked my merger they would be pretty apt to win, but the question seemed to be whether they would attack it in the first place."

In antitrust litigation, as with all areas of federal law, the ultimate arbiter is the Supreme Court. Enforcement policy decisions of the antitrust agencies, and the decisions of the lower courts or the FTC, must reckon with this greater authority. Donald Baker, a former Antitrust Division chief, has aptly observed: "Antitrust law embodies a broad commitment to competition in a few general provisions. Congress has left the details to the courts. Thus the exact state of antitrust law at any particular time depends mostly on the approach of the courts—and most particularly the Supreme Court—to that underlying commitment to competition."

It was not until almost 1960 that a case brought under Section 7 of the Clayton Act, as amended, made its way to the Supreme Court. For more than a decade thereafter, in the crucial formative period of the antitrust law of mergers, a majority of the Supreme Court displayed an open hospitality to merger enforcement under Section 7. During that period the enforcement agencies never really lost a merger case in the Supreme Court. Needless to say, the business community's legal advisers were unhappy over the direction followed by the Supreme Court, and the belief was widely expressed that the Court was doing violence to economic principles in order to ease the task of the antitrust enforcers. Robert L. Stern, a former government antitrust attorney, commented that "sometimes the [Supreme] Court goes further in favor of the government than even the trial court did in accepting the government's position."

Following the 1950 amendment of Section 7, the enforcement agencies found in the lower federal courts a reluctance to give Section 7 an expansive reading. Faced with this recalcitrance, the enforcement agencies felt they must appeal to the Supreme Court to vindicate their merger policy. When they learned how receptive the Supreme Court would be, they would then appeal to increment their authority.

From 1950 through 1968 the Supreme Court rendered decisions in 29 merger cases appealed to it. The astounding scorecard was: government 28, defendant 0; no decision (evenly divided Court) 1. In 19 of its 28 decisions in favor of the government, the Supreme Court was reversing a lower court decision.

The heyday of the activist Supreme Court was the period 1960-68, when all but one of the Court's 29 pre-1969 decisions were rendered. The Supreme Court of the 1960s, of course, was referred to in popular parlance as the "Warren Court" for Chief Justice Earl Warren, himself an antitrust activist. He enjoyed the consistent support of Justices Hugo Black, William O. Douglas, William Brennan, and Tom Clark. These five justices were, in fact, on the government's side in every one of the cases decided during their tenure. And all five were there from 1960 to 1968 except for Justice Clark, who resigned in 1967 when his son Ramsey Clark was appointed attorney general. Clark's successor, Thurgood Marshall, also lined up with the antitrust majority. In short, the Court throughout the 1960s had a solid majority for the government in merger cases.

The leaders of the antitrust enforcement agencies were, of course, pleased with the direction of the Supreme Court. Not so the leaders of business. They contended that the Court was being inconsistent in its application of basic economic principles, with the sole apparent aim of giving Section 7 a maximum scope of applicability. Supreme Court Justice Potter Stewart, dissenting in 1966 from the majority's ruling in the Von's Grocery case, seemed to support this view in stating: "The sole consistency that I can find is that in litigation under Sec. 7, the Government always wins." The Court's critics accused it of gerrymandering the "market" in which the effect of competition must be measured in order to put a particular acquisition in its worst possible light. For example, when Continental Can Company, a producer of metal cans, acquired Hazel-Atlas Company, a maker of glass bottles, the district court had dismissed the government's suit, finding that the two firms were not competitors, and that the merger constituted a diversification from which no anticompetitive effects would ensue. When the government appealed to the Supreme Court, the majority of that Court said the district court was wrong, that the relevant market included both metal cans and glass bottles because, over the long run, they were interchangeable by packers (although not without an expensive conversion of packaging equipment); therefore, the two firms *were* competitors in this combined market, and since each had a significant share of that market, the merger was unlawful.

But, pointed out the critics, when Aluminum Company of America, in defending its acquisition of Rome Cable Company, which resulted in a 1.3 percent increase in Alcoa's share of aluminum conductor sales, argued that copper conductor was interchangeable and therefore part of the same relevant market (on the theory that the broadening of the relevant market would minimize the possible competitive impact of the acquisition), the Supreme Court majority, again reversing the district court, said no. While aluminum-copper conductor combined could be a relevant market, yet aluminum alone could be a relevant *submarket* of that overall market, and the submarket could be used for Section 7 purposes. To many business critics this seemed inconsistent.

Nor did the critics of the Supreme Court like what Justice John M. Harlan referred to as the Court's "'numbers game' test for determining Clayton Act violations." The Court seemed determined to streamline merger cases by announcing simplistic rules. Where it found a market to be concentrated, i.e., oligopolistic, said the Court, any merger causing an "undue" rise in concentration could be stopped. In Alcoa's acquisition of Rome Cable, this was Rome's 1.3 percent added to Alcoa's 27.8 percent. This rule manifestly left little room for horizontal mergers in such an industry. Even if the industry was not concentrated, if the Court perceived that a trend was underway by which the leading firms were increasing their market shares, it showed little hesitation in stepping in. In the Von's Grocery–Shopping Bag merger between Los Angeles retail grocers, the combination of market shares of 4.7 percent and 4.2 percent was held unlawful under that rationale.

The most scathing public critic of the Supreme Court of the 1960s undoubtedly was Milton Handler, part Columbia university law teacher, part defender of corporate antitrust defendants. Handler has delivered a lengthy succession of antitrust writings, most of them with puzzling but intriguing titles. Handler showed no mercy to the 1960s Supreme Court. He accused the Court of developing "a network of mechanical rules, all designed to invalidate corporate acquisitions." Indeed, he charged, "the Court at times starts with the answer rather than with a question, thus placing its own policy predilections above statutory language and legislative history. . . . The Court has gone out of its way to rest its decisions on the broadest possible grounds."

Herbert A. Bergson, a former Antitrust Division chief who had entered law practice, distilled "the chief lessons to be learned from the Supreme Court decisions" as follows:

First, if the Supreme Court wants to strike down a merger, it can find a way.

Second, it's going to want to strike it down.

And third, the trial court is only a way station on the way to the Supreme Court.

Bergson concluded that the Supreme Court had given the Antitrust Division all the chips: "It is there that the shape of the merger movement is going to be determined, because once you get into court and the case gets to the Supreme Court, the Supreme Court is going to find the merger illegal."

4

LAW AND THEORY

Probably the most portentous developments under antitrust in terms of its future course and that of the structure of American business in general and consequences for the American economy will arise in connection with enforcement decisions and cases involving growth by product, geographical and functional diversification, now the most prevalent form of growth by acquisition.

E. T. Grether
Antitrust Law Journal, 1963

Even by 1969—almost twenty years after amendment of Section 7 of the Clayton Act—the enforcement-oriented Supreme Court of the 1960s had spoken surprisingly little on the legality of conglomerate mergers. This was because that Court had little opportunity to do so. The enforcement agencies had filed few complaints against conglomerate mergers; therefore, there were few chances for a conglomerate merger case to filter its way through the trial process up to the Supreme Court. During this formative period of merger law, from 1950 through 1968, only two mergers involving clear-cut diversification into new product lines reached the Supreme Court, and neither of these involved what have became known as "pure" conglomerate mergers. Hence, even in 1971 Solicitor General Erwin Griswold pointed out that despite the government's success in merger cases before the Supreme Court, "we have never won nor lost in the Supreme Court a conglomerate merger case, because there haven't been any yet, largely because until fairly recently people didn't really think it was covered by the Clayton Act."

Since 1950 economists and the enforcement agencies have labored mightily to attempt to figure out how a conglomerate merger diminishes competition. A horizontal merger is easy—it is the ultimate form of collusion between independent competitors and has the same effect as if they decided by agreement to cooperate in their competitive efforts. Also it did not take long to conclude that vertical mergers interfere with the supply stream; vertical integration shrinks the free market in which suppliers can sell and customers can buy. But what about conglomerate mergers? As the FTC has stated: "Such a merger . . . does not have the effect of automatically foreclosing to competitors any market outlet or source of supply as in a vertical merger, nor does it have the effect of automatically eliminating a competitor as in a horizontal merger."

A conglomerate merger thus appears to be merely a change of ownership without ostensible competitive significance. One competitor is substituted for another. How, then, might this substitution lessen competition in the marketplace?

In its 1948 report urging amendment of the original Section 7, the FTC had stated its view of the evils of conglomerate mergers:

There is present in most conglomerate acquisitions a simple drive to obtain greater economic power. With the economic power which it secures through its operations in many diverse fields, the giant conglomerate corporation may attain an almost impregnable economic position. Threatened with competition in any one of its various activities, it may sell below cost in that field, offsetting its losses through profits made in its other lines— a practice which is frequently explained as one of meeting competition. The conglomerate corporation is thus in a position to strike out with great force against smaller business in a variety of different industries. As the Commission has previously pointed out, there are few greater dangers to small business than the continued growth of the conglomerate corporation.

The FTC report's view was followed in a succession of economic writings arguing the anticompetitive effects of conglomerate mergers; these were delivered by a plethora of liberal economists, of whom the most vociferous probably have been Corwin Edwards and Willard Mueller (each of whom served for a time as chief economist of the FTC). The premise of their arguments was the sheer economic power said to flow from corporate bigness, and the numerous sinister ways in which that power might be misused. The aggregation of assets, they argued, would have a chilling effect upon market competition, would portend deleterious changes in market structure, and would invite emulation by other firms feeling the need to merge to grow big.

It is beyond our scope, however (and probably beyond the reader's patience), to explore all the flights of economic fancy which have been exercised to tag conglomerate mergers. Those that have sifted through to achieve some degree of judicial acceptance can be divided into three general categories.

One theory was that the conglomerate merger eliminated "potential competition." The reasoning of the propounders of this theory goes as follows. If a new company enters an industry or a marketing area on its own, by building a new plant, store, etc., it introduces another competitor in the market. The additional capacity will sharpen the competitive battle as the new entrant strives to gain a share of the market by making price reductions, quality improvements, and so on. Entry by internal expansion, the argument goes, is far more promotive of aggressive competition than is entry by merger. The latter form of entry constitutes a mere substitution rather than an enhancement of competition. Hence, in an industry in which competition is sticky, a diversification merger by a potential competitor should be disallowed. The acquiring firm should be made to go back and start over, with its entry to be by internal expansion.

The judges of the lower courts initially had a hard time swallowing this. They expressed incredulity over the notion that a firm could be required to diversify only by internal expansion. True, it might be a nice, altruistic gesture on its part, but where was the lessening of competition if it didn't want to? The prevailing attitude was expressed colorfully by a law professor, James Rahl, who stated: "To treat an election not to augment competition as a lessening of competition is a neat trick, perhaps facilitated by the enveloping propensities of the phrase 'potential competition.' It is, however, plainly not authorized by the language of the statute, nor by the philosophy of antitrust, which does not affirmatively seek to compel competition."

But the strongly pro-antitrust Supreme Court of the 1960s had less conceptual difficulty. In a series of decisions beginning in 1964, the Court held that a merger between potential competitors could be held unlawful. Most of these decisions involved geographic expansion mergers. But that the same rule could be applied to conglomerate mergers as well is shown by the Supreme Court's decision in the celebrated Procter & Gamble (P & G)–Clorox merger case. P & G had longed to enter the liquid bleach industry, as a natural fit with its soap, detergent, and cleaning products. It had conducted the usual market and feasibility studies but, so it claimed, concluded that it did not want to go head-to-head against Clorox, whose name had become almost synonymous with liquid bleach (a chemically standardized product of which every brand was exactly the same). The better solution was to acquire Clorox, which P & G proceeded to do. The Supreme Court, in reversing the court of appeals which had viewed the FTC's case as "based on merely possibility and conjecture," held the merger unlawful, because, for one reason, P & G was a potential competitor which theretofore exercised some competitive restraint over the liquid bleach producers. The merger manifestly eliminated Procter & Gamble as a potential competitor, and this was sufficient reason to bar it. P & G's own protestations that it would not enter the industry by internal expansion if it could not acquire Clorox were self-serving and not entitled to be accorded any weight.

A second theory, usually called "decisive competitive advantage," was also applied in the same P & G case as an additional reason for branding that merger illegal. Association with P & G would make Clorox, which already had 50 percent of the national liquid bleach market, so formidable a competitor that its smaller rivals would find it difficult to survive. Such an eventuality manifestly would lessen competition, since the number of firms would be reduced, and moreover new firms would not enter to replace those that disappeared because no one would be foolish enough to put up money to go into business in competition with Procter & Gamble and Clorox combined. Hence, Clorox would receive a "decisive competitive advantage" from the merger. The Court further noted that "the products of the acquired company are complementary to those of the acquiring company and may be produced with similar facilities, marketed through the same channels and in the same manner, and advertised by the same media." The Court found, for example, that P & G could integrate Clorox into its own tremendous national advertising program, and Clorox therefore could get the benefit of volume discounts that other bleach companies could not.

The antitrust enforcement agencies' third major judicially accepted theory was proceeding apace. This was the reciprocity theory. The FTC had found a neat case when Consolidated Foods acquired Gentry, a producer of dehydrated onion and garlic. Consolidated was a grocery wholesaler and retailer, and some of its suppliers (particularly soup companies) used onion and garlic in their products. After the merger Consolidated started to pressure the soup companies to buy Gentry products if they wanted to continue selling their soup to Consolidated. This is what economists call reciprocity: if you buy from me, I will buy from you—or, if you don't buy from me, I won't buy from you. If Consolidated had not acquired Gentry, this reciprocity pressure could not have been brought to bear; hence, the merger was held unlawful by the Supreme Court because it led to reciprocity practice which in turn led to disadvantage to Gentry's competitors, which (in turn) was a lessening of competition. (Here again, the Supreme Court was reversing the court of appeals which had found the FTC's case unconvincing.) The Supreme Court brushed aside Consolidated Foods's argument that its reciprocity efforts had produced slim results, noting that Gentry had at least been able to maintain its market share despite an inferior product.

What of efficiencies and economies? Would the Supreme Court give credit to cost savings from the combination of complementary product lines—the synergism of the conglomerates—which might well bring pressures on competitors and result in lower prices or higher quality to consumers? In the first major Supreme Court decision under amended Section 7 of the Clayton Act, involving a merger of Brown Shoe Company and Kinney, shoe companies which both manufactured and sold at retail, the Supreme Court obliquely cast doubt on the status of economies by noting that while manufacturer-retail chain integration perhaps "in some of the results . . . are beneficial to consumers," still "Congress appreciated that occasional higher costs and prices might result from the maintenance of fragmented industries and markets. It resolved these competing considerations in favor of decentralization." Later, in striking down a proposed merger of Philadelphia National Bank and Girard Trust, the Court brushed aside the asserted need of the City of Philadelphia for a large bank to finance local industry and commerce. The Court made the following often-quoted observation:

We are clear, however, that a merger the effect of which "may be substantially to lessen competition" is not saved because, on some ultimate reckoning of social or economic debits and credits, it may be deemed beneficial. A value choice of such magnitude is beyond the ordinary limits of judicial competence, and in any event has been made for us already, by Congress when it enacted the amended Sec. 7. Congress determined to preserve our traditionally competitive economy. It therefore proscribed anticompetitive mergers, the benign and malignant alike, fully aware, we must assume, that some price might have to be paid.

Businessmen began to assume that the price to be paid included operational efficiency. This view was expressly confirmed by the 1967 Procter & Gamble decision where bulk advertising efficiencies were not merely discounted but were affirmative grounds for striking down the merger. The Supreme Court put the matter bluntly enough: "Possible economies cannot be used as a defense to illegality. Congress was aware that some mergers which lessen competition may also result in economies but it struck the balance in favor of protecting competition."

The diversifying firms got the idea. Synergism would avail little in the courts. On the contrary, if the competitive position of the acquired firm were strengthened by the efficiencies, this itself might be considered anticompetitive, particularly if the increased effectiveness would divert sales from smaller companies. This meant that the diversifying corporations had to change their tactics: they would have to argue *against* efficiencies once they were haled into court. Thus, when the FTC brought suit against the acquisition by Kennecott Copper Corporation of Peabody Coal Company, Kennecott went to great lengths to disclaim the bringing of any added efficiencies to the acquired firm. The acquisition, it said, was merely a diversification opportunity which would leave competition in the coal industry exactly as it was, neither more nor less. According to its counsel, "You couldn't save any money by having a copper company buy a coal company because you couldn't ship by the same freight cars or the same trucks. Kennecott had no advertising program, no TV program." In that case, the FTC disagreed and held the acquisition unlawful, in part because the addition of Kennecott's resources would considerably strengthen Peabody's competitive position by enabling it to finance additional acquisition and development of coal properties, to the disadvantage of other, less well-endowed coal companies.

As 1969 approached, the leaders of big business were faced with a dismal record before the Supreme Court. Many observers felt that the Court had subordinated efficiency and price competition to the preservation of small businesses at the ultimate expense of the consumer and of technological progress. Some also claimed that the Court had fashioned tools which the antitrust enforcers could wield and manipulate to channel economic growth to their liking.

Comfort could be taken perhaps only in the area of conglomerate mergers, which still remained as a frontier yet to be fully explored by the Supreme Court. Fortunately, from the business standpoint the enforcement agencies' relative lack of interest in conglomerate mergers had denied the Supreme Court the opportunity to make a full sweep of those mergers. The conglomerate corporations could live, with a fair degree of comfort, with the three theories which had been approved by the Supreme Court— at least in the terms in which those theories had been framed thus far. Professor E. T. Grether observed that the decisions applying those theories had involved no more than "peripheral determination" of the legal status of diversified corporate growth. All these theories would, it seems, require a close and peculiar product relationship between the merging corporations. Reciprocity would require at a minimum that those who are customers of the acquired firm be suppliers, normally in substantial quantities, to the acquiring firm, and, so it seemed, that the merged companies attempt to exploit that relationship to enhance their sales. The competitive advantage theory expressed in Procter & Gamble must require products which were integratable in advertising, promotion, or selling. And to conclude that the acquiring firm was a potential competitor normally should require that the new market be a logical extension of the acquiring firm's present product lines.

But if these product relationships were absent—as they most often were in the conglomerate merger wave—theories of illegality could be found only in the economic journals and not in the judicial reports. Diversification mergers, therefore, as the end of the 1960s approached, were still relatively free of constraints imposed by the enforcement-oriented Supreme Court. The business community hoped to keep it that way until the leanings of the Court could be modified by changes in its composition.

5

THE KENNEDY–JOHNSON
POLICIES

> *It is significant to note—and I would hope that the members of the press would report this, because I have not seen this in many stories—it is significant to note that ITT became the great conglomerate that it was in the two previous administrations primarily, the Kennedy administration and the Johnson administration. It grew and grew and grew, and nothing was done to stop it.*

> Richard M. Nixon
> March 24, 1972

In so saying, President Nixon was not far off the mark, if indeed at all. In fact, he could, with equal accuracy, have expanded his coverage to include the Eisenhower administration (although, to be fair, conglomerate merger activity was less frenetic during the Eisenhower years).

The growth of ITT and other conglomerate firms from 1960 to 1968 indeed did occur under a relatively benign antitrust enforcement policy. Despite a great deal of furor in economic and legal journals, and protestations from pro-antitrust senators and congressmen, the antitrust enforcement officials seemed unclear about the extent of their power to halt diversification acquisitions and reluctant to test that power.

While it is true that the Democratic administrations in office from 1961 to 1969 filed in total over one hundred merger complaints—more than twice as many as had been filed during the Eisenhower adminstration— those complaints predominantly challenged horizontal and vertical mergers. The Antitrust Division during the Kennedy-Johnson years filed but ten complaints against conglomerate mergers. Of these, only two involved conglomerate mergers by corporations which would appear on the FTC's list of the twenty-five most active acquiring corporations in the 1960s. In both these complaints, moreover, the government tried to cast these acquisitions as horizontal by claiming that the merging corporations were actual competitors. In the case of the government's complaint against Ling-Temco Electronics's merger with Chance-Vought, the district court, after trial, found the merger to be a diversification, seeing only insubstantial actual competition between the firms. With that finding, the government dropped the case, choosing not to appeal to the Supreme Court. Similarly, in the case of the complaint against FMC Corporation's acquisition of American Viscose, where the government also claimed horizontal effects, the judge who heard the case on the government's motion for a preliminary injunction found that the merger was purely a diversification and denied the preliminary injunction. In this instance the government then dropped the case without ever going to trial. In at least two cases, therefore, the government voluntarily gave up the opportunity for Supreme Court review of conglomerate mergers.

Thus, the growth of the large conglomerates went virtually unchallenged. The chain of mergers which brought them to the top of the acquisition lists were not attacked. Of course, a conglomerate probably would face antitrust attack if it attempted to build upon its prior acquisitions by making an additional acquisition of a competitor. For example, when Gulf & Western acquired Desilu Productions following its unchallenged 1966 acquisition of Paramount Pictures, the government filed suit and forced divestiture of Desilu.

The large conglomerates were also fully aware that certain types of diversification mergers were to be avoided. The circumstances which were present in the handful of merger complaints filed against less-active acquiring companies were shunned by the large conglomerates. Those complaints involved two kinds of factual situations. One was where the industry was susceptible to the practice of reciprocity and where the acquiring firm, according to the Antitrust Division, had demonstrated a proclivity for reciprocity. Allegations of reciprocity were contained, for example, in the complaints against General Dynamics's acquisition of Liquid Carbonics, and in R. J. Reynolds Tobacco Company's acquisition of Penick & Ford. This theory was premised upon the Supreme Court's strong criticism of reciprocity in the Consolidated Foods case. The other situation was where the acquired product line could be integrated neatly into the marketing and promotional activities of the acquiring firm, and would eliminate potential competition between the two firms or result in advantages which were unattainable by single-line competitors, i.e., a "product extension." This was the theory, for example, of the complaints against Wilson Sporting Goods's acquisition of Nissen Corporation, and First National City Bank's acquisition of the Carte Blanche credit card operation of Hilton Hotel Corporation. This theory followed from the Supreme Court's decision against Procter & Gamble's acquisition of Clorox, which had brought into issue Procter & Gamble's advertising power and its potential competition in the liquid bleach industry.

THE KENNEDY-JOHNSON POLICIES / 39

During this same period, the other antitrust enforcement agency, the FTC, was little more active in bringing complaints against conglomerate mergers. The FTC did initiate both the Procter & Gamble and Consolidated Foods cases, the only product diversification merger cases to reach the Supreme Court in the 1960s (although both cases had been started during the Eisenhower administration). But of the dozen conglomerate merger cases initiated by the FTC from 1960 through 1968, only one complaint involved one of the twenty-five most active acquiring companies; that was Occidental Petroleum's acquisition of Hooker Chemical, where the FTC also claimed a competitive overlap in chemical fertilizers. (This case was settled by a consent order.)

Nor did the FTC's complaints—with one possible exception—seek to plow new ground. The complaints rather were premised upon the basic theories of potential competition, and (to a lesser extent) reciprocity and the "decisive competitive advantage" of product extension. The exception was the August, 1968 complaint against the acquisition by Kennecott Copper Corporation, a large copper producer, of Peabody Coal Company, one of the leading coal producers. The product relationships appeared to be sufficiently remote to escape censure under the law as it had developed to that time. Nevertheless, FTC Chairman Paul Rand Dixon, apparently sensing an opportunity for the FTC to move toward the forefront in conglomerate merger enforcement, brought that case to the commission even after the Antitrust Division chief, Donald F. Turner, had indicated a lack of enforcement interest.

If during the Kennedy and Johnson administrations conglomerate mergers on the whole did enjoy an hospitable enforcement policy—and it certainly seems they did—where was the policy making focus? Was this White House policy or did it reflect the propensities of the Antitrust Division chief? To be sure, antitrust rarely has appeared as a subject of high presidential interest. The extent of direct concern usually has been evidenced by a sentence or two in the State of the Union message, tying antitrust abstractly to some cure of an economic ill such as inflation or depression. The principal exception probably was Theodore Roosevelt, who tried with some success to instill life into the Sherman Act, little more than ten years old when Roosevelt assumed office but already apparently moribund. Woodrow Wilson also publicly supported antitrust; he was influential in the 1914 enactment of the Clayton Act— which included the original antimerger prohibition in Section 7—and the Federal Trade Commission Act which created that agency.

Generally speaking, however, the tenor of antitrust policy at any particular moment has depended primarily upon the philosophy and fervor of the Antitrust Division chief (and sometimes the attorney general).

The principal imprint of presidents has been in their selection of the occupants of those offices.

It seems fair to say that the Kennedy and Johnson administrations followed this expected form. President Kennedy's first appointment as Antitrust Division chief was highly regarded. He was Lee Loevinger, a Minneapolis lawyer of varied government experience (including five years early in his career as a trial attorney with the Antitrust Division), who had become a justice of the Minnesota Supreme Court. In June, 1963 Loevinger left the Antitrust Division (to become chairman of the Federal Communications Commission), and was succeeded by William H. Orrick, Jr., a well-known San Francisco lawyer who had already been in the Justice Department in other positions since the beginning of the Kennedy administration.

After President Johnson assumed office, he retained Orrick as Antitrust Division chief until April, 1965. Then just after Orrick had promised the Senate Antitrust Subcommittee that he intended to devote greater enforcement attention to conglomerate mergers, Johnson announced that he was replacing Orrick.* As Orrick's successor Johnson selected Donald F. Turner, a Harvard Law School professor with a wide reputation as an antitrust scholar. If Johnson indeed wanted to hold back on enforcement against conglomerate mergers, while at the same time installing an antitrust enforcement chief whom liberals would find difficult to fault, he had, in Turner, made a shrewd choice. For Turner not only was a lawyer (a graduate of Yale Law School) experienced in antitrust, but also held a doctorate in economics from Harvard. He had, moreover, once served as law clerk to Supreme Court Justice Tom Clark who, it will be recalled, consistently voted in favor of the government in merger cases before the Supreme Court.

Turner was sworn into office in July, 1965, and served as head of the Antitrust Division for the next three years, during the white-heat period of the conglomerate merger wave. Turner's background, considered alone, might have led an observer to suspect that he probably would move with some force against conglomerate mergers. But the fact is that Turner was already on record with ambivalent views about the power, and indeed even the need, to take any vigorous action against the growth of conglomerate firms.

Turner had been one of the most active commentators on the antitrust scene ever to be appointed to serve as antitrust assistant. Together

---

*In the 1960s there was considerable speculation that President Johnson deliberately sought to downplay antitrust enforcement to hold business support for his Vietnam policies. If so, Johnson undoubtedly was shrewd enough to achieve this result by selection of amenable enforcement officials, rather than by direct orders.

with Carl Kaysen, he had authored a leading treatise entitled "Antitrust Policy." And his *Harvard Law Review* article in May, 1965 still remains as perhaps the most noted exploration of the legal-economic context of conglomerate mergers. Turner urged caution in moving into this still-uncharted territory; he suggested that a limited number of general rules should cover carefully defined situations, principally the three judicially accepted rules discussed previously, i.e., potential competition, reciprocity, and decisive competitive advantage. But he suggested:

> One cannot support an attack of much greater breadth on conglomerates without trenching on significant economic and other values, and therefore without an unprecedented reliance on judgments of an essentially political nature. There are indeed many who will rousingly make those judgments. There are many who firmly believe that "superconcentration" —further concentration of assets in the hands of large conglomerate firms— is a very bad thing, even if devoid of any anticompetitive consequences. . . .
>
> I do not believe Congress has given the courts and the FTC a mandate to campaign against "superconcentration" in the absence of any evidence of harm to competition. In light of the bitterly disputed issues involved, I believe that the courts should demand of Congress that it translate any further directive into something more formidable than sonorous phrases in the pages of the Congressional Record.

Turner also indicated disagreement with the proposition that a conglomerate merger should be subject to attack on the ground that it gives rise to economies, even promotional economies; to his mind, efficiency is one of the benefits of competition that the antitrust laws are intended to promote. Turner thus, it would appear, might disagree with some of the Supreme Court's reasoning in the Procter & Gamble-Clorox decision.

After taking office as assistant attorney general, Turner said, "I think the approach I took in that [*Harvard Law Review*] article would more or less indicate the approach that I would continue to take." This furnished the conglomerates' antitrust advisers with a fair roadmap, and the *Harvard Law Review* with a spate of orders for its May, 1965 issue. While the conglomerates had always, it seems, enjoyed a low level of antitrust enforcement interest, never before had they possessed a planning document as authoritative as Turner's article.

Given his announced views on conglomerate mergers, the conglomerates also liked Turner's approach to antitrust policy making. Turner did not conceive it to be his function merely to offer up novel cases to the Supreme Court just because the Antitrust Division career staff, or some senators and congressmen, thought that a class of mergers could be swept up under the pervasive language of Section 7 of the Clayton Act. Turner took the political view of his office (as contrasted to the more hard-line bureaucratic view), by which he would seek to judge the ultimate economic benefits (or detriments) of the Antitrust Division's enforcement decisions. Thus, Turner said:

> It is the duty of the Department of Justice not to bring a case simply on the basis that it thinks it *can* win, but to bring only those cases that it thinks it *should* win. ... It is inconceivable to me how anybody can operate in this position under the assumption he is going to throw everything at the Court that he can give any conceivable basis for, on the chance he will make out with it. I think this is far too important an element in our national economic policy to be handled that way.

In short, in Turner the president had chosen a man who, on the basis of his own prior utterances, would be quite comfortable with an enforcement policy which, by and large, left alone conglomerate mergers. This expectation in fact was borne out by subsequent events—the Antitrust Division during Turner's three-year tenure filed only five complaints against conglomerate mergers (none involving the twenty-five largest acquiring corporations of the 1960s). All five complaints were against mergers having seemingly close product relationships: two of the mergers involved electric razor producers merging with safety razor manufacturers; another involved the acquisition of an independent credit card operation by a commercial bank; the fourth was acquisition of a gymnastics equipment maker by a manufacturer of a diversified line of sporting goods equipment; and the fifth (which probably was closer to horizontal than conglomerate) was the acquisition of a trust business by a commercial bank. All five were quite ordinary cases in the context of existing conglomerate merger law; Turner was not attempting to penetrate any new frontiers. Indeed, on those rare occasions when a conglomerate contemplating an acquisition asked for Turner's advance blessing (a practice not followed by most conglomerates), it was usually received, as in Continental Oil's merger with Consolidation Coal. Similarly, Turner approved the North American-Rockwell merger, the only condition being that they eliminate, by sale, existing competition between certain of their subsidiaries.

The tranquility of Turner's conservative approach to conglomerate merger policy was disturbed only when Ramsey Clark became attorney general of the United States.

In October, 1966 Ramsey Clark assumed leadership of the Justice Department, succeeding Nicholas Katzenbach, who had been content to leave antitrust enforcement policy in Turner's hands. Clark, however, was not so compliant. Not only did he have a good knowledge of the role of antitrust in industrial performance, but he also had some definite ideas of how the antitrust laws should be enforced. His view went considerably beyond the enforcement limits favored by Turner. Ramsey Clark's father, Justice Tom Clark (for whom, ironically Turner had once served as law clerk), was one of the five justices who had consistently voted in favor of the government in merger cases before the Supreme Court. (The elder Clark, however, resigned from the Supreme Court after Ramsey Clark became attorney general, on the ground that their relationship might create an appearance of conflict of interest when government suits came before the Supreme Court.)

Almost immediately upon Ramsey Clark's assumption of control in the Justice Department, an antitrust policy conflict between him and Turner occurred. That conflict happened to relate to a case involving ITT, i.e., its proposed merger with American Broadcasting Corporation (ABC). That merger was agreed upon in 1966, with ITT to issue shares valued at some $400 million in exchange for all ABC shares. ABC was best known for its television network, which had some 135 affiliated stations, and its radio network, but it also owned five television and twelve radio stations, as well as the Paramount movie theater chain, the nation's largest. Geneen saw a chance to rival RCA, which owned NBC, as an industrial-communications-broadcast complex which would reach into every American household.

The Antitrust Division investigated the proposed ITT-ABC merger at some length, but Turner decided not to file an antitrust suit. The merger still needed the approval, however, of the Federal Communications Commission (FCC) for transfer of ABC's broadcast licenses; that agency had held its hearings in September, 1966, one month before Clark took over leadership of the Justice Department. Clark took heed of the complaints from a number of senators and congressmen who opposed the merger, and of the rumblings of the Antitrust Division's career staff, whose members generally favored a much harder line against conglomerate mergers. With this support, and from his own personal interest in the case, Clark directed Turner to intervene in the FCC proceeding to try to prevent that agency from approving the merger. Reluctantly Turner did as he was instructed. In December, 1966—three months after the FCC hearings— Turner delivered a letter to the FCC expressing concern over the competitive effects of the merger. Turner's letter went on to point out, however, that "the possibilities of such anticompetitive consequences seem sufficiently speculative that we are not presently contemplating an action under the antitrust laws." The FCC rejected this appeal, and approved the merger that same month. Clark was dissatisfied and, taking virtually personal control of the case, had the Justice Department ask the FCC for a rehearing, claiming that the agency had given inadequate attention to competitive considerations. While the FCC majority felt that this belated request came with poor grace, they felt obliged to listen to another government agency, and a rehearing was held in April, 1967.

The Justice Department's stance against the merger now toughened considerably. At the rehearing before the FCC the department's objections fairly ran the gamut of the established Section 7 theories, i.e., that the merger would remove ITT as a potential competitor of ABC in network television, either by establishment of a fourth network or by a national cable television (CATV) grid; and that ITT would employ reciprocity to induce its suppliers to advertise over the ABC network. The Justice Department also feared that ITT would, for some reason, cease development of new broadcast technology because of its affiliation with ABC (although ITT was not in the United States broadcast equipment market). Finally, the department and other critics complained that ITT's economic interests would threaten the independence of ABC's news and public affairs programing, because ABC's activities necessarily would be controlled so as not to endanger ITT's relationships with major customers or foreign governments from which ITT had obtained concessions. (This latter argument would appear to be a considerable stretching of the concept of "competitive considerations," but under the FCC's public interest standard practically any kind of argument would be received.)

There was also evidence introduced which, according to some observers, foreshadowed the activities of ITT public relations personnel in the later merger cases. Thus, there were charges of ITT's attempting to influence newspapers to avoid unfavorable stories about the merger. (The FCC majority felt, however, that ITT generally did no "more than ask reporters covering tne proceeding to be factually accurate in their reporting.") Antitrust Division staff members also complained of the flood of letters received from congressmen urging approval of the merger, most of which they presumed were spurred by ITT and ABC lobbying efforts.

The Justice Department's opposition to the merger was unavailing. In June, 1967 the FCC, by the same 4-3 vote as its original decision, reaffirmed its approval of the merger. The majority rejected the Justice Department's charge that ITT was a likely independent potential competitor of the major networks. True, Geneen had been interested in broadcasting and once had even vowed to make "a sizeable entry" into television. But the FCC found the economic prospects of a fourth television network or a competing CATV grid so dismal that not even ITT— particularly lacking, as it did, broadcast knowhow—would have dared to attempt independent entry. As for reciprocity, ITT was found to have no desire or real power to influence its suppliers in their placement of television advertising, and the theoretically possible foreclosure from any practice of reciprocity was in any event minimal.

Rather than being anticompetitive, the FCC majority found that ITT would bring needed technological strength and financial resources to ABC's weakened television network operations and ease its competitive disadvantage. ITT, as "a large diversified company with strong financial resources," could supply the funds needed for conversion to color programing and modernization of facilities. Geneen had committed himself that ABC would remain autonomous and would have a majority of independent directors; the FCC majority therefore found no reasonable doubt that "the integrity and independence of ABC's activities in the news, information and public affairs field will be maintained after the merger."

The Justice Department under Clark, now in for a fight to the last, decided to appeal the FCC's decision to the court of appeals, which could be counted on to drag the matter out for at least another year. In January, 1968, however, before any decision on appeal, ITT withdrew from the merger agreement. ITT announced simply that the past and prospective delays had made the merger no longer in the interests of the stockholders. Various explanations have been put forward as the real reason. One is that Geneen by that time was angry and fed up with the whole affair. A more plausible reason is that ITT did not want its reserved shares tied up any longer, as the pendency of the unconsummated ABC merger made difficult the negotiation of any other substantial mergers. Coupled with this was the fact that in the almost two years since the merger agreement the relative share values had changed to the disadvantage of ITT's shareholders, i.e., ITT's shares had increased in a greater proportion than had ABC's. Finally, it may be noted that ITT, in common with other large conglomerates, was anxious to keep conglomerate merger issues out of the Supreme Court, and it was beginning to look as though ITT would end up there if it continued with the merger.

Except for the ITT-ABC case, however, Clark was unable, in the face of Turner's opposition, to bring about an aggressive enforcement policy against conglomerate mergers. Turner stuck to his position that the antitrust laws, as presently written, were not sufficient in any event to deal effectively with conglomerate mergers; if Congress wanted to stop the conglomerate merger movement, new legislation should be passed. The solution to the problem—if there were a problem—was therefore in the hands of Congress rather than of the Justice Department. Clark was unable to budge Turner on this point, and perhaps felt that his hands were tied in view of Johnson's personal role in the selection of Turner.

Just after taking office Turner had promised that he would give the business community more concrete guidance than was then available in the merger area. He proposed to do this by issuing a set of guidelines detailing the circumstances under which the Antitrust Division would bring suits against mergers. These guidelines, of course, would be considerably more specific than the general language of Section 7 of the Clayton Act. Not until June, 1968, on the eve of Turner's departure from the Antitrust Division, were the guidelines issued. While the guidelines, though more specific than the statute, still left large gray areas of flexibility for the Antitrust Division, nevertheless the section on conglomerate mergers hewed rather closely to the judicially accepted theories which envisioned close product relationships giving rise to elimination of potential competition, or the creation of undue competitive advantages, or reciprocity. Despite the rather emphatic tone of these guidelines, they were far less than a call to arms against the conglomerate merger movement. One Antitrust Division staff member, who had hoped to see a greater sweep to the guidelines, was quoted as saying, "If the guidelines had existed three years ago, I know of no case we did not bring that we would have brought had we had the guidelines." One antitrust lawyer in private practice observed that "the Guidelines are really Nonguidelines in the conglomerate field."

In June, 1968, coinciding with the release of the merger guidelines—and only seven months before Johnson's term of office was scheduled to end—Turner unexpectedly resigned his position in the Justice Department to return to Harvard Law School. By that time Clark had succeeded in having President Johnson appoint a nongovernmental commission to study conglomerate merger policy (of which more will be said in the following chapter), and perhaps Turner had the uneasy feeling that he was being second-guessed. For the balance of Johnson's term the Antitrust Division was headed by Edwin Zimmerman, a former Stanford law professor who had served as Turner's deputy.

The public record of the Kennedy-Johnson years, while replete with merger announcements, contains scant criticism of the Antitrust Division's conglomerate merger policies. Generally speaking, antitrust nonenforcement is not particularly newsworthy, unless a specific merger strikes the fancy of a critic (such as a senator or congressman) who can catch the attention of the news media (as was the case with Continental Oil Company's acquisition of Consolidation Coal Company). The pro-antitrust economists and professors (the private antitrust bar can hardly be expected to complain of antitrust inattention) lack the clout to generate public outrage. Former Federal Trade Commissioner James M. Nicholson has noted "the indifference that antitrust seems to engender in the collective public consciousness."

Nevertheless, by 1967 there were beginning to be heard murmurs of dissatisfaction over the Democratic policies. The *Washington Post* complained that antitrust policy had "fallen into an innocuous state of desuetude"; the Justice Department's merger enforcement "is noteworthy for its inaction." An article in the *Wall Street Journal* seemed to confirm the *Post*'s factual premise: "Antitrust enforcement in the traditional sense is becoming an anachronism in this era of the Great Society; the declining number of significant antitrust suits attests to that." A *Time* report told its readers that the Justice Department had grown "more cautious" in antitrust enforcement (it probably would have been more accurate to say it had remained cautious).*

Richard J. Barber noted in *The American Corporation:* "Since 1960 more than 80 percent of all the major mergers that have taken place have been of the conglomerate variety, yet this category of mergers has received strikingly little, only spasmodic attention from the antitrust enforcement agencies." Barber went on to charge: "For Kennedy and Johnson no less than Eisenhower and Truman, the corporate behemoths that roam American industry were too big, too dangerous prey."

Save for the uncertainty felt after Clark became attorney general, the leaders of the conglomerates were pleased with the Antitrust Division's inaction. But, of course, it was not in their interests to say so. On the contrary, the conglomerates' public stance would be dissatisfaction even with the minimal Kennedy-Johnson enforcement. Thus, in 1968 Roy L. Ash, president of Litton Industries—which had never been sued for any of its 1960–68 acquisitions, totaling some $610 million in acquired assets —was complaining: "Unhappily, the application of the antitrust laws, particularly in cases of conglomerate mergers, seems to be aimed directly at making sure that a minimum number of bridges are built between different industries and the technologies that they employ."

It was part of the game that the conglomerate corporations would continue to protest even while being treated gently; by keeping the pressure on, they hoped to avoid future policy changes in their disfavor. Given the Supreme Court's demonstrated progovernment leanings in merger suits, it was manifestly important to influence the executive branch to continue holding to a low-key merger enforcement policy.

In summary, the Kennedy-Johnson antitrust assistants kept a low profile on the conglomerate merger issue, even while the merger wave was

---

*In a 1966 column Art Buchwald took a swipe at antitrust inaction by hypothesizing a 1978 scene where, after due study, the Justice Department was persuaded to approve a merger between the only two companies left in the United States on their assurance that it would increase efficiency and was "the American way." Supreme Court Justice Douglas reprinted this column as his concurring opinion in the Pabst-Blatz merger case.

reaching unprecedented heights. From 1965 to 1968 Turner greeted outcries for more vigorous enforcement action against conglomerates with the observation that this determination should await completion of his merger guidelines and that congressional action probably would be needed. This, of course, was tantamount to a green light for the conglomerates.

6

THE NIXON PROMISE

Antitrust law has seemed to some a convenient weapon with which to attack large conglomerate mergers. If one interprets "elimination of potential competition," "reciprocity," and "foreclosure" as threats to competition, one can always bring and usually win a case against the merger of two large companies, however diverse their activities may be. These are often make-weights.... We seriously doubt that the Antitrust Division should embark upon an active program of challenging conglomerate enterprises on the basis of nebulous fears about size and economic power. Vigorous action on the basis of our present knowledge is not defensible.

Report of President Nixon's Task Force
on Productivity and Competition
February, 1969

Only a year before President Johnson's term of office would end, at the urging of Attorney General Ramsey Clark, Johnson appointed a commission of nongovernment economists and lawyers to study antitrust law enforcement policies with regard to conglomerate mergers. This commission, which came to be referred to by the name of its chairman Phil C. Neal, University of Chicago law dean, included a majority of persons who were known generally to favor vigorous antitrust enforcement. The tenor of the commission's report was predictable.

Ten members of the Neal commission voiced concern over the conglomerate merger trend:

Current data confirm that the number and scale of mergers, and particularly of conglomerate mergers, have been accelerating rapidly and continue to accelerate. Individual firms have achieved spectacular growth in this way. There is no comparable trend toward reduction in corporate size through spinoffs of assets. The current rate and pattern of mergers is causing significant and apparently permanent changes in the structure of the economy, and the long-run impact of these changes cannot be readily foreseen.

But even this pro-antitrust group expressed some puzzlement over what to do about conglomerate mergers. The problem was, they said, that "the antitrust laws leave relatively wide latitude for conglomerate mergers." The solution, they suggested, would be new legislation to prohibit a "large firm" (i.e., one having annual sales of $500 million or assets of $250 million) from acquiring a "leading firm" (i.e., one of the top four firms with a 10 percent market share) in any market with a four-firm concentration ratio of more than 50 percent. This recommendation drew dissents from only three members (including Robert H. Bork, later to become solicitor general).

The Neal commission did not rule out stepped-up antimerger enforcement under Section 7 of the Clayton Act. The thrust of its report clearly was anti-large conglomerate mergers. (Indeed, the proposed new legislation would merely supplement, rather than replace or modify, Section 7.) Presumably this "midnight" commission was intended by Attorney General Clark to set the stage for a move toward stronger antimerger enforcement under a succeeding Democratic administration. The election of Nixon in November, 1968 nullified that purpose.

After his election Nixon's economic advisers, fearful of being saddled philosophically with the Neal commission report, persuaded the president-elect to appoint his own independent commission to study antitrust enforcement. This body, named the White House Task Force on Productivity and Competition, was composed of persons generally considered to be more conservative in their leanings than the members of the Neal commission.

The chief architect of the Nixon-appointed commission was Arthur Burns, Nixon's principal economic adviser. If Burns wanted a conservative yet credible report on conglomerate mergers and industrial concentration, his choice of a chairman was inspired. Burns selected another University of Chicago professor, economist George J. Stigler, as the man whose name would grace this commission's report. But Professor Stigler was not known as a friend of big business; on the contrary, in 1952 he had written a widely read article in *Fortune* entitled "The Case against Big Business" in which he called for dissolution of large firms in concentrated industries. Obviously, Stigler's views had mellowed over the years, and presumably Burns knew this beforehand. A conservative report bearing the name of a foe of big business, manifestly, could hardly be criticized as "stacked."

The Stigler commission's nine members unanimously concluded that the growth of conglomerate firms posed little, if any, competitive threat based on known economic hypotheses and observations, and recommended a continuing hands-off policy toward diversification acquisitions unless and until someone (of unspecified identity) were able to come forth with more proof of anticompetitive effects. The conglomerates, said the Stigler commission report, "almost by definition . . . pose at most a minor threat to competition." The report concluded:

We strongly recommend that the Department [of Justice] decline to undertake a program of action against conglomerate mergers and conglomerate enterprises, pending a conference to gather information and opinion on the economic effects of the conglomerate phenomenon. More broadly, we urge the Department to resist the natural temptation to utilize the antitrust laws to combat social problems not related to the competitive functioning of markets.

Against the background of a relatively hospitable conglomerate merger policy under the Democratic administrations from 1961 to 1968, and given the findings of the Stigler commission manifestly designed to counteract the more hawkish sentiments of the Johnson-appointed Neal Commission, the business community could reliably anticipate a lenient antimerger policy in the coming four years.

It was not so much that Nixon himself had said so; he had himself spoken little on this issue. Only once during his campaign had Nixon, adverting to the unsettled law on conglomerate mergers and the fuzziness of the Turner guidelines, vowed "to clarify this entire 'conglomerate' situation." The business community, of course, read this to mean a construction even narrower than Turner's. (This view was confirmed by the Stigler commission's criticism of Turner's guidelines as overly stringent.) Specific promises by Nixon did not seem even to be necessary.

There would be a Republican administration, headed by a president with extensive contacts in the business community and who had most recently practiced law in a Wall Street firm which principally represented business clients. The anticipation of leniency was heightened with the appointment as attorney general of Nixon's campaign manager, John Mitchell, who had spent his professional career practicing corporate law, most recently with the same law firm as Nixon. After the election Mitchell had remarked, perhaps hyperbolically, that "this country is going so far right you won't recognize it." And Mitchell's deputy would be Richard Kleindienst, a Phoenix attorney who was a protégé of Senator Barry Goldwater and who had worked in both the 1964 and 1968 Republican presidential campaigns. Could it be doubted that diversification mergers would have easy going?

Nor would it appear that Nixon would have any difficulty in translating his views into the policy of the Antitrust Division. Nixon was an avowed believer in a "strong presidency"; a major promise was to instill in the federal government managerial competence. Nixon scoffed at the Kennedy-Johnson efforts; the "New Frontier" and the "Great Society" had been slogans without substance, promising much but delivering little. It was time to emphasize execution and efficiency rather than unattainable schemes, to introduce problem solving methods, which worked in the business world, into the world of government.

Management and control were to become the bywords of Nixon and the executives who made up the White House staff. Their approach was remarkably similar to the personalized style of business management practiced by Harold Geneen; like Geneen, Nixon would delegate to others the responsibility of administration, but not of determining what to administer. H. R. Haldeman, the president's top assistant, approached government as a matter of managing the world's largest corporation. Haldeman was to guide the process of management—he would be, in corporate terms, the executive vice president, seeing to movement, orchestrating the determination of policy, the decisions to be made, and the execution of the White House commands. The substantive areas—the vice presidential level—would be two, foreign and domestic affairs. (In the corporate world, these would be considered rather unwieldy divisions.)

According to the Nixon plan, all important policy decisions were to be made in the White House. Leaving policy determinations to the individual departments of government resulted (so Nixon believed) in a splintered national policy under which competing interests were not sufficiently evaluated and coordinated. The role of the departments would be solely to execute and administer given policy; they would not formulate policy.

In late 1969 John Ehrlichman (then presidential counsel) was promoted to domestic "vice president," to succeed Arthur Burns and Daniel A. Moynihan, who had jointly acted in that capacity. Nixon was dissatisfied with the lack of organizational strength displayed by the latter men (especially when compared with Henry Kissinger's thrust in foreign affairs). Ehrlichman, who had been Haldeman's classmate at UCLA, virtually matched Haldeman in his zeal for managerial efficiency.

The Justice Department, under the charge of John Mitchell, appeared to be the department least likely to buck the policy centralization scheme. For one thing, Mitchell himself, as Nixon's closest adviser, occupied a dual role as a member of the White House policy making group as well as attorney general. For another thing, the Justice Department theoretically by definition should have little room for policy making (although of course the case selection process and the allocation of enforcement resources may be a form of policy making.) Probably the Nixon White House saw little need to concern itself with enforcement of the antitrust laws. The enforcement by the Kennedy and Johnson administrations had not ruffled business feathers (except perhaps at the very end when Ramsey Clark began to take an interest); the Stigler commission report had effectively dealt with the outcries of critics for more action on concentrated industries and conglomerate mergers, the main areas of policy concern. Mitchell and Kleindienst could be counted on to see that the department would strike out in no new antitrust directions that might bring business wrath down upon the administration. Mitchell of course would choose his antitrust assistant, as all his assistants, for their fealty to the basic policies for which the administration would stand. It was unthinkable, needless to say, that any assistant would have much influence on policy, much less be able to make it on his own. If an aberrational assistant should appear, he would not be able to work past Mitchell, who would have ultimate authority for the department's case selection.

With the advent of the Nixon administration, the conglomerate merger movement stepped up from its already frenetic pace. The last quarter of 1968 surpassed any other similar period in history in the number of mergers recorded, and 1968—with its $15 billion in acquired assets—was the record year to date. (The first quarter of 1969 was to surpass even the hectic 1968 pace.) Of course, diversification mergers were already much in evidence, particularly since the late 1950s. But it seemed that the conglomerate firms had exercised some voluntary self-restraint in generally avoiding "supermergers" which they feared might force the Democratic administration to take some action from the sheer force of public opinion. The conglomerate firms were anxious to keep merger policy out of the Supreme Court. The only two decisions by that Court involving conglomerate product diversification mergers, Procter & Gamble's acquisition of Clorox, and Consolidated Foods's acquisition of Gentry, were viewed as relatively limited in effect because of the close and peculiar product relationships involved in the mergers. The conglomerate firms could live with those decisions, but they wanted to avoid a broader test of conglomerate mergers by the Supreme Court as it was then composed. There was reason to believe—as borne out by subsequent events—that President Nixon would have the opportunity to change the Supreme Court's composition in the direction of a less severe attitude toward mergers.

In late 1968, following Nixon's election, and continuing after the change of administration in 1969, ITT picked up its merger activity and in short order entered into agreements for three of its largest acquisitions to date. These were, in chronological order, Canteen Corporation, Grinnell Corporation, and Hartford Fire Insurance Company.

Canteen was the nation's second largest operator of vending and on-site feeding services. Its 1968 revenues were $322.3 million, and it had assets of $141 million. It could provide factories and offices with complete food and snack services for their employees, from candy and cigarette machines up to full operation of cafeterias and dining rooms. ITT agreed to issue $245 million in value of its stock for the Canteen acquisition.

Grinnell, one of the nation's three hundred largest industrial firms with 1968 revenues of $340 million and assets of $185 million, was the leading producer of automatic sprinkler fire protection systems for factories, office and apartment buildings, warehouses, etc., and engaged in several other lines of business (e.g., pipe systems and hangers). Grinnell had only recently emerged from a protracted government antitrust suit in which it was accused of monopolizing the market for accredited central station fire and burglary protection services. The case ultimately went to the Supreme Court; Grinnell lost and was forced to divest its entire interest in that business and to refrain from future acquisitions of other firms in the same business. The demoralizing effect of this setback may have contributed to the Grinnell management's willingness to cast its lot with ITT. For this acquisition ITT agreed to issue some 1.6 million shares of its common stock plus some 1.7 million shares of convertible preferred stock, valued in total at $250 million. ITT was offering a premium (excess of preexisting ITT common stock price over Grinnell common stock price) of $53 per share of Grinnell stock, or a total of $75 million.

The pinnacle of ITT's acquisition plan to date would be the acquisition of Hartford; according to the *Wall Street Journal,* this would be the largest business combination up to that time in the nation's history. Hartford was the sixth largest property and casualty insurance company, with total revenues (premium receipts) of $968.8 million in 1968. Hartford's assets were $1.9 billion, almost half those of ITT itself. Hartford also had excess surplus of $400 million, which made it especially appealing to ITT. The fact was that ITT's acquisition program had made its balance sheet "debt-heavy," that is, the ratio of debt to equity was higher than optimum. Melding Hartford's more favorable debt-equity ratio into ITT's balance sheet manifestly would improve the latter. For this acquisition ITT agreed to issue one share of convertible preferred stock for each share of Hartford common stock, a total of some 21.7 million shares, at an aggregate market value of slightly over $1 billion (based upon the market price of ITT common stock into which the preferred stock would be convertible). ITT would be paying a premium of $28 per Hartford common share, or a total of $600 million. (Because of a ruling of the Connecticut insurance commissioner, the form of the transaction had to be changed from a statutory merger, as originally agreed in April 1969, to an exchange offer. By the time of the offer, in May, 1970, the spread had closed to a premium of $11 per share, still 28 percent.)

Together these three acquisitions would increase ITT's revenues by some 40 percent and would give it an immediate position among the leaders in three important industries. While these acquisitions were to be among ITT's largest, they also appeared to ITT's counsel to be outside the special circumstances present in the Supreme Court's Procter & Gamble and Consolidated Foods decisions. Hence, ITT could confidently expect that an antitrust attack upon these mergers—which would require the advocacy of new theories—would not be forthcoming from the Nixon administration.

7

RICHARD McLAREN
A Different View

The problem is McLaren's a nice little fellow who's a good antitrust lawyer out in Chicago. Now he comes in and all these bright little bastards that worked for the Antitrust Department for years and who hate business with a passion—any business—have taken him over. . . .

Richard M. Nixon, April 19, 1971

The business community saw little reason to change its expectations of the Nixon antitrust policy with the appointment of Richard McLaren as assistant attorney general in charge of the Antitrust Division. McLaren, then fifty-one years of age, was a recognized antitrust law expert. A 1942 graduate of Yale Law School, McLaren had spent almost twenty years with a large Chicago law firm, Chadwell, Keck, Kayser, Ruggles & McLaren. His career had been devoted for the most part to advising and defending corporate clients against charges of antitrust law violations. In 1967-68 McLaren had served as the chairman of the Antitrust Section of the American Bar Association, claimed by some to champion the interests of the business world. A nominal Republican, McLaren was one of several names developed as likely candidates for the antitrust position. McLaren met with Mitchell and Kleindienst in New York in December 1968; they liked him and offered the position. McLaren accepted, but only, he later said, after Mitchell had agreed that "we would have a vigorous antitrust program," and "that we would decide all matters on the merits, there would be no political decisions." Nevertheless, nothing in McLaren's public background would suggest that his philosophy of antitrust law enforcement would not be consonant with the views expressed by the Stigler commission.

McLaren moved into his new office in the Justice Department in February, 1969. The professional career staff of the Antitrust Division greeted his coming with a conspicuous lack of enthusiasm. Many of the career professionals were exasperated by the merger wave and frustrated by the enforcement inaction. They did not expect that their feelings would be ameliorated by the actions of the new administration. But, to their surprise, they found in McLaren an unexpected ally.

In preparation for his new assignment McLaren had begun to refresh himself by extensive review of the literature on antitrust enforcement and issues. While he was already well versed in antitrust law and economics, his prior viewpoint had been almost wholly that of warding off and defending antitrust attacks against his corporate clients. He had to shift his focus to an overview of the functioning of the antitrust laws as a regulatory mechanism in the performance of the United States economy. He believed that he must approach the antitrust laws afresh, by determining for himself the public interest implications of various antitrust policy choices.

After accepting the position, and even before his confirmation, McLaren spent much of his time in study and discussion of the conglomerate merger phenomenon. This was the hottest item in antitrust. It had been at the forefront of the Neal and Stigler commission reports. The FTC economic staff was engaged in a massive study of economic and sociopolitical effects. Numerous congressional hearings had been held, and the pro-antitrust segment of Congress was becoming ever more vociferous in calling for more vigorous merger enforcement. Hardly a week passed that a critique or defense of diversification mergers did not appear in an economic or legal journal.

The more he read in the voluminous literature of conglomerate mergers, the more McLaren began to be swayed by the reasoning of their critics. Since the late 1940s the subject of diversification had been hotly disputed, and this debate had reached a crescendo in the late 1960s. Critics worried that the merger wave was increasing the concentration of productive assets to a degree which seriously threatened nondiversified firms and gave big business an unduly strong voice in governmental policy. The diversified firm was thought to gain a major competitive advantage by its ability to use its larger purchasing power to induce sales of its products (i.e., reciprocity); by its ability to sustain intensive national advertising and promotion; and by its power to support and expand one product line from profits earned in other product lines. Not only were single-line firms disadvantaged, but the conglomerate firms by acquisition removed themselves as potential competitors to one another by internal expansion into new product lines.

These critics worried about how much longer the United States economy could tolerate the continuing wave of conglomerate mergers without suffering perhaps some irreversible damage. The top two hundred United States manufacturing firms now controlled 59 percent of production assets, versus 54 percent in 1960 and 48 percent in 1948. Did not this trend portend ominous, if hard to define, consequences for the United States economic system?

A major difficulty confronting McLaren, of course, was that opinion was sharply divided, and there was very little in the way of empirical analysis of the effects of conglomerate growth. Arrayed against the conglomerate critics such as Corwin Edwards, Willard Mueller, and Walter Adams, were the defenders such as Sumner Slichter, Jesse Markham, and Alfred Kahn. The latter would argue that, in general, conglomerate mergers provide a healthy capital movement mechanism which encourages new business formation, affords a market for business sellouts, and introduces new competition into stagnant industries.

And, of course, McLaren well knew that those who came down on the permissive side of conglomerate growth included not only the antitrust assistants, including Donald Turner, who had served under Presidents Kennedy and Johnson, but also the members of the Stigler commission appointed by President Nixon. In the face of this impressive group of experts who at least found it difficult to disfavor conglomerate mergers, McLaren had to question how much weight his own growing anticonglomerate opinion should carry. Should he attempt to expand the bases for attacking conglomerate mergers? Was his personal assessment of the possible long-range damage from conglomerate mergers a sufficient reason to adopt a stepped-up enforcement policy? McLaren himself posed the broad issue: "The economy of the country is undergoing a radical restructuring. Are the underlying reasons for the change valid ones?" McLaren later cast as follows the dilemma that confronted him:

Early in 1969, we were faced with a growing merger trend and a serious debate about what steps, if any, should be taken to meet it. We were acutely aware of the difficult choices we faced. If our response was not cautious and well-considered, we might have expended vast amounts of our limited resources without producing any lasting public benefit. On the other hand, if we failed to utilize existing law and did nothing, we might by default have allowed a vast and potentially harmful restructuring of our economy to take place now, with little effective means of correcting matters later.

Had McLaren been willing to follow the reasoning of the Stigler commission, he probably would not have undertaken to resolve these questions on his own. Obviously, reasonable men could differ; the questions were difficult and important and properly the subject of economic analysis. Despite the outcry from legislators and economists who favored stronger conglomerate merger enforcement, an easy out for McLaren would be to commission another study, as suggested in the Stigler report. McLaren could hardly have been criticized if he had followed that approach, in view of the ambiguous enforcement policies of his predecessors and the views of the Stigler commission, which included highly reputed economists. Needless to say, a new study group would mean that little or no action would be undertaken against diversification mergers pending the outcome of the study.

But McLaren, from his intensive review of the subject, knew that conglomerate mergers already had been extensively studied, not only by the Neal and Stigler commissions but also by a number of reputable economists acting on their own, and by the FTC's capable Bureau of Economics. Thus, there was already an extensive body of literature authored by recognized antitrust experts. Since these prior studies had not resulted in agreement on appropriate enforcement policy, could another study be expected to contribute anything further, either in empirical data or economic hypotheses?

The main problem with another study, McLaren felt, was that the conglomerate issue was, in a sense, a philosophical matter rather than one of interpretation of available data. The adverse effects feared from conglomerate mergers were a long-term proposition. The effects of those mergers probably could not be determined in the scant twenty years since the phenomenon had begun to gain momentum. Rather, the effects would be more indirect and insidious; perhaps not for a generation could it be told on the basis of observable data whether or not the conglomerate merger wave had weakened our economic system.

McLaren, with considerable encouragement from Antitrust Division career professionals, reached the ultimate conclusion that more intensive enforcement against large conglomerate mergers was called for despite the recommendations of the Stigler report. He came to the belief that "the merger movement was leading to what I felt, at least, and I know many economists feel, was a very serious concentration. I think that a strong economic case can be made against those mergers." Indeed, McLaren characterized the conglomerate merger wave as involving "the restructuring of industry that I thought was coming about in an almost idiotic way."

A key element in McLaren's thinking was his assessment that there was little virtue to conglomerate growth to offset its possible adverse consequences. McLaren did not buy synergism: "It is fair to suggest," he later said, "that those who see an incompatibility between efficiency and low concentration are in error." On the contrary, "Market power and the security of bigness, with the concomitant vested interest in the status quo, may have a stultifying effect [on research and innovation]." McLaren sided with those economists who believed that the benefits possibly obtainable from a permissive view of conglomerates were insufficient to offset the serious risk of long-range damage to a freely functioning competitive economy. A more stringent policy toward conglomerate mergers, McLaren concluded, would itself not harm our economic functioning; by restricting large firm growth, ample opportunity for diversification still would be left to the medium sized and small firms, which would improve their competitive significance and preserve capital-movement and sellout opportunities.

It was therefore important, McLaren thought, to intervene in the conglomerate merger process before it went further, in order to "protect our political system by promoting a broad dispersion of economic power among the many, rather than concentration in the hands of a few." McLaren's reasoning certainly resembled more closely the philosophy expressed in the Neal commission report than that of the Stigler commission report designed to offset the former. Thus, by a curious anomaly, the Nixon appointee came to embrace the philosophy avowed by the antitrust advisers appointed by Nixon's predecessor.

Having determined his preferred enforcement policy on economic grounds, McLaren still faced the question, would the courts accept an expanded attack upon conglomerate mergers? Or would a new enforcement attack be no more than a waste of enforcement resources?

There were acknowledged difficulties in stopping conglomerate mergers, as McLaren's predecessor had often pointed out. There was little question that Congress intended Section 7 of the Clayton Act, as amended in 1950, to apply to conglomerate mergers; indeed, the committee reports specifically said so. And the Supreme Court in general terms, and in the specific circumstances of the Procter & Gamble and Consolidated Foods cases, had affirmed this coverage. But Congress had provided little or no guidance on the standards by which the legality of a conglomerate merger should be tested. It had spoken in generalities, leaving to the courts the matter of determining how conglomerate mergers might lessen competition, and the courts thus far had decided relatively few conglomerate merger cases.

It seemed clear by 1969 that the courts might find a lessening of competition if the merging firms had theretofore been potential competitors of each other in a particular market, or if there was a close and unique interproduct relationship between the merging firms which would lead to an unusual competitive advantage for one of the merging firms, or if the merger probably would lead to the practice of reciprocity.

But those theories were limited. Where the products of the merging firms were not closely related, these theories seemed to furnish little basis for a legal attack. In about one-half of the conglomerate mergers in the 1960s, the products of the two firms had borne little or no relationship to each other, as reported by the FTC. The remainder did involve some significant product relationships, to varying degrees, but most of these probably were not sufficiently close to bring the merger under the decided cases. The conglomerate firm already knew that if it wanted to continue to grow, it must forswear reciprocity and must seek acquisitions which did not fit hand-in-glove with existing product lines. This limitation seemed to have little adverse impact upon the conglomerate firms' ability to find attractive—and apparently legally safe—acquisition opportunities.

McLaren knew, therefore, that the existing judicially accepted theories must be expanded considerably if the conglomerate merger wave were to be stopped. The conglomerate situations which had been involved in past cases were simply too narrow for his purposes. At the outset of his new merger policy, McLaren recognized this limitation: "I anticipate that we will be bringing cases that seem to us to be logical next steps, i.e., somewhat beyond what the Supreme Court has already decided, in the development of the law. . . . This effort may require us to ask the courts to adapt established theories to new circumstances, or to fashion new tests to meet new needs, in order to insure that the objectives of the Congress are achieved."

Still, McLaren believed that he could not afford to rest an expanded attack on conglomerate mergers simply on assertions of possible unspecified future damage to our economic system, on theories of mutual interdependence or forbearance among the largest firms, upon sheer data as to asset control by the largest firms, or upon theories of undue power to influence governmental actions. True, these were the ultimate effects which were feared, but McLaren knew that they were too speculative and untried for the courts to accept in one fell swoop. While McLaren "shared the concern of those who stressed the financial, social, and political implications of the merger movement," he recognized that "the principal emphasis had to be placed on the competitive implications of this trend." Hence, the Department of Justice must ease toward its ultimate position by starting with an intermediate position tied to precedent. This intermediate position was available and spelled out in the literature: it was "reciprocity effect." This theory did not depend upon a showing of actual use of reciprocity, or of intent to benefit from reciprocity. Rather, it proceeded from the presumption that if the product relationships made reciprocity possible, the suppliers of one of the merging firms would naturally turn to the other merging firm for their purchases in order to maintain good will. Hence, competitors of the merging firms would lose an opportunity to make sales in a freely competitive market. The market would be clogged by reciprocity; the unrestricted demand level would be shrunk; and new entrants would be discouraged since they would have to capture a larger share of a smaller unrestricted market in order to achieve minimum efficient scale.

McLaren could take some comfort from the virtually universal sentiment that reciprocity as such was antithetical to our notion of free competition (though not necessarily unlawful). In Consolidated Foods the Supreme Court had thoroughly condemned reciprocity practice as a bad thing. Even in the literature the few apologists for reciprocity did not go so far as to defend it, but rather claimed that it had little real impact upon purchasing decisions and was so slight as not to produce any anticompetitive effect.

Economic commentators observed that reciprocity was the domain of the diversified, multiproduct firm. The reciprocity practitioner had to bestow substantial dollar volumes of business to its suppliers, and also had to be making a product (or products) purchased by those suppliers. This profile fitted nicely the multiline producer of industrial goods. (Consumer goods of most types were unsuitable for reciprocity because of their dispersal characteristics; reciprocity works best where purchases are concentrated.) Indeed, some economists claimed that diversification decisions were often impelled by the opportunity to add a product line which would enable a firm to make reciprocity use of its purchasing power. And many, such as the Columbia law professor Harlan M. Blake, believed that "reciprocity is as inevitable a result of widespread conglomerate structure as price rigidity is a consequence of oligopoly structure."

Before 1969 the Justice Department had initiated two cases in which it tentatively sought to stretch the reciprocity theory, one against Ingersoll-Rand Company and the other R. J. Reynolds Tobacco Company. McLaren's predecessors, however, seemed to have limited their efforts to circumstances where an historical use of reciprocity could be claimed to furnish support for a prediction of its future use. In preliminary injunction rulings the court in the Reynolds case refused to accept this prediction; the government did obtain a preliminary injunction, and some language in its favor, in the Ingersoll-Rand preliminary injunction ruling, but the factual setting included strong horizontal merger overtones, and the reciprocity discussion appeared superfluous. In neither of those cases was a final decision rendered, both being settled by consent judgments. The pre-Nixon Antitrust Division had made no further efforts to expand the reciprocity theory.

Even though McLaren recognized that his support was slight and that he would be making a considerable leap, he decided to go with an expanded reciprocity—or "reciprocity effect"—theory. This was to be the first string in McLaren's bow. His broader theory of the dangers inherent in sheer economic concentration and the interdependence, forbearance, and power stemming therefrom would be a tag-along. But if McLaren could gain judicial acceptance of the latter theory (usually referred to as an "aggregate concentration" theory), he knew that a giant step toward halting the merger wave would have been taken. McLaren acknowledged that this was his real interest: "Basically, what we were shooting for, from the beginning of 1969, was to stop this merger trend that was leading more and more toward economic concentration."

To that time, the aggregate concentration theory had had no definite judicial acceptance; but neither had it been definitely rejected. Indeed, there were numerous judicial dicta in which increasing economic concentration had been branded undesirable. The legislative history of amended Section 7 was almost totally premised upon general concerns over increasing economic concentration, and the Supreme Court had sweepingly condemned, in passing, the growth of concentration. The FTC studies had indicated that virtually the entire 11 percent increase in aggregate concentration within the two hundred largest manufacturing firms from 1948 to 1968 had come about by mergers. Hence, the conglomerate merger critics reasoned that since Congress was most concerned with preventing increases in concentration, and since Congress intended amended Section 7 to apply to conglomerate acquisitions, Congress must have intended that increases in economic concentration generally, rather than merely in a specific market, would be a highly pertinent consideration in the enforcement of Section 7.

Manifestly, the targets of McLaren's new policy would hardly be industrial pygmies. To the contrary, they would be among the nation's largest firms, leaders in a number of different industries. McLaren was setting his sights upon large diversification mergers, which generally would mean the five hundred largest industrial firms (or nonindustrial firms of comparable size). It might be anticipated that firms of that size would have considerable political influence, and that they might try to exercise it. To McLaren, however, any thought that political considerations should enter into his decisions was unthinkable. He perceived antitrust as an integral part of our economic system, mandated by the Congress and nourished by decades of administrative and judicial thinking. While particular aspects of that policy might be the subject of genuine disagreement on economic grounds, McLaren felt that antitrust was the last place that political considerations should intrude. But neither was

McLaren naive. The subject of political considerations had occurred to him when he was first approached for his interest in the position. He then told Mitchell that he would accept only on the condition that antitrust policy and enforcement decisions were to be made "on their merits" and without reference to "political" factors. Mitchell responded that this condition was satisfactory and that it would be honored.

Hence, McLaren had little concern that any backlash from the business community, including attempts to lobby to change his policy, could have any effect.

Even as early as his Senate Judiciary Committee confirmation hearings in January, 1969, McLaren was beginning to voice publicly, in preliminary fashion, his concerns over the conglomerate merger wave. He went on to say, however, that he had not yet made up his mind and that the subject would be under continuing study. McLaren perhaps gave some inkling of his leanings when he cautioned businessmen against relying very heavily on the Turner merger guidelines; "We may sue even though particular mergers appear to satisfy those guidelines," McLaren said. Two months later, in another appearance before a congressional committee, McLaren's thinking had further crystallized, and his position was stated more strongly:

My predecessors at the Antitrust Division took the position that "purer" forms of conglomerate mergers could not be reached under Section 7 because, in their view, where merging firms are commercially unrelated, proof cannot generally be made of a reasonable likelihood of a substantial lessening of competition as called for by the Act's provisions. They suggested that conglomerate mergers which threatened undue concentration of economic power should be dealt with through new legislation. . . . I was not persuaded that Section 7 will not reach purer types of conglomerate mergers than have been dealt with by the courts thus far. . . . I am by no means opposed to amendatory legislation, but I feel that the matter is too pressing to wait, and we are willing to risk losing some cases to find out how far Section 7 will take us in halting the current accelerated trend toward concentration by merger and—as I see it—the severe economic and social dislocations attendant thereon.

McLaren's comments received wide circulation in the financial press. The conglomerates were now on notice of McLaren's policy, so it would seem, although, as we shall see, there was considerable incredulity in the business community that this could be the antitrust voice of the Nixon administration.

8

THE SUITS

The three cases against ITT are extremely important to our program of maintaining a competitive market structure. I have every expectation that we will ultimately prevail in these cases, thus obviating what probably would be rather inflexible legislation in this area by the Congress.

Memorandum from Richard McLaren to
John Ehrlichman, July, 1970

McLaren proceeded to put into action his new merger policy. In 1969 the Department of Justice was to file five complaints against large product diversification acquisitions. Three of the cases were against ITT, and one each against LTV and Northwest Industries. A sixth case, against White Consolidated Industries, would be filed in 1970.

ITT barely escaped the dubious distinction of being the first corporation to face a suit under McLaren's new policy. That honor rather went to LTV, which in 1968 had announced its intention to acquire Jones & Laughlin Steel Company (J & L), the nation's sixth largest steel producer, with assets of $1.1 billion. LTV proceeded to acquire some 60 percent of J & L's common stock via tender offer. The Antitrust Division, still under the Johnson administration, began an investigation—a usual move in the case of any large merger and not significantly indicative of enforcement intention since most investigations (which are usually initiated by the career staff) do not result in complaints. When McLaren took office, the investigation was still plodding along, and in March, 1969 LTV made an offer to acquire the balance of the J & L common stock still held by the public.

This spurred McLaren into action. On April 14, 1969 McLaren filed a complaint against this acquisition, alleging elimination of potential competition, enhancement of reciprocity effect, and anticompetitive increase in aggregate concentration. (Attorney General Mitchell routinely approved the filing of this complaint.) The LTV-J & L complaint was a precursor of the ITT complaints, and McLaren's first court filing based upon his expanded theories of conglomerate merger illegality. This complaint, however, never resulted in a judicial decision because, as noted later, it ended in a settlement bearing some similarity to the ITT settlement.

Exactly two weeks later, on April 28, 1969, McLaren filed the first ITT complaint, against its acquisition of Canteen. ITT had earlier made public "negotiation" announcements of all three of its large mergers. The Canteen acquisition was the first scheduled for closing, and McLaren had followed it closely. In March, 1969 he asked ITT and Canteen to supply information about their businesses and the expected impact of the merger. This was the first ITT knew of the Antitrust Division's interest, but it was not yet alarmed. A request for information by the Antitrust Division (or the FTC) was almost standard procedure after announcement of any large merger proposal.

The real sting came, however, when McLaren advised ITT's counsel that he had serious reservations about the Canteen acquisition and asked that its closing be postponed so he could complete his study. ITT, still disbelieving or complacent, agreed to a brief postponement. After completing his study McLaren, on April 7, sent to Mitchell a memorandum describing the ITT-Canteen merger, and requesting authorization to file suit. McLaren also sought permission to ask the court to enjoin preliminarily the merger, pending completion of the trial and the court's final decision. Upon receiving the memorandum Mitchell decided to disqualify himself from this case. He did this, he later explained, because his former law firm, while he had been a partner, had done legal work for Continental Baking Company, which had been acquired by ITT. Responsibility for the case now fell upon Kleindienst, the deputy attorney general, who would function in the role of attorney general with regard to this case.

Having agreed to postpone the merger, ITT's attorneys now asked for a conference with Kleindienst in hopes of dissuading him from approving McLaren's request to bring suit against the Canteen acquisition. This is another of the normal, and usually unsuccessful, precomplaint maneuvers by a company about to be sued. Kleindienst granted the request and, with McLaren present, received the ITT and Canteen attorneys on April 14. At that meeting Howard Aibel, ITT's general counsel, suggested that it was unfair to apply McLaren's new theories to a merger which had already been agreed upon and publicly announced even before the Nixon administration took office. Aibel also charged that McLaren was espousing "a radical construction of the Clayton Act which went way beyond the language of the act and legislative history to have the Clayton Act apply to any merger which involved companies of large size."

The Canteen lawyers said that Canteen faced a "very bad situation"; it had lost some good management people and badly needed the dynamism which ITT would bring. Without ITT's help, Canteen might well suffer a serious competitive decline. At least, they asked, forgo the preliminary injunction request so that Canteen could obtain immediate help. Aibel added that ITT would be perfectly willing to negotiate a "hold-separate" agreement to preserve Canteen as a separate entity and not intermingle its assets with those of other ITT businesses, so that Canteen could be readily separated from ITT in the event a court held the acquisition unlawful.

A short time after this meeting Kleindienst received a call from John Ehrlichman, counsel to the president, asking for a report on the proposed suit against the ITT-Canteen merger. It had come to his attention, said Ehrlichman, that the suit might extend beyond the merger rules applied during the Johnson administration, and if so, the wisdom of such an extension should be considered.

McLaren, when apprised of this request, was taken aback, but only momentarily. He reacted quickly by having one of his assistants, Donald Baker, prepare a memorandum concluding that the ITT-Canteen merger would fall within the Turner merger guidelines. Thus armed, McLaren prepared a memorandum to Ehrlichman, to be signed both by McLaren and Kleindienst, in which he claimed that the proposed complaint fell within the Turner merger guidelines and also had support in prior judicial decisions. While McLaren admitted that his approach went beyond that of the previous administration with regard to "conglomerate mergers involving very large firms," he noted that this approach had been favorably received by Congress, the public, and by business; had been supported by the Council of Economic Advisers; and well might ward off any movement toward unduly restrictive legislation.

Kleindienst and McLaren telephoned Ehrlichman to tell him of the forthcoming memorandum. McLaren said that he was very firm that the suit should proceed. He had, however, concluded that the Justice Department should not seek a preliminary injunction, but rather would accept ITT's proposal to enter into a hold-separate agreement. McLaren later explained that in reaching this decision he considered the problems Canteen was having, and also took into account that "the Chicago court was not known for its sympathy to antitrust," and hence "we would have a good chance of starting out my program with a loss on a preliminary injunction." The memorandum to Ehrlichman, which at his insistence was framed as a request for approval of a suit against the ITT-Canteen merger, was delivered on April 23. Two days later one of Ehrlichman's assistants, Egil Krogh, notified McLaren of Ehrlichman's concurrence in the proposal as modified to eliminate the request for preliminary injunction.

ITT now entered into the hold-separate agreement with the Antitrust Division, and proceeded to consummate the Canteen acquisition. On April 28 the Justice Department filed its suit against the merger in the United States District Court in Chicago. The complaint asked that the acquisition be declared unlawful and that ITT be ordered to divest itself of Canteen.

There no longer appeared to be any doubt about McLaren's direction, and the business world was highly perplexed. Could this really be the voice of the Nixon Republican administration?

It appeared so, for McLaren in May, 1969 filed the third of his complaints against large conglomerate acquisitions, namely Northwest Industries's proposed takeover of B. F. Goodrich Company (which was also opposed by Goodrich management). Northwest had started as a railroad, had formed a holding company, and thereafter made a number of acquisitions which had diversified its operations to include chemicals, steel, wire, and other industrial and consumer products. Goodrich, from its original tire business, had also greatly diversified. The Justice Department's request for a preliminary injunction against the continuation of the exchange offer was denied in July, 1969. The court's opinion basically found that the data presented had not yet been developed sufficiently to show probable illegality under McLaren's reciprocity effect theory; the court also expressed some doubt over the department's aggregate concentration theory. This case was to proceed no further, however; Northwest succeeded in acquiring only 20 percent of Goodrich's stock, and abandoned its attempt to gain control. Because of that abandonment, the Justice Department subsequently dropped the suit.

McLaren's attention turned back to the ITT acquisition proposals for Grinnell and Hartford. From information supplied by ITT McLaren knew that the earliest either could be consummated would be in the late summer. Nevertheless, he instructed his staff to speed up their evaluation with a view toward reaching an early decision. McLaren in fact had promised ITT counsel that he would advise them of his enforcement intention by the end of June.

ITT's counsel, of course, argued vigorously against the filing of the complaints. They claimed that any suits against the mergers would be a considerable stretching of existing antimerger law. This same argument had been made against the Canteen suit, however, and McLaren had tried to justify that suit as within the authority of the Turner merger guidelines. ITT thought that McLaren was deliberately equivocating on this subject: to obtain authority to file the suits, he would say they fit within existing rules (which ITT believed was wholly incorrect); but later, so ITT thought, McLaren would want to take credit for a revolution in merger law.

To head off McLaren's argument of consistency with the Turner guidelines, ITT went to Turner himself, now back teaching law at Harvard. ITT procured from Turner his written opinion that the Hartford merger was unequivocably lawful and there was no basis for a suit against it. McLaren politely answered that he did not agree with Turner and would let the courts decide who was right. He had, he said, determined to file suits against the Hartford and Grinnell mergers.

This time McLaren had little difficulty in obtaining authorization to file complaints, together with requests for preliminary injunctions. Mitchell, having been advised of Ehrlichman's demand for clearance through him of the Canteen complaint, had admonished Kleindienst to rebuff any such suggestions in the future. A subordinate White House official, Mitchell held, was not to have a power of approval over the complaints to be filed by the Justice Department. Kleindienst quickly approved the new complaints.

On August 1, 1969 the Antitrust Division filed two separate complaints against the Hartford and Grinnell acquisitions. Both complaints were filed in the federal district court in Hartford, Connecticut. Both complaints were accompanied by requests for preliminary injunctions against the mergers, pending trial and decision.

With the filing, over a period of three and one-half months in 1969, of his five big cases, McLaren's theories had been translated into concrete language in legal pleadings. The legal documents followed closely the thought process which McLaren had gone through in the early months of 1969. These cases, said McLaren, were "in effect, tests of our policy" that Section 7 applies to "conglomerate mergers, and particularly the mergers that were contributing to and really proliferating a merger trend." In requesting approval of his initial complaint against ITT, McLaren stated his theories:

It has been our position (contrary to that taken by the prior Administration) that conglomerate mergers involving very large firms violate Section 7 of the Clayton Act where (1) significant potential horizontal competition is eliminated; (2) the merger will create reciprocity power which will substantially lessen competition in lines of commerce occupied by either the acquired or the acquiring firm; and (3) where economic concentration and the triggering of further mergers may be anticipated, with effects condemned by Congress when it amended Section 7 of the Clayton Act in 1950.

None of the complaints against ITT made any claim that the merging firms were potential competitors in any specific market, which was the theory most accepted by the courts. All included some product integration claims, along the lines of Procter & Gamble-Clorox. For example, it was claimed that Hartford Insurance personnel could be used to promote Grinnell sprinkler systems; and Levitt would steer the purchasers of its houses to Hartford for their fire insurance.

But the real first strike in all the cases was to be reciprocity effect. ITT was an enormous purchaser of goods and services, in the magnitude of $550 million. It purchased at least $100,000 from each of some 750 suppliers. Practically all these suppliers would need property and liability insurance; many would from time to time construct plants and offices requiring sprinkler systems; and many others would have need for in-plant feeding services of the kind provided by Canteen. Hence, these ITT suppliers were susceptible to pressures or suggestions that they purchase Hartford's insurance policies, Grinnell's sprinkler systems, and Canteen's food services in order to become or continue as suppliers to ITT.

But McLaren was not concerned merely with ITT pressures. If ITT were to utilize its purchasing power to induce suppliers to buy ITT products and services, that would constitute "reciprocity" of the kind present in Consolidated Foods. McLaren was after "reciprocity effect," which he defined as "the tendency of a firm desiring to sell to another company to channel its purchases to that company." In McLaren's view, ITT need do nothing affirmative to pressure its suppliers; those suppliers would favor ITT's products and services in the natural course in order to maintain the good will of ITT. McLaren noted: "Where the large diversified company makes substantial purchases from many suppliers, these suppliers are going to feel a 'reciprocity effect' even without affirmative use of reciprocity by the purchaser. . . . The creation of such power, regardless of whether it is overtly exercised, may have a serious anticompetitive effect."

Finally, McLaren's complaints naturally included his aggregate concentration theory, still somewhat amorphous and evolving. As the Antitrust Division later told a court, this series of cases "is predicated in part on the claim that Section 7 of the Clayton Act prohibits acquisitions by large conglomerate corporations in the course of, and which tend to proliferate, a merger movement where concentration of control of manufacturing assets will be substantially increased and the trend to further concentration will be encouraged."

Apparently seeking to forge some measure of affinity with the established potential competition theory, the complaints asserted that the mergers would reduce the number of potential firms capable of entering concentrated markets. And the combined economic strength of the merging firms would tend to entrench them against their less well-endowed competitors and possible newcomers to the industry, and would force competitors, in self-defense, to seek mergers with larger companies to offset the ITT competitive advantages.

McLaren expanded on his aggregate concentration theory in the following language:

> The present conglomerate merger movement has substantially contributed to the rising level of concentration in the economy. As a result of this trend, many large firms which are substantial competitors in concentrated markets have been acquired by other similar entities. The effect has been to place a steadily increasing percentage of the nation's industrial wealth in the hands of a few giant companies.
>
> The disappearance of many large firms has substantially reduced the number of potential sources of entry into concentrated markets. In addition, the merger movement, which is causing an increasing number of leading firms in concentrated industries to become affiliated with leading firms in other concentrated industries, is entrenching these leading firms and raising barriers to entry. It is thus making deconcentration of those industries less and less likely. The overall result is that leading firms are becoming even more entrenched and barriers to entry are rising.

With the August 1, 1969 filing of the Hartford and Grinnell cases, the die was cast. There had been set in motion the mechanism for a legal test of McLaren's expanded theories, and the signal had been clearly sent to the business world that the Antitrust Division's merger policy had changed.

Even though McLaren's request for authorization to seek a preliminary injunction in the Canteen case had not been granted, McLaren nevertheless decided to request similar authority in the Grinnell and Hartford cases. This time, with Ehrlichman excluded from the cases upon Mitchell's order, McLaren obtained the authority he sought. In retrospect, this may have been a questionable decision.

It is not easy for the government to obtain a preliminary injunction in a merger case, and this normal difficulty is exacerbated when the suit involves novel legal issues. To obtain a preliminary injunction, the Department of Justice must prove that it is likely to succeed in its case upon final decision, and that the public interest requires that the merger be stopped before it can be consummated. The defendant will espouse the position that a preliminary injunction would wreak inordinate hardship upon the merging companies and their stockholders (the stock prices usually having been inflated by the merger announcement with the likelihood of a precipitous decline if the merger is stopped.) Further, it will usually say, there is no real public interest in prohibiting the merger pending final decision because, if the government wins, the illegal merger can be easily remedied by an order of divestiture. As one court had already stated, in refusing to enjoin the proposed FMC Corporation-American Viscose merger, in the case of a conglomerate merger "ordinarily . . . divestiture is a complete and adequate remedy."

The government's main difficulty at this stage is that it has not yet had the opportunity fully to develop and refine its case. Usually a substantial part of its evidence is developed in pretrial discovery where it has the powers of the court to use in obtaining documents and testimony from the merging firms. Hence, if its complaint has a substantial basis, it can expect to strengthen its case through discovery. At the least, its preliminary injunction presentation usually will be raw and weaker than its final evidence.

But if the Department of Justice does not seek a preliminary injunction, it may be subject to the criticism that it should have sought such relief to protect the public interest and even indeed for the benefit of the merging firms—i.e., so that they would not have to undergo the expense and loss of executive time involved in completing an acquisition which later must be undone. Moreover, the divestiture remedy for a completed acquisition has been likened to unscrambling an egg—it is often incomplete, unsatisfactory, and messy.

The preliminary injunction proceeding in theory is a limited, self-contained inquiry which should have no effect upon final decision. But the attorneys know that the evidence and legal theories propounded at the preliminary injunction hearing can make an impression upon the judge and condition him in the direction of the position of one or the other of the parties.

Both the Hartford and Grinnell merger cases were assigned to Judge William H. Timbers, a Republican who had been appointed to the federal bench by President Eisenhower in 1960. Judge Timbers, who had graduated from Yale Law School only two years before McLaren, was to handle the cases from their inception nearly to conclusion.

Both the government and ITT filed with Judge Timbers a number of affidavits, documents, and legal memoranda with regard to the preliminary injunction motions. The court also scheduled hearings beginning September 18, at which the testimony of several witnesses was taken. Both sides made the usual arguments, disagreeing of course upon the probable outcome of the cases at the conclusion of trial. The government argued that, since there was at least a serious question concerning legality, the sheer size of the mergers favored preliminary injunctions. For, it said (prophetically as we shall see), the size of the transactions—and particularly the Hartford merger, as the largest in the nation's history—would make divestiture extremely difficult.

To this, ITT countered that, in the unlikely event it lost the cases, it was agreeable to facilitating divestiture by holding separate the acquired corporations. Thus, a clean break could be made readily if and when the time came. ITT had, it pointed out, voluntarily made this same agreement in the Canteen merger suit and the government had then deemed it sufficient. Why, then, would not the same procedure be adequate in the Hartford and Grinnell cases?

Moreover, ITT argued, a preliminary injunction against either of the mergers would be the death knell for it. The parties to the merger agreements had already publicly announced that the mergers would be abandoned if a preliminary injunction were issued. Both Grinnell and Hartford management agreed with ITT on this. If the mergers were abandoned, the spreads between the stock prices, which had been narrowed by arbitrage transactions, would revert to the former levels. The Grinnell stockholders, therefore, would be deprived of their premium of $53 per share, and the Hartford stockholders of theirs of $28 per share.

Judge Timbers found ITT's arguments the more persuasive at this stage. He denied the government's requests for preliminary injunctions. But he did not simply rest his decision on findings that the possible injury to the merging corporations and their shareholders outweighed the need for an injunction. He went beyond this; he ruled, both as to the Hartford and the Grinnell acquisitions, that the government had shown an insufficient probability of likely success upon final decision. He found the case as thus far developed by the government to be too weak and expressed preliminary doubts about the viability of the government's legal theories. In support of his rulings, Judge Timbers issued a detailed opinion of some thirty-five printed pages which was highly favorable to ITT's legal position, and of course discouraging to the government. (Since ITT had made the offer, however, the court said it would require ITT to hold separate the acquired firms as viable entities to facilitate eventual divestiture should it come.) Thus, the government had not simply lost its preliminary injunction motions, but had lost them in a manner which indicated extensive study of the case by the judge and a negative attitude by him toward the government's case, which would now have to be overcome.

It was now October, 1969. It would take another year for the ITT cases against Canteen and Grinnell to come to trial. After Judge Timbers's decision ITT proceeded to consummate the Grinnell acquisition on

October 31, 1969. The Hartford acquisition continued to be delayed by regulatory proceedings before the Connecticut insurance commissioner. That acquisition ultimately would be completed in May, 1970.

Notwithstanding its elation over Judge Timbers's forceful denial of the government's preliminary injunction motions, ITT knew it still could not afford to rest easy. It had to present a case in court which would be persuasive to the nine Justices of the Supreme Court (who, it was assumed, would be the ultimate arbiter), or else ITT had to persuade the administration that these merger suits were ill-advised and ought to be withdrawn.

9

THE FIRING LINE

The idea was to tell anyone who would listen that we thought the antitrust policy being pushed by the administration was not in the national interest.

Edward Gerrity, vice president for
public relations, ITT, March, 1972

McLaren had moved on the legal front, and the merger cases themselves were now in the hands of the lawyers. But Geneen was both perplexed and incensed; he felt that somehow the business community had been betrayed. For this antimerger policy to come from the Nixon administration was wholly unbelievable and unacceptable.

Geneen did not stand alone; his ire was shared by the leaders of big business, and particularly of the conglomerates. McLaren's new policy was discussed with vehemence not only inside those corporations but also in the councils where business leaders meet to consider business and economic matters of mutual interest.

The complaints filed by McLaren were of concern beyond those having an immediate interest—i.e., ITT, LTV, and Northwest. For the complaints represented more than routine law enforcement; they represented the making of new antitrust policy. The complaints and the ensuing decisions would be a mandate and a guide to the business community. McLaren had said: this is the department's merger policy; all other corporations contemplating mergers are advised to guide themselves accordingly. Antitrust lawyers would no longer be so free in rendering opinions that diversification mergers not involving reciprocity or close product relationships could be lawfully consummated. Account would have to be taken of McLaren's position in the new cases. McLaren had sent an antitrust enforcement policy signal which could not be ignored. *Business Week* noted: "The new team is upsetting the merger plans of multimarket companies by taking a much broader view of the Clayton Act than did their Democratic predecessors. For businessmen, the administration's merger guideline is indeed clear: it says: STOP."

McLaren certainly knew that the signal of his new conglomerate merger policy would not pass without considerable comment. Observers of the antitrust scene were quick to note the enforcement change. Milton Handler said, "There has been a marked intensification of enforcement under the new administration, which has trained its fire principally at conglomerate mergers." Handler went on to express his doubt that "the antitrust laws are the proper vehicle for accomplishing social reforms which bear little or no relationship to the preservation of competition." Kenneth Dam, a University of Chicago law professor who had been a member of the Nixon-appointed Stigler commission, complained, "Never have proposals to an administration been so resoundingly rejected as the Stigler Report's recommendations on conglomerates."

The proponents of stronger conglomerate merger enforcement, after their initial surprise, expressed gratification that their long unanswered pleas had been heeded, without expectation. The heads of the congressional antitrust subcommittees, Senator Philip A. Hart and Congressman Emmanuel Celler, together with some of their colleagues, applauded; they were joined by a smattering of economists and professors. Celler commented, "This development is one that I have long encouraged." And the staff of the House Antitrust Subcommittee commended McLaren for undertaking his conglomerate campaign: "Judicial delineation of the reach of the antitrust laws to changing economic conditions and new corporate organizational structures is a necessary ingredient in resolution of the problems of increasing concentration of economic power."

But the opposition, as is usually the case, was considerably noisier. James J. Ling, chairman of the board of Ling-Temco-Vought—the first target of McLaren's new policy—led off with the charge that the suit against LTV's acquisition of J & L Steel was a "tainted and suspect lawsuit"; it was not "a responsible act"; McLaren was "a legal vivisectionist." Noting that the Johnson administration had not moved against the merger, Ling plaintively queried: "What happened within the Justice Department in its first sixty days under the new Administration to change all of this? What new studies were developed? Who were the expert witnesses called during this time period?"

The antitrust lawyer Howard Adler sympathized with Ling: "There are many problems where one administration issues guidelines under which an acquisition is perhaps all right and that administration probably is not going to sue, and then another administration takes a different view of the antitrust laws and decides that it is not quite sure about the law but it is going to test it out. . . . When you have got $434 million cash invested in a company with a billion dollars in assets, I can see why one would be a little perturbed with that kind of procedure."

Geneen was only somewhat more restrained than Ling in his public statements. There was, said Geneen, "an impression in the business community that a large-scale offensive war has been declared on American business growth, business change and business diversification." Geneen's tack was defense of conglomerate efficiency coupled with allusions to the specter of foreign competition—fast-growing foreign technology supported by lower wage rates and affirmative government assistance. He told his stockholders: "To be able to compete with full effectiveness in overseas markets [ITT] cannot be hamstrung at home. We will resist any attempt to deprive us of our proper rights. It is clear that whatever the guise, by imaginary and strained legal theories, what we are experiencing is a direct attack on bigness as such."

McLaren's conglomerate merger policy, said Geneen, was obsolete: "We must not be hampered with artificial strictures against diversification or against size. We must not be hampered by yesterday's myths in concentrating on today's needs."

Beyond those having an immediate economic interest in the subject, the legal and business periodicals witnessed a spate of comments usual to any antitrust offensive. Of particular note for its scholarly yet acerbic tone was a *Fortune* article by Robert H. Bork, who as a member of the Johnson-appointed Neal commission had been a vigorous dissenter from the majority report's anticonglomerate bias. Bork's article, revealingly titled "Antitrust in Dubious Battle," claimed that "in antitrust policy the Nixon Administration has sprinted away to a fast start in the wrong direction." Bork charged that McLaren's "creative flair" exceeded the bounds of the statute he was given to enforce. Indeed, Bork concluded, "The Nixon Administration's announced determination to wage war on conglomerate mergers . . . must rank as one of the bleakest, most disappointing developments in antitrust history."

The two best-known Kennedy-Johnson antitrust chiefs, whose more moderate enforcement policies McLaren was now, by implication, criticizing, joined forces with the conglomerates in opposing McLaren's new merger policy. Lee Loevinger, President Kennedy's first Antitrust Division leader who now was practicing law, struck hard; indeed, compared to Loevinger's biting attack, Robert H. Bork was a voice of moderation. Loevinger held McLaren's theories of increased aggregate concentration and reciprocity effect to be unsupported by accurate data, unproven in their cause-effect relationships, foreign to the desired goals of antitrust, and reflecting an "emotional attack on business size and diversification." Loevinger labeled McLaren's approach a "potentiality theory," improperly directed to the *mere possibility* of abuses of economic power. The effects of judicial acceptance of the "potentiality theory" would be highly damaging:

If it is accepted by the courts, it will subvert some of our most important legal principles, with consequences far beyond the field of antitrust. . . . It seems clear that potentiality theory has been devised in an effort to block conglomerate and other mergers which have no adverse effect on competition but are objected to on grounds of other social goals or views. . . . Under potentiality theory the size of monopolies found and prosecuted by the government will surely and progressively diminish until any expansion of business without advance permission comes to be regarded as potential monopolization or restraint of trade and illegal. . . . It threatens our economic welfare in both domestic and world markets.

Thus spoke the Kennedy assistant attorney general of the Nixon assistant attorney general. Donald F. Turner, Johnson's assistant attorney general, was less vocal; Turner for the most part kept a public silence, perhaps figuring that it would be unseemly to become embroiled in a public debate on antitrust policy making. Only once—at the inception of the McLaren policy—did Turner slip and let himself be quoted as implying his disagreement with the suit against LTV's acquisition of J & L Steel. But Turner let it be known where his sentiments lay when, at the request of ITT, he furnished an opinion letter stating his view that the ITT-Hartford merger was unequivocally lawful. And Turner was later to confirm to a House subcommittee that, in his judgment, "there is no substantial probability of anti-competitive practices resulting from conglomerate mergers."

Some observers viewed McLaren's new conglomerate merger policy with open suspicion. Coming from a Republican, business-oriented administration, it must have an ulterior motive. After some pondering these observers concluded that the administration must be endeavoring to protect entrenched companies from the spur of aggressive new competition. Hence, reported *The Economist*, the LTV–J & L Steel suit "can be criticized as protecting established industry (and the highly concentrated steel industry at that) against a newcomer. . . . A raider like Ling-Temco-Vought is an instant and unwelcome competitor to the established giants." Others echoed this sentiment, pointing to the unhappiness caused in the steel industry by the conglomerate Norton Simon's previous diversification acquisition of Wheeling Steel, which was followed by some innovative pricing practices. The columnist Milton Viorst observed that McLaren was moving against the new-money "conglomerate builders" (usually, he said, Democrats) who "were challenging the entrenched economic power of the 'blue chip' corporations like steel and railroads."*

---

*In answer to the government's complaint against it, LTV charged that the "static condition of the steel industry, over an uninterrupted period of two decades, indicates that the acquisition, by a newcomer in the industry, promises beneficial competitive effects, rather than a lessening of competition."

The *Wall Street Journal* reported that McLaren "was cheered by big, establishment-type companies that were already targets for conglomerate take-overs or feared they would be." And, speculated *Business Week,* the Justice Department "could hardly have been unaware that many executives, even in big companies, were uncomfortable over the idea of being dragged into a conglomerate marriage." Congressman Celler, perhaps unwittingly, furthered this theory when he noted the phenomenon of

the business community pleading with the Federal Government for an investigation of business. . . . That is exactly what has resulted from the merger practices of some of our leading corporations, particularly the tactics of some of the so-called conglomerate corporations. From all sides we hear complaints about corporate "raiders" and "buccaneers." There are even worse adjectives used to describe take-overs from non-willing managements.

It is a fact that Section 7 of the Clayton Act does produce something of a schism among business, depending upon whose ox is being gored at any particular time. It is a standard, albeit usually unsuccessful, merger defense that the consolidation is needed to compete with industry leaders who, it is often pointed out, became industry leaders by past, unassailed mergers. This is what Bethlehem Steel said when it tried to acquire Youngstown Steel, pointing to United States Steel's dominance. (This defense was rejected, however, by the court.) Businesses which want to merge but are prevented from doing so curse Section 7 of the Clayton Act. The businesses which might suffer a competitive disadvantage—or a sharpening of the competitive battle, depending upon one's point of view—may look to Section 7 as a salvation in the particular case. It is not unusual to see the target of a hostile takeover attempt defend with claims that the takeover would violate Section 7 even though the target itself has a long history of acquisitions. This is what B. F. Goodrich Company, for example, said in defending against an attempted takeover by Northwest Industries. One of the marvels of Section 7, of course, is its flexibility. In view of the great number of economic variables which are present in mergers, it is not difficult for a company's lawyers to seize upon differences in some of these variables to claim a controlling legal distinction between mergers. Indeed, ITT itself, in October, 1967, before it began to feel the sting of McLaren's merger policy, filed an antitrust suit against General Telephone & Electronics Corporation seeking to break up the latter's vertical integration between telephone communications equipment and telephone operating companies. Part of ITT's claim was that GT & E had achieved this status by a series of unlawful acquisitions. (Incredibly, this case is still making its way through the courts.)
John Kenneth Galbraith in his book *The New Industrial State* had

already furnished a theoretical framework for the conglomerates' claim of protectionism. Galbraith's thesis was that antitrust serves mainly to prevent newly emerging companies from gaining some position of equality with the industrial establishment. He explained: "If a firm is already large it is substantially immune under the antitrust laws. . . . If a firm is already large, it has as a practical matter nothing to fear under antimerger provisions of the Clayton Act. . . . But if two medium-sized firms unite in order to deal more effectively with this giant, the law will be on them like a tiger." What we really have, said Galbraith, is "gross discrimination as between those who already have and those who aspire to market power. . . . The antitrust laws give the impression of protecting the market and competition by attacking those who exercise it most effectively." Galbraith's solution would be to abandon reliance upon antitrust in favor of governmental and industrial planning. Somewhat surprisingly, FTC Commissioner James Nicholson seemed supportive of this view when he noted that antitrust indeed appeared concerned with "the builders of new centers of power" to the exclusion of "the problems of existing power and concentration."

The University of Chicago law professor Kenneth W. Dam, noting the charges that "the purpose of the present enforcement policy is to protect the industrial establishment from being rendered unemployed by brash upstarts," concluded: "The anti-merger law should not be used to shield entrenched managements from the market in corporate control. Whether the present enforcement policy has such a purpose is beside the point because it tends to have that effect."

Even Edwin Zimmerman, Johnson's last Antitrust Division chief, was moved to comment: "I suggest it is bizarre to concoct a particular antitrust doctrine in order to contain the emerging political power or social impact of a Northwest Industries but not a General Motors—social and political problems do not segregate themselves nicely into such antitrust categories as that of the conglomerate merger."

Geneen sounded a similar theme in wondering why McLaren was going after conglomerates instead of doing something about the AT & T stranglehold on the United States telecommunications industry. Certainly, said Geneen, it was more procompetitive to have an ITT made up of a number of smaller companies than to continue to have "the $4 billion Western Electric [AT & T's manufacturing arm] dominating one industry." He went on to say: "What we feel is really at stake is the question of allowing meaningful new competition to be brought into established industries. By meaningful, I mean rapid, broad and effective additions to the competition which are on a scale sufficient to provoke economies for the consumer and strengthen the industry. . . . It is clear that if you stop this new kind of competition by new people entering old industries that the status quo would be all that would remain. And, in our opinion, this would be lessening of the competitive growth in industry."

McLaren appeared to be unperturbed by the criticism of his new policy. With characteristic good humor, tongue-in-cheek, he took note of his critics: "Of course, antitrust being a somewhat abstruse and specialized field, our critics are usually eminently responsible, careful, temperate and constructive. Consider, for example, the gentle and unrestrained comment one friendly observer recently delivered: 'McLaren,' he said, is 'destroying the last vestiges of rationality in the antitrust laws.'" McLaren shrugged off the charges of protectionism, pointing out that most of the conglomerate mergers that he had witnessed (including four out of his five big cases) appeared to be true affairs of the heart rather than shotgun weddings. The only one who seemed to need protection, he pointedly noted, was the public.

In a more serious vein—and one which some of his critics thought duplicitous—McLaren claimed that he was simply enforcing the law as written: "We are a law enforcement agency. While, of course, we have a measure of discretion as to the cases we will bring and the investigations we will pursue, we are not authorized to rewrite the law. The law is written by the Congress, and definitive interpretation comes from the Supreme Court."

This seemed to state an inflexible, bureaucratic approach, in contrast to the political style of Turner, who freely admitted that he would tailor his enforcement efforts toward desired economic ends. Turner had not felt constrained by the law to bring suits against mergers which technically (i.e., by expansive construction by the Supreme Court) could be brought under Section 7. Nor did his critics find McLaren's disavowal of a policy making function to be credible; under a statute as amorphous as Section 7 of the Clayton Act, in an area as untested as conglomerate mergers, it was impossible to divorce pure law enforcement from policy making.

McLaren made no effort to hide his disagreement with Turner on the conglomerate merger issue, but he would not go so far as to say that Turner had shirked his responsibilities. Rather, said McLaren somewhat enigmatically, Turner "had analyzed the thing in terms of an economist looking at markets. I look at it perhaps more as a lawyer interpreting the legislative history going back to 1950 and the Supreme Court decisions."

There are three well-accepted methods of meeting an antitrust suit. One is to try to get the Antitrust Division chief to reverse himself and dismiss the suit. This course is, almost invariably, futile. The second is to offer to compromise on terms that the company can live with. This is often successful if the right combination can be reached. The third is to defend the suit vigorously. This is, especially if the suit goes to the Supreme Court, unsuccessful most of the time (at least, it was during the 1960s).

ITT decided to follow all three of these accepted methods of defense. It found that McLaren was uninterested in withdrawing the suits; as for compromise, the combination could not be agreed upon. This left ITT with the vigorous judicial defense which it indeed intended to pursue.

There is a fourth, less well-accepted, borderline method of response to an antitrust suit (or any other kind of government suit). This is the twilight zone of political muscle—to bring to bear pressures which will cause the Antitrust Division to withdraw the case or to accept the settlement combination proposed by the defendant. Antitrust lawyers usually caution against the political approach because historically it has not usually done much good, and there is the risk of embarrassing public revelation. But despite these negative aspects, it is done.

George D. Reycraft, a former Antitrust Division official, has observed: "I would assume that the use of political influences may be like going into the Bay of Pigs. You probably shouldn't do it. But, if you are going to do it, you'd better do it right."

"Political" influence, in the sense of using strategy or intrigue to obtain a position of power or control (in this instance, vis-à-vis McLaren), manifestly depends upon gaining the ear of someone who has the authority to modify McLaren's policy. The line of authority ran upward from McLaren to the attorney general—in the ITT cases, to Kleindienst as acting attorney general, Mitchell having disqualified himself—and thence directly to the president. The only other avenue of political influence would be through the Congress, which has the power to modify Section 7, even on a retroactive basis. While ITT and the other conglomerates did not ignore the possibility of congressional relief, they clearly felt that their prospects of influencing a Republican administration were better than those of moving a Democrat-controlled Congress in a probusiness direction.

Whether ITT paused for even a moment before deciding to use the fourth line of antitrust defense—political influence—is unknown; probably not. Geneen had experienced what he saw as the bureaucratic intractability of the Antitrust Division in the aborted ITT–American Broadcasting Corporation merger. There the Antitrust Division, acting under Attorney General Clark's lead, had dug in harder as the suit progressed. While both ITT and ABC had worked successfully to gain congressional support, Geneen had seen how little that counted for when the bureaucracy had gained momentum. Geneen believed, in retrospect, that the ABC transaction could have been salvaged if ITT had done a better job of selling it to the White House.

This time there appeared to be no question what ITT should do. It would go straight to the White House from the start. Geneen was personally convinced that Nixon had not approved, and would not approve of, McLaren's policy. Indeed, the business community generally believed that Nixon had on his hands a runaway antitrust assistant. Geneen believed that something should, and could, be done about the situation. The president and his advisers must be informed of McLaren's perfidy, and Geneen was convinced that once they knew and understood the facts, McLaren's policy would be changed.

ITT was not unequipped to present its grievances to administration officials. It already maintained one of the largest corporate Washington offices, which served as its liaison with the executive branch and Congress. ITT's multinational character and its substantial defense contract business gave it need of considerable interchange of information with the government. Many of its Washington personnel functioned essentially in a business sense in negotiating with government procurement officials. Others acted as "lobbyists" in the broad sense of that term, keeping management informed of relevant Washington developments and presenting ITT's views and information where indicated.

ITT's Washington office was headed by William Merriam, who bore the title of vice president. Merriam reported to Edward Gerrity, ITT's public relations director and an ITT vice president headquartered in its New York executive offices. Gerrity had gained some unwanted public attention in connection with the attempted ITT-ABC merger by his calls upon the *New York Times* correspondent Eileen Shanahan. Gerrity's action had been termed "improper" by the FCC in his apparent attempt to try to convince Miss Shanahan to treat ITT more favorably in her articles about the ABC merger proposal. (The impropriety consisted of supplying erroneous information about one of the FCC commissioners' asserted support of legislation to prohibit newspaper broadcast cross-ownership.)

The ultimate director of ITT's efforts, however, would be Harold Geneen himself. Geneen believed, not without some justification based upon his past record, that he could overcome practically any resistance by sheer force of persuasion, whether that resistance came from the management of a prospective merger partner or from a government official. Geneen characteristically wanted to start high. In the summer of 1969, with the Canteen suit on file, and under imminent threat of suits against the Hartford and Grinnell mergers, Geneen decided that he must speak to the president himself. Geneen felt, with considerable cause, that pointing Nixon toward McLaren's insubordination would do the trick, and that a personal talk would most directly accomplish this result. Geneen therefore instructed Merriam to make an appointment with the president. With the assistance of California Congressman Bob Wilson, Merriam tried to do as instructed, but the president's advisers would not have this. Peter Flanigan, a White House adviser on business matters, believed that it would be "inappropriate," and so rejected the suggestion. Geneen had to content himself with telling his story to Arthur Burns, then the White House official in charge of domestic economic affairs, and to Secretary of Commerce Maurice Stans.

In late 1969 Geneen himself for the most part was preoccupied with other things, mainly the need to obtain the Connecticut insurance commissioner's consent to the Hartford acquisition (approval was finally received in December, 1969). In addition, Geneen was heavily involved on the congressional front. Conglomerates were under study in hearings during that period before both the Senate and House antitrust subcommittees. Naturally, the views of ITT were sought, and the conglomerates generally were eager to make a good case for the beneficial effects of conglomerate mergers. The hearings also gave Geneen suitable opportunity to visit with a number of senators and congressmen. While these hearings were not overly popular with ITT, inasmuch as it was one of the targets of the investigation, nevertheless ITT thought some use might be made of them. Geneen suggested that Congress adopt legislation to cancel out the Justice Department's conglomerate merger program (including, of course, the suits against ITT) pending completion of the hearings and congressional resolution of the conglomerate merger controversy. Unfortunately for ITT, it could find no takers willing to put their names to this bill, so nothing came of the suggestion.

In the meantime ITT's Washington office was availing itself of every opportunity to present ITT's point of view to any government official who conceivably might be of help. Sometimes this effort took on an almost comical aspect. For example, Dita Beard, whose principal function was liaison regarding ITT's government contracts business, determined to try to get the message across to Secretary of Defense Melvin Laird. After hearing enough of this, which he did not understand anyway, Laird referred Mrs. Beard to Colonel James Hughes, the president's military assistant, to whom Mrs. Beard vented ITT's frustration at being unable to discuss the suits with McLaren or Mitchell. In passing, Mrs. Beard made reference to the "heavy financial support given by ITT to the president's election." Hughes, who was as puzzled as Laird, passed this message on to Ehrlichman, no doubt figuring that he, as counsel to the president, must know what she was talking about.

ITT's approach was based upon what it conceived to be a "new" antitrust policy adopted by McLaren. ITT's arguments had the same basic ring whoever the audience, but the emphasis differed to suit the occasion. It had a basic economic argument—diversification mergers were necessary to preserve a market for capital assets, to introduce new competitors into industries which were stagnant or dominated by a few complacent market leaders, and to smooth out business cycles by a balance of different products and services. ITT management also sought to develop new considerations. If protectionist influences—the "industrial establishment"—were at work in the administration, ITT must have an offsetting point, one which would overshadow the political appeal of the old-line companies. ITT settled upon the "foreign implications" of McLaren's merger policy. By diversification United States firms forged a strong base which would enable them to compete more forcefully overseas with foreign cartels or (said to be the same) firms unhampered by antitrust laws. (The ITT spokesmen were always quick to point out that ITT was one of the largest private contributors to the United States balance of payments.) A virtually total ban on large diversification acquisitions—which McLaren manifestly sought, according to ITT—would undermine the position of United States firms in foreign markets and harm the United States balance of payments.

ITT further argued that McLaren's position was without legal precedent, was considered to be unwarranted by many leading economists, and was contrary to the findings and recommendations of the president's own policy commission, i.e., the Stigler commission. McLaren was going far beyond the antimerger enforcement policy of the Johnson administration, and the Nixon administration was fast gaining an antibusiness image.

ITT anticipated the argument that its proper recourse was in the courts. In a memorandum prepared for circulation to administration officials, ITT predictably struck at the Supreme Court:

The Supreme Court is not "making" these decisions. They are in most cases merely affirming the "invitation" to these decisions as sent up by the Antitrust Division of the Department of Justice. In fact since the advent of the Warren Court, 62 out of 65 cases in this area have been affirmed for the government.* The Supreme Court, therefore, is endorsing and confirming what it conceives to be the economic policy desired by the government almost precisely as presented by the Antitrust Division. In short, the Antitrust Division is writing, in this method, its own economic

---

*ITT was counting all antitrust cases. Had it confined its survey to merger cases, as described in a previous chapter, its point would have been even more dramatic in percentage terms (28 out of 29 cases decided for the government).

policy for the nation. . . . The cases sent by the Antitrust Division to the Supreme Court are therefore in many instances "invitations" to spell out increasingly restrictive economic policy based on the exceedingly vague process of "interpreting" the *intention* of Congress when passing this amendment in 1950.

ITT registered its views with a large number of executive branch and legislative officials beginning in 1969 and continuing through April, 1971. ITT early concluded, however, that further appeals to McLaren himself would be futile. Its attorneys had attempted vigorously to dissuade McLaren from filing the complaints; the policy, legal, and economic arguments had been heard and rejected by McLaren. It would be necessary to have McLaren overruled. And ITT had a notion how to do this; it was not unaware certainly of Nixon's desire to centralize and coordinate national policies.

In the spring of 1969, even while ITT's lobbying campaign was barely underway, McLaren, although short on political experience, made a countermove which showed considerable political savvy. McLaren was aware from the very beginning, as he said, that "certain companies of the conglomerate type have mounted a rather comprehensive campaign to criticize this program." McLaren already had Mitchell's promise, made in December, 1968 when McLaren was offered the antitrust position, that antitrust enforcement decisions would be made "on the merits." But McLaren had soon learned, in the ITT-Canteen suit in which Ehrlichman had intervened, how chimerical such a promise could be in the complex of government policy interplay. He wanted more; he wanted a public expression of support from Mitchell, which McLaren hoped would head off further White House intervention. McLaren wanted something which would bring home to his public critics and to Ehrlichman just where the antitrust power lay.

McLaren caught Mitchell at a good time. Mitchell had learned of Ehrlichman's move in the ITT-Canteen case, and was not pleased over it. The Justice Department was Mitchell's turf, and a low-level White House official (Ehrlichman at that time was only counsel to the president) had no business interfering in Mitchell's department. McLaren convinced Mitchell to give him public support. Whether Mitchell acceded from a true belief in the McLaren approach is problematical; to Mitchell it was probably a matter of sticking with his own people, coupled with his ire over Ehrlichman's maneuver. That Mitchell did not want to create too much of a public stir was shown perhaps by his choice of a rather obscure forum (from an antitrust standpoint) to voice his public support of McLaren. Mitchell delivered the speech given to him by McLaren at the

Georgia Bar Association meeting in June, 1969. The speech reviewed the "dangers posed by the conglomerate merger": reciprocity effect; elimination of potential competition; entrenchment and raising barriers to entry; and the power attendant upon increasing aggregate concentration. The Mitchell speech concluded: "The danger that super-concentration poses to our economic, political and social structure cannot be overestimated.... The Department of Justice may very well oppose any merger among the top 200 manufacturing firms . . . [or] by one of the top 200 manufacturing firms of any leading producer in any concentrated industry."

If Mitchell hoped to avoid wide public circulation, he was to be disappointed. His speech was reported in practically every important financial and legal journal; it brought further despair to the conglomerates. ITT management read Mitchell's speech "as strong support for Mr. McLaren's policy." Whatever slight chance there may have been of reversing McLaren's policy within Justice Department channels now seemed to be gone. McLaren had to be pleased that his policy had received the public imprimatur of one of the most powerful individuals in the administration. From that time forward the aggressive antitrust campaign against conglomerate mergers was often referred to as the Mitchell-McLaren policy.

ITT's pretrial contacts with the Nixon administration reached their zenith in the late summer of 1970, in anticipation of the Grinnell trial scheduled for September 15. ITT, believing that its chances of undoing McLaren's campaign would diminish after the beginning of trial, worked to achieve administration action before that date.

This time Geneen decided to ask to see Ehrlichman, now the president's domestic policy chief, instead of risking another rebuff from the president. The request was made through Charles Colson, who, as a general contact with outside groups, was well known to ITT. Colson asked if he could not handle the matter himself; Geneen insisted that he must see Ehrlichman, and the appointment was made. The meeting took place on August 4, 1970 in Ehrlichman's office, with Geneen and Merriam present for ITT. According to Colson's recollection:

Mr. Geneen made the argument that the administration, he felt, was pursuing an antitrust policy or pursuing an antitrust case against ITT based on a policy of "bigness" per se, simply because the concerns were so large that antitrust actions would be brought, notwithstanding any of the other statutory criteria.

Mr. Ehrlichman at that meeting did say that the President did not favor the policy that bigness alone, just the mere size of a corporation, should be grounds for an antitrust action.

On the same day, in fact preceding the Ehrlichman meeting, Geneen had also met with Attorney General Mitchell even though he had disqualified himself from the ITT cases. Mitchell later described the meeting as short—not more than thirty-five minutes—and recalled the substance of it as follows:

> The meeting was held at Mr. Geneen's request to discuss the overall antitrust policy of the Department with respect to conglomerates. I assented to the meeting on the express condition that the pending ITT litigation would not be discussed at this meeting.
>
> At the meeting Mr. Geneen contended that the Department's antitrust policy with respect to conglomerates was to bring suits solely on the bigness theory. I told him this was not the Department's policy and advised him that our policy was to bring litigation only where there was a showing of anticompetitive practices.

ITT came away from these meetings with a claim of greater assurance than the government participants voiced. ITT's understanding was reported by Gerrity to his long-time friend, Vice President Spiro Agnew. Gerrity had met with Agnew (also on August 4) to solicit his support in overturning McLaren's campaign; Gerrity followed up this meeting with a letter reporting on the Mitchell-Ehrlichman meetings:

> You will recall at our meeting on Tuesday I told you of our efforts to try and settle the three antitrust suits that Mr. McLaren has brought. Before we met, Hal had a very friendly session with John, whom, as you know, he admires greatly and in whom he has the greatest confidence. John made plain to him that the President was not opposed to mergers per se, that he believed some mergers were good, and that in no case had we been sued because "bigness is bad." Hal discussed this in detail because McLaren has said and in his complaints indicated strongly that bigness is bad. John made plain that was not the case. Hal said on that basis he was certain we could work out something. John said he would talk with McLaren and get back to Hal.
>
> While you and I were at lunch, Hal and Bill Merriam, who runs our local office, met with Chuck Colson and John Ehrlichman, and Hal told them of his meeting with John. Ehrlichman said flatly that the President was not enforcing a bigness-is-bad policy and that the President had instructed the Justice Department along these lines. He supported strongly what John had told Hal. Again, Hal was encouraged.

In a single day Geneen had presented his arguments to two of the administration's most powerful figures, Mitchell and Ehrlichman, and Gerrity had sought to enlist his friend Agnew. Geneen's confidence in his own power of personal persuasion may have colored ITT's view of the outcome of those meetings. ITT expected, presumably, that McLaren would be appropriately instructed on the administration's desired conglomerate merger policy.

McLaren knew of Ehrlichman's meeting with Geneen; indeed, at Ehrlichman's request McLaren, albeit reluctantly, had prepared for him a briefing paper on the ITT cases. McLaren, mindful of Ehrlichman's previous interference with the filing of the Canteen complaint, wanted to know what was going on; he telephoned Ehrlichman's office and was routed to Tod Hullin, an Ehrlichman assistant. Hullin checked with Ehrlichman, who disliked dealing directly with officials who were down the line in the chain of command, and reported back to McLaren that "there was nothing of significance to be passed along." Hullin went on to say that Ehrlichman "had discussed some of the content of this meeting with the Attorney General. Perhaps the Attorney General could give you more specific guidance."

ITT wasted little time in attempting to follow up its contacts of August 4. Several days later ITT's counsel in the Canteen case, Hammond Chaffetz, had a meeting with McLaren. Chaffetz was instructed by Geneen to raise the possibility of that case being dropped or settled by a consent decree not requiring divestiture. Naturally, he would be expected also to test the winds on the matter of overall disposition of all three cases.

If ITT had expected that McLaren would be more receptive after the August 4 meetings, it was to be sorely disappointed. ITT's counsel still ran into a stone wall in McLaren. Gerrity indignantly relayed, to Agnew, McLaren's response:

McLaren, ignoring the evidence, said that ITT must be stopped, that the merger movement must be stopped, etc., in effect saying he was running a campaign based on his own beliefs and he intended to prosecute diligently. It is quite plain that Mr. McLaren's approach to the entire merger movement in the United States is keyed into the present cases involving ITT. Therefore, it is equally plain that he feels that if a judgment is obtained against ITT in any of these cases then the merger movement in the United States will be stopped. His approach obviously becomes an emotional one regardless of fact.

Concurrently Thomas Casey of ITT's Washington office complained to Colson that despite Ehrlichman's statements McLaren had rebuffed ITT's request to have the Canteen suit dropped. Casey continued: "It seems plain that Mr. McLaren's views were not and are not consistent with those of the Attorney General and the White House as expressed to us. Apparently, we are going to be prosecuted, contrary to what the Attorney General, Mr. Ehrlichman and you told Mr. Geneen, not on law but on theory."

Colson relayed this message to Ehrlichman with the observation that "we may be riding one horse and McLaren another." Colson suggested "another discussion" with the attorney general; Ehrlichman duly sent the Casey letter to Mitchell for handling, apparently assuming that Mitchell was staying on top of the situation. In fact, Ehrlichman was wrong; Mitchell was doing nothing. Indeed, according to both Mitchell and McLaren, ITT's lobbying efforts failed to spur any discussion between the two on the subject of the ITT cases or conglomerate merger policy.

Mitchell's inaction was brought to White House attention a month later, when ITT complained to Colson that nothing had been done and that now the Grinnell trial had started. In the by now familiar chain of communications, Colson passed up this complaint to Ehrlichman, noting, somewhat superfluously, that the White House had a "serious problem which is manifesting itself in Mr. McLaren's conduct of the ITT case." Ehrlichman in turn fired off another memorandum to Mitchell, expressing his disappointment "that the ITT case had gone to trial with apparently no further effort on the part of Mr. McClaren [sic] to settle this case with ITT." He had received word from ITT, said Ehrlichman, that the gravamen of the case was "largeness"; McLaren's approach "is contrary to the understanding that I believe you and I had during the time that we each talked to Gineen [sic]." Ehrlichman concluded: "I think we are in a rather awkward position with ITT in view of the assurances that both you and I must have given Gineen [sic] on this subject.... I would appreciate your reexamining our position in the case in view of these conversations. Gineen [sic] is, of course, entitled to assume the Administration meant what it said to him."

This wave of ITT's lobbying efforts was now, in mid-September, 1970, at an end. For the next three months ITT would be occupied in the trial of the Grinnell and Canteen cases. Whether from this occupation or from a sense of decorum, or perhaps of frustration, ITT avoided any further intensive lobbying until 1971, after the completion of the trials.

From ITT's standpoint the 1970 round of meetings had little discernible immediate impact. The initial spurt resulted in no reversal of McLaren. But Geneen had caught the interest of Ehrlichman; ITT had gotten its message out, and had set the stage for its later renewed efforts.

Ehrlichman probably felt as frustrated as ITT. The chain of command was not working as it was supposed to. Colson was feeding to Ehrlichman requests from citizens for policy actions, as he was supposed to. Ehrlichman was attempting to execute his responsibility for policy making in the area of domestic issues, of which the Antitrust Division's merger policy, to his mind, clearly was one. But the Department of Justice was not implementing the policy decision as it was supposed to; Ehrlichman was tugging on the reins, but was receiving no response. His messages to Mitchell were being shunted aside; Mitchell was not directing McLaren to comply with White House policy on conglomerate mergers.

10

IN COURT: Trial and Decision

> This case is not so much a contest between the
> United States Department of Justice and the two
> defendant companies as a skirmish in a broader battle
> over the direction American economic life will take
> in the coming years. At the center of this struggle
> is the concept of the conglomerate corporation—
> not a particularly new development, but one which
> lately has gained great momentum. One reason for
> its recent popularity is the attempt of companies
> to expand through acquisition of other firms, while
> avoiding the antitrust problems of vertical or hori-
> zontal mergers. The resulting corporations have had
> none of the earmarks of the traditional trust situa-
> tion, but they have presented new problems of
> their own. Although the market shares of the several
> component firms within their individual markets
> remain unchanged in conglomerate mergers, their
> capital resources become pooled—concentrated into
> ever fewer hands. Economic concentration is
> economic power, and the Government is concerned
> that this trend if left unchecked will pose new
> hazards to the already much-battered competitive
> system in the United States.
>
> Judge Frank Battisti, in United States
> v. White Consolidated Industries
> February, 1971

The battle now was joined in the courts; it had become evident that
ITT could not head off judicial consideration. The legality of ITT's acquisition of Grinnell Corporation would be the first case to be tried. As
the Antitrust Division's chief trial attorney in the case, McLaren designated Joseph Widmar, a career attorney who had been with the Antitrust
Division since 1961. Within the Antitrust Division hierarchy another
career man of long tenure, Robert B. Hummel, deputy director of operations, had the responsibility for coordination and planning for all three
ITT cases. McLaren himself would not handle the actual trials in any

of the cases, but kept in close consultation with his trial attorneys. ITT was represented by Covington & Burling of Washington, D.C., a large, nationally known law firm with extensive experience in antitrust cases. Judge Timbers, who had rejected the government's preliminary injunction motions, was to be the trial judge.

The first trial testing McLaren's new theory thus began on September 15, 1970 in Bridgeport, Connecticut (moved from Hartford for reasons of courtroom availability). The occasion most certainly lacked the suspense of a sensational murder case (and probably even a third-rate burglary). There were no jurors, for the simple reason that government antimerger cases are tried and decided solely by the presiding judge. There was no standing room crowd seeking to elbow into the courtroom for a view of the proceedings. The press coverage consisted of two or three financial reporters who would duly report the beginning of the trial, and not much after that. Mainly there were lawyers. To all outward appearances, then, this was not drama.

But in fact, economic drama was taking place, which could have a widespread impact on business growth. This was to be a test of antitrust policy—to shape, perhaps, the parameters of diversification mergers for the foreseeable future, perhaps to determine whether the conglomerate phenomenon could continue at all.

A spectator sitting in the courtroom in Bridgeport would have had a difficult time following the progress of the antimerger case. Government antitrust cases tried before a judge have been aptly termed a battle of papers. Usually much of the evidence is in the form of documents—letters, memoranda, economic studies, etc.—which are simply identified and placed in the record. Unlike a jury, which is obliged to rely upon its collective memories of most of the evidence presented, the judge will later peruse this documentary evidence and the transcripts of the testimony of witnesses in the confines of his chambers.

The fruits of pretrial preparation and discovery furnish much of the paper evidence in an antitrust case; a major source of paper evidence is in the form of depositions. These are transcriptions of oral testimony taken outside the courtroom, and usually without a judge in attendance. Deposition activity ordinarily is quite active in an antitrust case, and thousands of pages may be transcribed. The testimony of lesser witnesses often is put before the court through their deposition transcripts.

Naturally, neither side will want to rest its case without presenting its major points through live witnesses appearing before the judge. In the Grinnell case fifty-three witnesses testified before the court; the testimony of an additional fifty-nine witnesses was presented in the form of extracts from their deposition transcripts. And, to complete the picture, there were 498 documentary exhibits introduced into the record.

It was Widmar's assignment to shape a factual presentation which would provide a foundation for application of McLaren's expanded theories of conglomerate merger illegality. In the context of the Grinnell acquisition, Widmar must portray a milieu in which "reciprocity effect" would act as a natural force to drive ITT suppliers (or potential suppliers) to buy Grinnell products. (While Grinnell made several products which were specified in the complaint, the main product of Widmar's concern, and to which he would devote the bulk of his evidence, was automatic sprinkler systems and components used for fire protection.) Widmar then must draw as terrifying a picture as he could of the overall damage to the American economy and American values from continued conglomerate growth.

The basic evidentiary foundation for McLaren's reciprocity effect theory was readily laid by Widmar. The Antitrust Division presented a list of large suppliers to ITT, and their volume of sales to ITT over the past three years. It had a corresponding list of Grinnell's customers, some of whom also appeared on the list of ITT suppliers. But dual appearance was not the key to the government's case. Its proof was directed to the proposition that the ITT suppliers were within the *class* of firms likely to be customers for sprinkler systems, and that the Grinnell customers were within the *class* of firms which could be ITT suppliers. Indeed, the potential firms susceptible to reciprocity effect might not yet appear on either list—there was yet another list of sprinkler customers which had purchased from Grinnell's competitors and which were, or could be, suppliers to ITT.

Widmar did not stop with those basic facts. Considerable time was spent raking over past attempts by some ITT personnel to promote sales of an ITT product to an ITT supplier. The objective was to show a proclivity within ITT to attempt to make sales to its suppliers. At the other end of the stream, Widmar also presented evidence intended to show that Grinnell, and some of its competitors, had previously tried to use reciprocity to make sprinkler sales. This would show, contended Widmar, that an automatic sprinkler was a reciprocity-sensitive product; customers would be likely to accept reciprocity suggestions if it would promote the sale of their own products.

While reciprocity effect and aggregate concentration were the legal theories by which McLaren hoped to gain an extension of existing merger law, still Widmar sought to "flavor" the case with perhaps more traditional evidence of competitive advantages to Grinnell from integration into the ITT system. To pinpoint more specific anticompetitive relationships would not hurt the government's case; indeed, a cumulative showing of anticompetitive probabilities might create an atmosphere of receptivity toward

McLaren's more novel theories. In view of Judge Timbers's prior expressed skepticism toward the government's case, it seemed that additional evidence certainly would be needed if the government hoped to obtain a victory in the district court. And a strong blend of possible anticompetitive consequences would point up the dangers of the conglomerate movement when the case reached the Supreme Court.

Thus, Widmar undertook to trace the sales methods for automatic sprinklers, how customers were found, and what role insurance agents played in the process—all to the end of demonstrating that Grinnell stood to gain sales leads from an affiliation with Hartford Insurance Company, by now, of course, another ITT subsidiary. Also, Grinnell's sprinkler systems, together with plumbing, heating, and air conditioning equipment already made by ITT, could be "packaged" for sale or installation, to the detriment of sprinkler companies which lacked such an affiliation, claimed Widmar. Finally, ITT's sheer financial resources and technical expertise would enable Grinnell to expand its business, at the expense of its competitors, by financing customer purchases, by participating in ITT advertising programs, by expanding overseas operations, and by affording reentry into the central station business (which Grinnell had been ordered out of as a result of the government's prior monopolization case against it). These points, while time-consuming in evidentiary presentation, nonetheless were peripheral. By the government's own claim, the "major marketing and promotional competitive advantage" to Grinnell would come from reciprocal dealings with ITT suppliers or potential suppliers.

When it came time for the aggregate concentration phase of its case—the theory which McLaren believed, if accepted, would virtually stop in its tracks the conglomerate movement—the government's presentation was almost anticlimactically brief. Widmar depended solely upon the statement of the government's expert witness, Willard Mueller, a former FTC Bureau of Economics director. Mueller's statement, complete with charts and tables, traced the post–World War II merger movement in detail, documented the rising trend of industrial asset concentration, and concluded with his opinion that further large conglomerate mergers—such as ITT-Grinnell—posed a probability of substantially lessening competition throughout the United States economy. Mueller contended that the trend toward economic concentration and the increasing diversification of large firms nurtured a system of conglomerate interdependence and forbearance which caused anticompetitive consequences in numerous product lines.

The counterstrategy of ITT's counsel, led by Henry Sailer of Covington & Burling, was to concede virtually nothing, but rather to meet head-on every factual and legal point raised by Widmar. These were good, sound, and expected tactics. When, for example, Widmar presented evidence of prior reciprocity practice by ITT, Sailer would later smother that presentation by testimony that any such practice was isolated, unauthorized, and ineffective: reciprocity was just not ITT's style, declared Sailer, as Geneen testified and had proved by an edict banning any reciprocity practice within ITT. And so it went with each line of attack pursued by Widmar; ITT would not let the smallest point of alleged anticompetitive effect escape thorough rebuttal. ITT's counsel wanted to leave not a single inference of unmet evidence for the Supreme Court to seize upon. ITT did indeed put forth the vigorous legal defense which had been expected of it and which Geneen had promised.

The Grinnell trial took eighteen court days, ending on October 30, 1970. The court scheduled posttrial proceedings, with each party directed to file proposed findings of fact and briefs. These steps were completed and the case submitted for decision by Judge Timbers on December 14, 1970.

Only a month after the Grinnell trial ended, the Canteen case was tried before Judge Richard Austin in Chicago, beginning on November 30, 1970. Lasting two weeks, the Canteen trial was a somewhat abbreviated version of the Grinnell trial. In Chicago the government presented only seven live witnesses, and ITT but nine. But both sides introduced voluminous paper evidence in the form of documentary exhibits and deposition transcripts. In total, Judge Austin's task of assimilating a heavy record probably was not appreciably less than Judge Timbers's burden.

In the Canteen trial the government presented essentially the same reciprocity effect evidence and arguments that it had put forth in the Grinnell trial. The government indeed had been able to come up with even more evidence that the acquired firm, Canteen, had a history of attempted reciprocity use. In the early 1960s Canteen had established what it euphemistically called a "trade relations" department to attempt to put the bite on its suppliers of food, snack, and tobacco items to avail themselves of Canteen's vending and feeding services wherever possible. Evidently Canteen lacked the purchasing power to carry this off, because its trade relations efforts had fizzled out, so Canteen claimed, without producing any consequential new business. The government, on the other hand, contended that in at least twenty-five cases reciprocity pressures had enabled Canteen to obtain or keep business.

In the aggregate concentration part of its case against the Canteen merger, the Antitrust Division narrowed its focus somewhat. Its purpose manifestly was to be able to present the Supreme Court with alternative versions of the aggregate concentration theory; if the Court would not accept the broader theory, the government would have a fallback position. Rather than complaining of the domination of United States industry as a whole by the conglomerates, the government claimed that the merger should be disallowed because Canteen's industry, the food service business, was becoming dominated by large diversified firms. To prove their point, the government attorneys introduced evidence of past mergers in the industry, including Litton's acquisition of Stouffer, Del Monte of Service Systems, Ogden Corporation of ABC Vending Company, Greyhound of Prophet, Standard Oil of Ohio of Cardinal Vending, and a Sears, Roebuck joint venture with Interstate United. The government argued that this trend toward conglomerate acquisitions should be stopped, at the ITT-Canteen stage, before it went any further.

To ITT this seemed to provide confirmation that McLaren's merger program was designed to protect the old-line established companies. The absorption of food service companies into diversified firms had not started with ITT. Why, then, should ITT's acquisition of Canteen, as merely the latest of a series of mergers, bear the brunt of the earlier mergers which the government had let pass unchallenged?

The trial completed, both sides filed their posttrial findings of fact and briefs, and Judge Austin took the case under advisement.

The ITT-Grinnell merger case came to final decision first. Judge Timbers handed down his decision, supported by a lengthy opinion, on December 31, 1970, only two weeks after he had received the final briefs (an extraordinarily brief interval for a case of this complexity). McLaren's move in 1969 to seek a preliminary injunction, which had been denied, now came back to haunt the Antitrust Division. Judge Timbers ruled decisively in favor of ITT. The reasoning of Judge Timbers's final decision followed closely his previous opinion rendered in denying the government's request for a preliminary injunction.

As an initial matter, the court questioned whether any of the government's theories were applicable where the acquired firm—here Grinnell—was not "dominant" in any product line sold by it. The court conceived the legal principle involved to be as follows:

The law is well settled that when a company which is the dominant competitor in a relatively oligopolistic market is acquired by a much larger company, such acquisition violates Section 7 of the Clayton Act if the acquired company gains marketing and promotional competitive advantages from the merger which will further entrench its position of dominance by raising barriers to entry to the relevant markets and by discouraging smaller competitors from aggressively competing. The effect of such a merger will be substantially to lessen competition.

But in the major product lines involved in the case—automatic sprinkler devices and systems used for fire protection—while Grinnell was the market leader, its market shares ranged around 20 percent. And Grinnell's market share had declined over the past five years in the face of competition from at least two other large national companies and a number of smaller regional firms which had grown rapidly. Grinnell's position was no greater in any of the lesser product lines involved. Judge Timbers concluded:

> The Court believes that it would be remiss if it did not state unequivocally that, in its opinion, this is not even a close case on the issue of Grinnell's dominance. It is not merely a case where the government has failed to sustain its burden of proof on that issue; it is a case where the overwhelming preponderance of the credible evidence clearly establishes that Grinnell is *not* the dominant competitor in *any* relevant market. Having lived with this case for nearly a year and a half, having heard scores of witnesses testify and having carefully studied hundreds of documents and thousands of pages of deposition and trial testimony, this Court is left with an unusually firm conviction that Grinnell, although a large and leading competitor, clearly is not a *dominant* competitor within the recognized meaning of that term in the antitrust field.

The judge noted that "a bolder Court would enter judgment for the defendant and proceed no further." But he was not so adventuresome. Foreseeing the likelihood of appellate review, he determined to decide the remaining issues in the case as though Grinnell were dominant. Thus, he passed on to consider whether Grinnell would gain anticompetitive marketing and promotional advantages from the merger. The prime issue raised by the government in this respect—reciprocity effect—turned, Judge Timbers held, upon whether the merger would create an opportunity for reciprocal dealing through a market structure conducive to such dealing *and* whether reciprocal dealing in fact is likely to occur.

On the latter point, the court made the key finding that ITT was not likely to attempt to induce its suppliers to purchase Grinnell products. ITT in 1966 had adopted a written antireciprocity policy; Geneen testified that he did not like reciprocity and considered it inefficient and uneconomic because it generally increased costs of supplies in an amount which offset the increased reciprocity sales. He considered it to be "a very costly, non-competitive, expensive practice." Consequently, ITT did not systematically compile purchasing and sales data which would be necessary to identify reciprocity opportunities. Furthermore, ITT's various divisions were organized into "profit centers" with separate operating managements. The managers of these separate centers were interested mainly in the profit performance of their own divisions; the court noted: "The management of one profit center has no motivation to tailor its purchasing decisions to facilitate the sales of another profit center."

The government's attempt to show the past exercise of reciprocity power by ITT was dismissed by the court as involving isolated instances which could occur in any organization of the size of ITT. The judge indeed thought these few examples to be the "exceptions which again prove the rule that ITT has had no substantial or significant reciprocal dealing practices."

Since ITT was not likely to practice reciprocity, it followed that the acquisition posed no serious threat of reciprocity. ITT's suppliers would find that ITT did not base its purchases on reciprocity, and hence would not purchase from Grinnell merely in hopes of selling to ITT.

Even if ITT were inclined to practice reciprocity, Judge Timbers found, the industry in which Grinnell was engaged was sufficiently competitive to preclude reciprocity from being an effective sales tool. Grinnell's main products—sprinkler systems—were sold principally to construction contractors on a competitive bidding basis. Thus, the owners of the buildings (who were the firms likely to be ITT suppliers) normally would have little voice in the selection of the sprinkler supplier. The construction contractor would be interested in the lowest responsible bid rather than in assisting an ITT reciprocity policy. The unsuitability of the sprinkler industry for reciprocity practice was confirmed by the absence of any substantial affirmative proof that reciprocity had been practiced by Grinnell or by any other companies in the industry. In other respects, Judge Timbers found that the government's evidence was simply too weak. Proof was lacking, for example, that ITT's business was sufficiently important to any supplier or group of suppliers to cause them to accede to any requests for reciprocity. Judge Timbers noted that a supplier which sells only a small portion of its total output to ITT is not likely to heed a reciprocity pitch, particularly if, by giving preference to Grinnell, it might lose sales it was then making to ITT-Grinnell competitors.

The court saved its most telling points for the government's second principal theory—the increase in aggregate concentration. The court said that the Department of Justice was in the wrong forum—it ought to be in Congress. Judge Timbers dismissed as irrelevant Mueller's testimony regarding the economy-wide dangers from further conglomerate growth; Mueller's assertions were legally defective, said Judge Timbers, because he failed to identify and pinpoint anticompetitive consequences in any particular product market. Judge Timbers explained:

The legislative history, the statute itself and the controlling decisional law all make it clear beyond a peradventure of a doubt that in a Section 7 case the alleged anticompetitive effects of a merger must be examined in the context of *specific product and geographic markets;* and the determination of such markets is a necessary predicate to a determination of whether there has been a substantial lessening of competition. To ask the Court to rule with respect to alleged anticompetitive consequences in *undesignated lines of commence* is tantamount to asking the Court to engage in judicial legislation.

The court refused to accept the government's invitation that it step forward as the innovator of a new and aggressive national posture toward conglomerate firms:

Despite the legislative history, the statute itself and the controlling decisional law, the government urges the Court to adopt an "expansive" reading of the statutory language "in any line of commerce" so as to read into the statute an interdiction of all mergers where the effect may be a substantial lessening of competition "anywhere, in the purchase or sale of anything" and thus to receive "proof of a merger or series of mergers which could be demonstrated to have a broad, anticompetitive effect upon 'markets' in general"—in short, to disregard the statutory requirement that alleged anticompetitive effects of a merger be examined with relation to a specific "line of commerce" and instead to conduct a roving expedition to determine whether "anticompetitive consequences will appear in numerous though *undesignated individual 'lines of commerce.'"*

The Court declines the government's invitation to indulge in an expanded reading of the statutory language and holds that the statute means just what it says. It proscribes only those mergers the effect of which "may be substantially to lessen competition"; it commands that the alleged anticompetitive effects be examined in the context of specific product and geographic markets; and it does not proscribe those mergers the effect of which may be substantially to increase economic concentration. Whatever may be the merits of the arguments as a matter of social and economic policy in favor of, or opposed to, a standard for measuring the legality of a merger under the antitrust laws by the degree to which it may increase economic concentration rather than by the degree to which it may lessen competition, that is beyond the competence of the Court to adjudicate. As the Court attempted to make clear in its preliminary injunction opinion, if that standard is to be changed, it is fundamental under our system of government that any decision to change the standard be made by the Congress and not by the courts.

It is hard to find in the judicial reports a more decisive loss for the government in a merger case. Not only had Judge Timbers rejected in toto McLaren's expanded legal theories, but he had found against the government on virtually all the critical facts. By following his self-described timorous instinct and anticipating appeal, Judge Timbers had traced through each element of the government's theories. Consequently, even had the government's reciprocity effect theory been acceptable, Judge Timbers had found no basis in the facts for application of that theory. His series of alternative holdings seemed to dispose of the government's reciprocity case beyond cavil. Only his rejection of the aggregate concentration theory, independent of its factual analysis, appeared to embody a pure legal ruling.

McLaren had lost the first major battle in his conglomerate merger campaign. At the beginning of 1971 the picture now looked like this. The Grinnell case had been finally decided against the government. McLaren had been denied preliminary injunctions in the Hartford and Northwest-Goodrich cases; the latter merger, however, appeared to have been effectively stopped, not by antitrust action, but by the failure of Goodrich's stockholders to accept the offer. The LTV-J & L merger case had been settled in 1970. The Canteen case had been tried but no final decision yet rendered. This accounted for all five of the 1969 cases; only the three ITT cases remained active. The Hartford case, which was also pending before Judge Timbers, was not scheduled for trial for another nine months. But it appeared that the government would fare no better than it had in Grinnell. There were no special factors in the Hartford merger to differentiate it from Grinnell, which Judge Timbers had decided against the government. And the judge had denied the government's preliminary injunction motion in a way which indicated it would take strong new evidence to change his views. The government did not have that evidence.

In January, 1971 McLaren filed the sixth, and final, complaint in his series of conglomerate merger test cases. That complaint challenged White Consolidated Industries's proposed acquisition of White Motors. Those companies, which many years before had split off from common ownership, were proposing to remeld. During their separation, however, both had been active in making diversification mergers, and White Consolidated was among the top twenty-five most active acquiring companies of the 1960s. From a sewing machine producer, White Consolidated had become a major seller of large home appliances and heavy industrial machinery. In 1968 White Consolidated had acquired Blaw-Knox Company, a major supplier of rolling mills and other production equipment to the steel industry. In 1969 White Consolidated attempted to follow up that acquisition with a takeover of Allis-Chalmers Company, but this effort was thwarted when Allis-Chalmers's management initiated a private antitrust suit to prevent the merger. White Consolidated's erstwhile sister corporation, White Motors, in addition to trucks and transportation equipment, also had expanded into industrial machinery. The White Consolidated complaint, while less startling and novel than the 1969 complaints, was to play an important role vis-à-vis the ITT cases in 1971.

11

ON APPEAL
The Solicitor General

*The Solicitor General bears a special relationship
to the [Supreme] Court. He owes it complete in-
tellectual candor even when that impairs his effectiveness as an advocate. The Court and its function
under our Constitution are far more important than
a Government victory in any given case.*

Solicitor General Robert H. Bork
August, 1973

The government had sixty days in which it could note an appeal from
Judge Timbers's decision against it in the ITT-Grinnell case. Under the
Expediting Act as then in effect, appeals in government antitrust cases,
unlike the vast majority of cases decided by the federal district courts,
were taken directly to the Supreme Court, bypassing the intermediate
federal courts of appeals. McLaren wanted to appeal, but he could not
make that decision on his own; he would need the concurrence of the
solicitor general.

The solicitor general serves, within the Justice Department, as the
government's advocate to the Supreme Court. The solicitor general must
approve before the government can appeal from an adverse judicial decision; the solicitor general's office itself handles all procedures in appeals
taken to the Supreme Court. It is a tradition of the solicitor general's
office that it has an obligation to present to the Supreme Court only those
appeals of substantial public importance, and to protect the Court from
the burden of considering cases which are of dubious merit or token
significance. As implied in Solicitor General Bork's statement quoted
at the beginning of this chapter, the solicitor general attempts to present
cases in a way that will assist the development of legal doctrine; the solicitor general disfavors appeals of cases which are in a posture unsuitable for
this purpose.

The post of solicitor general was held in 1971 by Erwin N. Griswold,
a holdover from the Johnson administration. Prior to his appointment
as solicitor general in October, 1967 (to succeed Thurgood Marshall, who

had been appointed to the Supreme Court), Griswold had been a Harvard law professor and dean, and early in his career had been a staff attorney in the solicitor general's office. Upon becoming attorney general, Mitchell, finding Griswold's credentials impeccable, asked him to stay on under the Nixon administration, and Griswold agreed.

The solicitor general's office, given its heavy responsibility, functions with a surprisingly small group of personnel. In 1971 it had only fifteen lawyers—the solicitor general himself, plus four deputies and ten staff attorneys under the supervision of the deputies. The four deputies were each assigned responsibility for a designated aggregation of legal subject matters. The antitrust category fell within the bailiwick of the deputy Daniel Friedman, a veteran Justice Department attorney who had once worked in the Antitrust Division's appellate section. Friedman's durability—he had been in the solicitor general's office since the Eisenhower years, a deputy since 1961—seems proof enough of his competence.

In January, 1971 McLaren duly sent to the solicitor general's office a copy of Judge Timbers's opinion in the Grinnell case, together with a memorandum prepared by the government's trial attorneys explaining the government's theories and the approach taken at trial to prove the theories. McLaren strongly urged that Griswold authorize appeal of the Grinnell case.

McLaren's submission to the solicitor general was reviewed, in time, by staff attorneys, by Friedman, and by Griswold himself. The solicitor general is solicitous of the views of the department's operating divisions, and, to the extent consistent with his perceived obligation to the Supreme Court, will give sympathetic consideration to a strong desire for appellate review by a division chief. But, in this case, despite McLaren's strong views, the reviewers were not persuaded that this case met the solicitor general's criteria for appeal. Said Griswold: "There was grave doubt in my office by members of my staff and by myself about the *Grinnell* case." The solicitor general noted that the district court had found all the material facts against the government. The district court's factual determinations left little room to frame a clear-cut legal issue. One of the principal considerations in determining whether a case is an appropriate one for appeal to the Supreme Court, Friedman had previously stated, is whether "the factual findings are so tied up with the legal issue that we would feel we would have great difficulty in getting the Court to reach the legal issue before we could overturn on the facts." This means simply that Supreme Court review is most effective when it can be argued that, even accepting the district court's finding of the facts, its ruling was wrong as a matter of law. In the Grinnell case the phrasing of a brief in those terms would be so extreme as to virtually read economic effect out of Section 7. While Griswold says that he personally thought that the growth of the conglomerates was not a good thing, still he was not prepared in his official capacity to go as far as McLaren thought the law might be stretched.

Griswold explained his view of the appeal:

We felt that it would be very difficult to win it, not only because the law with respect to conglomerate mergers is far from clear, but also because in this particular case there had been sharp conflict in the evidence before the District Judge, and the District Judge had found all the facts against us. And all experience shows that it is extremely difficult to win an antitrust case or another type of case in the Supreme Court when you have to attack the findings of fact.

There was even some feeling among Griswold's staff that it would be positively embarrassing to go before the Supreme Court with a case in which the Antitrust Division had presented such a paucity of evidence before the district court.

McLaren was persistent. He respected Judge Timbers, but believed that in this instance he had gone too far in the direction of accepting ITT's assurances that it would do no wrong. To let a defendant escape merely on its own say-so that it does not practice reciprocity seemed to McLaren to be an undesirable precedent. Nor was McLaren enamored of Judge Timbers's threshold ruling that a conglomerate merger could not be stopped on the basis of anticompetitive marketing and promotional advantages unless the acquired firm were "dominant" in its market. McLaren believed that adherence to this rule would insulate most conglomerates from attack altogether. Dominance, to begin with, was an amorphous concept, and however defined, single-firm dominance probably represents the exception rather than the rule in American industries.

McLaren contended to Griswold that Judge Timbers's decision as to those points at least was susceptible to attack. An outright victory in the Supreme Court might be unattainable, but the government could well—and McLaren thought should—win on some of the district court's legal formulations. That, at least, would result in some clarification of the law in the conglomerate merger area and assist the Antitrust Division in winning other cases in the future. On the other hand, to let Judge Timbers's decision pass without appeal not only would leave his troublesome legal rulings standing as precedent, but would also leave an erroneous implication that the government, by not appealing, was now expressing agreement with those rulings. It would be, to his thinking, a bad public relations move—in the usual manner (all too familiar to McLaren) taken by the antitrust bar as an antitrust policy signal.

McLaren also sought to convince Griswold that the Grinnell case was only one part of the whole picture. The same issues were involved in Canteen, which McLaren expected to be decided surely within the next few months. The solicitor general must also consider the interaction between Grinnell and Canteen. McLaren's trial staff was not wholly pessimistic over the Canteen case. They felt that they had presented a somewhat stronger case in Canteen (principally because of the evidence concerning Canteen's past reciprocity practices and the merger trend in the food services industry), and of course Judge Austin might adopt a wholly different perspective than Judge Timbers. The government could win in Canteen; if so, it would create a split in the district courts which would make the cases particularly appropriate for Supreme Court resolution. Even if the government lost in the Canteen case, its melding with Grinnell on appeal might help to remedy some of the factual defects which Griswold observed in the Grinnell case. And of course down the road was Hartford Insurance, which might eventually be combined with the other two cases on appeal, and the three cases together might have a cumulative impact upon the Supreme Court. McLaren said: "I felt confident that if we were able to get the three cases up together, there was no question, in my mind, what the result would be. I felt confident that we would win them."

Thus, appeal was a matter of high importance to McLaren. Without appeal, his options in the combined ITT cases would be severely curtailed, his power would be weakened, and there would be the public appearance of retreat from his conglomerate merger policy. From a personal standpoint, there might also be left the inference of a vote of no-confidence in McLaren himself. That McLaren was fighting hard for the appeal is not surprising.

In the midst of his negotiations with the solicitor general, McLaren received a stroke of fortune—a ruling in his favor on his preliminary injunction motion in his case against the White Consolidated–White Motors merger. In Cleveland, District Judge Frank Battisti, on February 24, 1971, preliminarily enjoined the merger on the ground of its probable reciprocity effect upon steel companies causing them to purchase White Consolidated's rolling mills in order to sell steel to the merged companies. In so ruling, the court followed the lead of another court which a short time before had enjoined White Consolidated from pursuing its attempted acquisition of Allis-Chalmers, an unwilling target which had initiated the suit. In stopping the White Consolidated–White Motors merger, Judge Battisti noted:

The result of a merger between the defendant corporations would be no less than a super-conglomerate, whose impact on the market can hardly be gauged. The undesirable effects of such a merger are totally unrelated to the motives of the parties; rather their mere size in the market will operate as a lever which in turn will lessen competition. Unquestionably, other firms will hesitate to compete too zealously with one division out of fear of antagonizing the entire firm and losing it as a customer for other goods.

This was a heartening development for McLaren; it was the first ruling in his favor in any of his six conglomerate merger test cases. And the acceptance of the essential premise of his reciprocity effect theory in the two White Consolidated cases (White Motors and Allis-Chalmers) were the first judicial rulings directly to favor that theory. These rulings appeared to show that the theory did have legal viability, and that it would not be improbable of acceptance by the Supreme Court.

The White Consolidated rulings, even though at the preliminary injunction stages, set up at least a philosophical judicial conflict, although not an actual conflict since there were no final decisions in those cases. (Nor were there ever to be, since, with its defeats at the preliminary injunction stage, White Consolidated abandoned both merger attempts.)

Time was running out for McLaren, however, on the Grinnell appeal. The deadline for filing the notice of appeal was March 1, 1971, but at the end of February Griswold had not yet been persuaded to approve the appeal. McLaren on his own went ahead and filed a "protective" notice of appeal in the district court. This was done on March 1; a protective notice is a not unusual step—the notice of appeal is a simple one-page document, and its filing would let the appeal go forward if Griswold finally decided in favor of appeal.

To perfect the appeal, the government must next file in the Supreme Court, within thirty days after filing the notice of appeal, a jurisdictional statement setting forth the basic facts and legal issues in the case; this document was Griswold's responsibility. On March 20, 1971 Griswold filed in the Supreme Court an application for a twenty-day extension of time to file a jurisdictional statement. The application explained: "The Solicitor General has not finally decided whether to proceed with the appeal. The additional time is needed for him to study the case further and, if he decides to proceed, to prepare and print the jurisdictional statement." Supreme Court Justice Harlan routinely granted this request. The deadline for perfecting the appeal was now April 20, 1971.

At about this time ITT's attorneys Henry Sailer of Covington & Burling and Scott Bohon from ITT came to see Griswold. Their mission was to argue against the filing of the Grinnell appeal. The solicitor general usually is willing to listen to those opposing an appeal, although it is problematical how much influence their presentation carries. In this instance ITT's attorneys were unsuccessful. In early April Griswold decided, "reluctantly," he said, to go ahead with the appeal. McLaren's drive had carried; Griswold was swayed by McLaren's "dogged determination to go ahead, and an engaging optimism." And the White Consolidated decision had furnished judicially sanctioned clothing for Griswold's inclination to honor McLaren's wishes consistent with his views of his own responsibilities. He instructed Friedman to prepare the jurisdictional statement for filing with the Supreme Court by April 20.

ITT did not know how close it had come to having the Grinnell appeal stopped in the solicitor general's office. Had the antitrust assistant been someone lacking in McLaren's fervor and tenacity, ITT's later efforts to stop appeal would have been unnecessary, and in all probability the ITT affair would never have become a cause célèbre (at least, not in the way that it did).

Geneen's elation over the district court win certainly was tempered considerably by the prospect of going before the Supreme Court. He had assumed from the start that the cases would wind up in the hands of that dread tribunal unless the administration could be persuaded to overrule McLaren's policies. In April, 1971 the Supreme Court still had four of the five justices who had uniformly decided in the government's favor in Clayton Act Section 7 merger cases in the 1960s. (Thus far, of that pro-antitrust majority, only Chief Justice Warren had left, to be replaced by Burger.) The usual pattern had been that the lower federal courts would rule in favor of the merging corporations, only to be reversed by the Supreme Court. Geneen feared that the pattern would be repeated in ITT's acquisition of Grinnell. The fervent hope of the growth corporations was to keep merger cases away from the Supreme Court until President Nixon had an opportunity to make additional appointments to the court.

Always vigilant for any possible help, Geneen decided to lobby for an amendment to the Expediting Act which might postpone ITT's appearance before the Supreme Court for two or three years. The Expediting Act required that appeals in government antitrust cases go directly to the Supreme Court rather than through the normal channel of intermediate court of appeals review. Enacted in President Theodore Roosevelt's tenure so that antitrust cases could be rushed directly to the more hospitable Supreme Court, the Expediting Act became, according to one observer, "the *bête noire* of the defense, and salvation of the

Government." But by the mid-1960s practically all the Supreme Court justices had concluded that any virtues of the Expediting Act were outweighed by the burdens that it imposed upon that Court. The Justice Department was compelled, reluctantly, to support repeal of the Expediting Act (although the department was sagacious enough to attempt to preserve to itself the option of taking a direct appeal in cases it believed important).

After the filing of McLaren's 1969 complaints against ITT, Geneen joined the Justice Department in this effort, hoping naturally for repeal of the Expediting Act before time for appeal of the pending merger cases. ITT disagreed, of course, with the Justice Department's proposal to keep for itself an option of direct appeal, figuring, no doubt correctly, that the Justice Department would exercise this option in the ITT merger cases. ITT's Washington office did considerable congressional groundwork, and Geneen himself met with Senators Philip Hart and Sam Ervin—no favorites of the conglomerates—to urge repeal of the Expediting Act.

ITT's work, however, was unavailing. The opposition of Congressman Emmanuel Celler, chairman of the House Antitrust Subcommittee, staved off repeal of the Expediting Act until 1974, which was too late to help ITT. That ITT even made the effort, however, may illustrate a quality which helps account for Geneen's success as a manager; he appears to overlook no possibility of advantage, however slight or improbable.

For his part, McLaren, despite his setback in the district court, maintained a public air of confidence. He indicated that his loss at the district court level was not wholly unexpected because of the relative novelty of the department's theories; he expected that Supreme Court review would result in a decision extending antimerger principles in favor of the government. *Business Week* reported: "When the conglomerate cases reach the Supreme Court, the Justice Department apparently expects 'friendly hearing.'" Given the Supreme Court's history in merger cases, McLaren's public optimism did not seem unreasonable. There were those even among the private antitrust bar who thought McLaren would probably win on appeal. George D. Reycraft, a member of a large New York law firm who had served on the Johnson-appointed Neal commission, noted: "I have the impression, myself, that the Government will probably be successful in the Supreme Court ... on general grounds of concentration of economic power and the fact that the concentration can be directed to anticompetitive results. . . . Theoretical perhaps, but I think the Government will be successful." ITT and the public had no way of knowing of Griswold's more pessimistic opinion of the government's chances before the Supreme Court.

12

TOWARD THE PRESIDENT

*You asked me to meet with Hal Geneen of IT & T
on anti-trust. In the course of that discussion, he informed me that Justice was about to make an appeal
to the Supreme Court that had very wide-ranging
policy implications.*
*I immediately called John Ehrlichman and I
understand action had been taken to at least postpone this action.*

Memorandum from Peter G. Peterson
assistant to the president
to Richard M. Nixon, April 23, 1971

John Ehrlichman had not forgotten the rebuff that he had gotten at
the hands of the Justice Department in the late summer of 1970. Certainly, Ehrlichman was nagged by the feeling that the White House must
stand aside, impotent, while the Antitrust Division furthered its own
policy, contrary to the declared policy of the president. Ehrlichman's
lack of success in dissuading the Justice Department from proceeding to
trial in the ITT cases, contrary he knew to ITT's faith in Ehrlichman's
power, caused him a loss of face. There was the appearance not of control
but of its absence. Ehrlichman's subordinates in the policy making scheme
had simply ignored his directives, and Ehrlichman had been able to do
nothing about it. For this he blamed Mitchell and McLaren; since Ehrlichman hesitated to beard Mitchell directly, he could not be sure where the
breakdown had actually occurred.

Following his embarrassment of 1970 Ehrlichman had set about trying
to devise means to bridle McLaren. It was clear to Ehrlichman at least
that Mitchell was not exercising the supervision over McLaren which
Ehrlichman felt was required. By the Nixon plan, the policies set in the
White House were supposed to be executed by the cabinet departments.
Ehrlichman, after all, was in charge of domestic policy, including antitrust,
and he believed he had the backing of the president on the ITT matter.
But Mitchell, by all appearances, simply refused to go along. And

Mitchell was still too powerful for even Ehrlichman to go head-to-head against.

Ehrlichman came up with the idea of a Domestic Council–controlled review of antitrust. Since this would be a general overview of policy process and content, and since, under Ehrlichman's plan, it would be conducted ostensibly by a committee composed of key administration officials (including Mitchell), this would avoid a direct confrontation with Mitchell over the ITT cases. Yet Ehrlichman was confident that, under his guidance, the committee would come out in favor of a conservative antitrust policy, including a reversal of McLaren's conglomerate merger enforcement efforts. Once the committee had reached its conclusions, Mitchell could hardly escape translating them into Department of Justice policy.

The means of Ehrlichman's approach to the president is not revealed. It is recorded, however, that by February, 1971 Ehrlichman had gained presidential authorization for the Domestic Council Committee on Antitrust Policy with responsibility to examine "existing Administration antitrust policy in all of its aspects ... as a foundation for further policy determinations." The committee, to function under Ehrlichman as director of the Domestic Council, consisted of five cabinet officers, with a working group of White House and departmental personnel. The cabinet officers appointed to the committee were Mitchell (attorney general), George Shultz (Office of Management and Budget), John Connally (Treasury), Maurice Stans (Commerce), and the secretary of labor. The working group, which was to generate policy option papers for the committee, included McLaren from the Antitrust Division; Peter Flanigan and Peter G. Peterson, both assistants to the president; Paul McCracken, chairman of the Council of Economic Advisers; and James Lynn, Commerce general counsel. As coordinator of the committee, Ehrlichman named Egil Krogh, an Ehrlichman assistant and a previous associate in Ehrlichman's Seattle law firm. Ehrlichman and Krogh began to set the working group in motion, with the idea of generating a final committee report by May, 1971.

ITT's contacts with the administration had subsided with the beginning of the Grinnell trial. After Judge Timbers's decision in December, 1970, Geneen made plans to renew his efforts. The immediate aim was to leave the Grinnell decision undisturbed—to prevent an appeal to the Supreme Court. ITT could now say that from the very beginning it had pointed out that McLaren's theory was bad economics and bad law, and that ITT had been wholly vindicated by Judge Timbers's decision. To carry McLaren's misguided campaign further would compound the original folly and would make it appear as though the administration were taking a punitive attitude toward big business. ITT's "image" argument would gather force as the 1972 elections began to assume greater immediacy within the administration.

ITT's renewed efforts to prevent appeal, like its earlier campaign, would not be directed at the man in the center, McLaren. ITT had early abandoned any hope that McLaren would change his policy voluntarily. Rather, ITT used an encirclement strategy. Its persuasion efforts were designed to involve the White House in the case; ITT sought those who had the president's ear. If they could be persuaded to speak up for ITT's position, it was believed that the president could be won over.

Geneen renewed his Washington campaign in early 1971. He met with Treasury Secretary David Kennedy and Economic Council Chairman McCracken. Geneen also attended a meeting between a group of business leaders and White House business adviser Peter Flanigan where the administration's antitrust policies were questioned. Not until two months after Judge Timbers's decision in the Grinnell case, however, did ITT's 1971 campaign heat up. Geneen earlier may have been under the misimpression that the White House was already seeing to it that McLaren could not appeal the Grinnell decision. (It is unlikely, however, that ITT would have been counting on Griswold to derail the appeal, as almost happened.)

Geneen received word on March 1, 1971 that McLaren had filed a notice of appeal in the Grinnell case. ITT now went back to work with vigor. Geneen's ability to gain quick attention is demonstrated by the fact that only two days later, at 10 o'clock of the morning of March 3, Geneen and Merriam were in Ehrlichman's office. Geneen reiterated his unhappiness with McLaren's merger policy and pointedly noted that the business community as a whole was unhappy. Geneen said that the Grinnell decision ought not to be appealed to the Supreme Court; the district court's decision was clearly correct, so there was no reason for appeal. Ehrlichman informed Geneen that the entire question of antitrust enforcement, including conglomerate mergers, was under study by the Domestic Council Antitrust Policy Committee. He fully expected that the Domestic Council project would bring about a change in conglomerate merger policy, and that this would also resolve ITT's problems regarding the three merger cases. Ehrlichman invited Geneen to confer with Krogh for more details on the workings of this project.

Ehrlichman was also seeking new allies within the government to aid him in making Mitchell responsive to White House policy. In February, 1971, with fanfare, the president had formed a new White House Council on International Economic Policy, to be headed by Peter G.

Peterson with the title of assistant to the president for international economic affairs. Peterson arrived at the White House after serving for almost ten years as chief executive officer of Bell & Howell Company (the same firm that Geneen had once worked for). Ehrlichman suggested that ITT should convey to Peterson its views on the detriment to the international position of United States business caused by McLaren's conglomerate merger policy. Ehrlichman noted that Peterson even then was putting together a presentation for the president on current problems in the international trade area. An approach to Peterson would be doubly beneficial since Peterson was also a member of the working group of the Domestic Council Antitrust Policy Committee.

Merriam's follow-up letter to Ehrlichman after this meeting said that he and Geneen "both came away from the meeting with the thought that you understand our position perfectly and are sympathetic." (While Merriam had to apologize for Geneen's having addressed Ehrlichman as "Chuck" on several occasions, this does not seem to have harmed ITT's case.)

Geneen himself next went to initiate John Connally, who had recently succeeded David Kennedy as treasury secretary, into the intricacies of the ITT merger cases. Geneen received a favorable response from Connally, who said that he would do what he could to help.

In the meantime Geneen dispatched Merriam in late March to see Peter G. Peterson, as Ehrlichman had suggested. Merriam and Thomas Casey, another ITT lobbyist, presented to Peterson ITT's views of the injury that McLaren's rigid antitrust policy would cause to the United States international trade position. The administration ought to consider resurrecting the Stigler commission report, with which, said Merriam, McLaren's conglomerate merger enforcement policy conflicted. Peterson suggested that ITT provide something in writing, and several days later Merriam sent to Peterson a memorandum which argued that the United States antitrust philosophy, unlike that of most foreign countries, ran counter to the salutary objective of increasing efficiencies and economies of scale in order to improve "competitiveness in world markets." On April 8 Peterson made his presentation to the president on international economic matters. This presentation included a review of antitrust policy with specific reference to the materials submitted by ITT.

By early April, 1971 ITT was coming closer to the presidential office in its quest for relief from McLaren's conglomerate merger policy. In addition to Peterson's presentation, which ITT understood was favorable to its position, Connally and McCracken spoke to the president personally, expressing sympathy with ITT. Another ITT contact, Stans, took time to prepare a memorandum for the president in which he faulted

McLaren's merger policy as counterproductive. But ITT's trump card seemed to be Ehrlichman, perhaps because he approached the cause not simply as a vindication of particular policy but as a power struggle to render the Justice Department responsive to White House command.

Several days after Peterson's April 8 presentation to the president, Ehrlichman told Peterson that the president wanted him to meet with Geneen personally to discuss antitrust policy and several other matters. Geneen, together with Merriam, went to see Peterson on the afternoon of April 16, only four days before the deadline for perfecting the Grinnell appeal in the Supreme Court. Geneen again complained of McLaren's "bigness" policy as exemplified by the ITT merger cases, and this time said that something needed to be done promptly in view of the impending Grinnell deadline. Geneen expressed his view that it would be dangerous to let that case go before the Supreme Court. When Peterson later that day reported to Ehrlichman on Geneen's concern over the Grinnell deadline, Ehrlichman responded, according to Peterson, that "the situation was well in hand, or under control, and, in any event, he indicated that action was underway to postpone the appeal."

In early April, 1971 Geneen had decided to bring a new actor into the drama of the ITT merger cases to make another appeal to the Justice Department. His reasons for doing so are murky. Some have speculated that Ehrlichman suggested it, to provide a cover for his own efforts to terminate the ITT cases. The story would then be told that the department yielded to reason as expressed to it by this new person. If a plan such as this were to be carried off, manifestly the new person would have to be one of considerable public standing.

The new actor brought in by Geneen indeed was a man of high reputation. He was Lawrence E. Walsh, a partner in the New York law firm of Davis Polk & Wardwell. Walsh was a man of extensive government service, most recently as deputy, with the rank of ambassador, in the United States delegation to the Paris peace talks on Vietnam, second in that assignment only to Averell Harriman. Walsh had also been a federal judge, appointed by Eisenhower, and had left the bench to become deputy United States attorney general from 1958 to 1960. As chairman of the American Bar Association federal judiciary committee (which reviewed prospective judicial appointments), Walsh had frequent contact beginning in 1968 with Kleindienst (now the holder of Walsh's old post), who had primary administration responsibility for judicial appointments. Walsh also had antitrust experience; he had successfully defended the Ling-Temco Electronics–Chance-Vought merger in the suit brought by the Justice Department in the early 1960s; he had also defended Gulf & Western, unsuccessfully, in a suit brought by one of its unreceptive take-over targets.

On April 8, 1971 Geneen, together with ITT's general counsel Howard Aibel, met with Walsh. They asked that Walsh prepare and present to the administration a position paper on conglomerate merger policy and the need to keep the Supreme Court out of the picture. Geneen's initial suggestion, according to Walsh, was that the presentation go directly to the president. But, said Walsh, "I thought it would not be effective because the antitrust field is too specialized and I didn't think the President would ever get into it." While Walsh has later said that he expressed doubts to Geneen and Aibel that the project could succeed, nevertheless he agreed to make a presentation within the Justice Department. Geneen informed Walsh that an interdepartmental committee within the government was studying the conglomerate question, and that he expected to receive support for ITT's position from that group. According to Geneen, his purpose in the new presentation was to spur an open discussion; "If McLaren could hear the other side of the problem perhaps there could be some recognition he was following a policy, which, in my mind, was not a good policy."

Walsh worked quickly. In little more than a week he had completed his written presentation, and Geneen and Aibel had approved it. On Friday, April 16 Walsh telephoned Kleindienst (who Walsh understood "had already been consulted") saying that he would deliver a memorandum on the ITT cases and conglomerate mergers to Kleindienst on that same day. Kleindienst countered that it would be more appropriate to deliver it directly to McLaren, who was in charge of the cases. Walsh responded that the presentation involved a policy matter which ought to be resolved at the department's highest levels; he would hope that both Kleindienst and Mitchell would give their attention to the presentation for ITT. Kleindienst, perhaps from deference to Walsh's past honors, finally said to go ahead and send the paper to him, but discouraged the suggestion that Mitchell, who was self-disqualified from the cases, be consulted.

The Walsh memorandum was delivered by an associate of Walsh's law firm to Kleindienst on the afternoon of April 16, 1971. Kleindienst received the memorandum without entering into any discussion with the bearer and, so Kleindienst claims, immediately sent his copy along to McLaren. On the same afternoon Merriam, having obtained Walsh's memorandum, delivered copies to the White House for Ehrlichman and Peterson.

The presentation, in Walsh's words, was addressed to the question of "prosecutorial responsibility." The arguments contained in Walsh's memorandum ran the gamut of reasons devised for permitting diversification by acquisition. This practice, according to Walsh, stimulates "new competitiveness in established industries." ITT "has been able to apply modern management skills in such a way as to increase very substantially the efficiency and competitiveness of the companies it acquired," he said, as illustrated by the growth and development of Avis and Sheraton. Walsh tried to turn to his advantage the recent high rate of diversification mergers, noting that the sheer number of such mergers "indicate[s] the importance of this 'capital market' for business." In ITT's case, moreover, its diversification was vital to the nation's balance of payments by permitting ITT to take the risks of doing business overseas while balanced by a stable economic base in the United States. Walsh's language almost soared: "Diversification by merger is the most important guarantee that every economic resource of the Nation will in fact be used to the best advantage."

Consequently, Walsh continued, the administration should not run the risk of "judicial legislation of a blanket condemnation of all significant mergers and diversification" which might ensue from the Grinnell appeal. This question should receive more input and study than is possible in Supreme Court review. The Supreme Court, after all, "has made clear that in merger cases it will look to the antitrust laws alone, and will disregard any economic or other public benefits resulting from the merger." And speaking of the Supreme Court, said Walsh, "if the government urges an expanded interpretation of the vague language of the Clayton Act, there is a high probability that it will succeed. Indeed, the court has at times adopted a position more extreme than that urged by the Department."

Before taking any conglomerate merger cases to the Supreme Court, the administration ought to heed the Stigler commission report: "The Department of Justice should initiate a comprehensive, Government-wide review of the national interest implications of diversification by merger," and should receive the views of the departments of the Treasury, Commerce, and Labor, and the Council of Economic Advisers, all of whom Walsh understood "have some views with respect to the question under consideration" (an obvious reference to the Domestic Council Antitrust Study Committee). The matter of putting the Grinnell case before the Supreme Court, in short, should be preceded by "all of the usual precautions that precede a recommendation for new legislation." To enable this review to go forward without the hindrance of pending litigation, Walsh suggested that the Grinnell case not be appealed, or at least be postponed "long enough to permit us to make a more adequate presentation on this question."

Walsh's presentation, while deftly assembled, added little to the arguments that ITT had already been making for more than a year (albeit the prior efforts were not as elegantly phrased). Walsh's different twist was that, for effect, he was virtually admitting the probability that ITT would be dealt a defeat by the Supreme Court. Walsh was saying, in an indirect way, that the Supreme Court simply did not, and could not, understand the functioning of the United States economic system. The executive branch was better equipped for that task and should not abdicate to the Supreme Court. (Naturally, Walsh was not publicly conceding the outcome of the Grinnell case before the Supreme Court; he assumed that his memorandum would never reach public view so there would be no way it could cut against ITT's legal position.)

On the morning of Monday, April 19, 1971—one day before the deadline for perfecting the Grinnell appeal to the Supreme Court—McLaren delivered to Kleindienst a one and one-half page memorandum expressing his disagreement with the Walsh proposal. McLaren thought Walsh had overstated his case; McLaren said he was not attempting to bar all diversification mergers as Walsh implied, and indeed the Grinnell case "will not necessarily plow new ground." McLaren's back seemed to stiffen a bit: "I know you have very much in mind the strong position I have taken with regard to using Section 7 of the Clayton Act to hold down the most anticompetitive kinds of conglomerate mergers." But, McLaren continued, Mitchell had expressed personal agreement with this program. (Or, ITT might have Walsh, but I have Mitchell.) What would be the effect of acceding to Walsh's request to solicit the views of other government departments? Said McLaren bluntly, it "would amount to abandoning a basic policy of the Department when the reasons for continuing it are just as strong as they ever were."

McLaren had just emerged from a protracted struggle to convince Griswold to authorize the Grinnell appeal. He was in no mood to give any quarter even to a fellow lawyer as respected as Walsh. Even a postponement would be unwarranted. "ITT's appeal comes at a very late hour"; having had one postponement, "it would be highly embarrassing to ask for another" on the day before the due date for the government's jurisdictional statement. Furthermore, "Any such request [for extension of time] certainly would be taken as a sign of weakness, and very possibly could undermine the big-merger deterrent which we have thus far developed."

In the face of McLaren's opposition there seemed to be little that

Kleindienst could do to assist ITT, even had he wanted to. Mitchell in his 1969 Georgia Bar Association speech seemingly had backed McLaren; intervention by Kleindienst at this point might precipitate an open struggle for Mitchell's favor. Kleindienst telephoned Walsh later in the morning of April 19 and left word that the answer to Walsh's plea probably was going to be negative. Walsh telephoned Aibel with this piece of bad news. The news quickly made its way to Ehrlichman, via Merriam.

At 2:30 in the afternoon of April 19, Ehrlichman telephoned Kleindienst. This was not characteristic of Ehrlichman; he did not like to deal with the second in command. But Mitchell obviously had pleaded his self-disqualification from the ITT cases to avoid being bothered further by Ehrlichman. This left Ehrlichman no choice but to go to Kleindienst. The president, Ehrlichman told Kleindienst, does not want the ITT appeal to proceed. Kleindienst responded that the decision to appeal was already made and it was too late to change it. Ehrlichman reminded Kleindienst that he was communicating a presidential directive. Kleindienst regretted having to disagree, but the department was now committed to the appeal; Ehrlichman should inform the president of the circumstances. Ehrlichman terminated the conversation with a vow that the matter was not closed.

It is not difficult to appreciate Kleindienst's dilemma. On the one side, there was McLaren invoking the blessing of Mitchell, who was Kleindienst's sponsor and the man Kleindienst hoped to succeed as attorney general. On the other side, there was Ehrlichman—who Kleindienst knew to have no bond with Mitchell—handing down supposed direct orders from the president. Kleindienst had to line up with Mitchell, not only because of his own ambition and his personal loyalty to Mitchell but also because of uncertainty about Ehrlichman's real authority. The staff of the Nixon White House freely, even loosely, purported to voice the direct wishes of the president in all manner of things. It was hard to be sure when the president had actually spoken on the subject, and when he had not. Kleindienst gambled that Ehrlichman was bluffing.

As for Ehrlichman, he made his way to the Oval Office.

13

IN THE OVAL OFFICE

The order is to leave the God damned thing alone. Now, I've said this, Dick, a number of times, and you fellows apparently don't get the message over there. I do not want McLaren to run around prosecuting people, raising hell about conglomerates, stirring things up at this point. Now you keep him the hell out of that.

Richard M. Nixon, speaking to
Richard Kleindienst, April 19, 1971

At approximately 3 o'clock on the afternoon of April 19, 1971, John Ehrlichman entered the office of the president of the United States. Present at the same time (whether by design is unknown) was George Shultz, director of the Office of Management and Budget, who, after Arthur Burns had moved to the Federal Reserve Board, became Nixon's principal adviser on economic matters. Ehrlichman initiated the discussion by saying that something had to be done at once about the ITT "antitrust thing:" "We are going to see the Attorney General tomorrow, and by then it may be too late, in a sense." The discussion continued:

Ehrlichman: God knows we have made your position as clear as we could to Mr. what's-his-name over there.

President: McLaren.

Ehrlichman: And, uh, John has said because ITT is involved, he's not involved because he's got a conflict of interest going back to the old law firm.

President: Huh [unintelligible].

Ehrlichman: Richard Kleindienst, uh, uh, has been supervising McLaren's work. It's the Grinnell case. It involves an attack on, uh, conglomerates, on a theory which specifically had been contemplated by the Johnson administration and laid aside as too antibusiness.

President: Kleindienst is in this?

Ehrlichman: Yes.

The president asked the White House operator to call Kleindienst.

Ehrlichman: They filed a notice of appeal. If we do not file a statement of jurisdiction by tomorrow the case is dead.

President: Who did?

Ehrlichman: Uh—the Justice Department.

President: They're not going to file.

Ehrlichman: Well, I thought that was your position.

President: Oh, hell.

Ehrlichman: I've been trying to give, I've been trying to give them signals on this, and, uh, they've been horsing us pretty steadily.

In introducing the subject Ehrlichman had played upon two aspects which were certain to pique Nixon's interest. One was that the Nixon administration was acting in an "antibusiness" fashion, extending further than the Johnson administration had been willing to go. The second was that the Justice Department in general, and McLaren in particular, were ignoring the directives communicated by the White House.

It is a fair inference that Nixon had given some attention to the ITT cases before. He could hardly have avoided it; McLaren's merger policy was the principal basis for Ehrlichman's request to form a Domestic Council Antitrust Policy Committee which had been approved by the president. Nixon now assured Ehrlichman and Shultz that his concern was a matter of principle rather than of politics:

I don't want to know anything about the case. Don't tell me a thing about it. I don't want to know about Geneen. I've met him and I don't know— I don't know whether ITT is bad, good, or indifferent. But there is not going to be any more antitrust actions as long as I am in this chair. God damn it, we're going to stop it.

Having placed the telephone call to Kleindienst (although only a couple of minutes had passed), Nixon became impatient.

President: Where's Kleindienst? Isn't he in town?

Ehrlichman: Yeah. He's in his office. I just talked to him about an hour ago.

President: Well, we'll take care of it.

The telephone rang the completion of the call to Kleindienst. This exchange occurred.

President: I'm going to talk to John tomorrow about my general attitude on antitrust, and in the meantime, I know that he has left with you, uh, the IT & T thing because apparently he says he had something to do with them once.

Kleindienst: [Laughs] Yeah. Yeah.

President: Well, I have, I have nothing to do with them, and I want something clearly understood, and, if it is not understood, McLaren's ass is to be out within one hour. The IT & T thing—stay the hell out of it. Is that clear? That's an order.

Kleindienst: Well, you mean the order is to—

President: The order is to leave the God damned thing alone. Now, I've said this, Dick, a number of times, and you fellows apparently don't get the me—, the message over there. I do not want McLaren to run around prosecuting people, raising hell about conglomerates, stirring things up at this point. Now you keep him the hell out of that. Is that clear?

Kleindienst: Well, Mr. President—

President: Or either he resigns. I'd rather have him out anyway. I don't like the son-of-a-bitch.

Kleindienst: The, the question then is—

President: The question is, I know, that the jurisdiction—I know all the legal things, Dick, you don't have to spell out the legal—

Kleindienst: [Unintelligible] the appeal filed.

President: That's right.

Kleindienst: That brief has to be filed tomorrow.

President: That's right. Don't file the brief.

Kleindienst: Your order is not to file a brief?

President: Your—my order is to drop the God damn thing. Is that clear?

Kleindienst: [Laughs] Yeah, I understand that.

President: Okay.

Nixon replaced the receiver and murmured, as if to himself, "I hope he resigns. He may." (Presumably referring to McLaren, not Kleindienst.)

Shultz, who up until now had been only a silent observer, announced that he was planning a speech to address the question whether "business has become more monopolistic." There was, said Shultz, indeed no evidence of any increase in monopoly in American business. In fact, "my friend Stigler" reported a decline over the past thirty years in industrial concentration. As if to buttress Nixon's action in stopping the ITT-Grinnell appeal, Shultz went on to say:

And in the conglomerate area is what I think we are witnessing, is, uh, a sort of a reaction to the buildup of conglomerates, which is perhaps affected somewhat by the antitrust. But basically, the marketplace is taken care of, in a sense that a lot of the firms that acquired businesses that they really didn't know anything about, are finding that they can't run those businesses very well, and they are getting rid of them. And, uh, so there is a cleansing process taking place. And where you have, uh, where you have a [unintelligible] of conglomerates, I believe, the case can be made, uh, rather readily in, uh, many, many instances, that they add to the sharpness of competition, because they acquire a relatively small firm, they give it muscle and they send it into, into competition and make the market work better. At least this is the, this is the general posture that I'm taking in this, uh, talk, I believe that evidence—I don't—I mean I don't—I'm not a lawyer and I don't know all of that side of it.

Ehrlichman: You're not the only one.

Shultz: From the standpoint of the economics of it, uh, I would be the last to say we should not continue, uh, to, uh, pursue the antitrust laws in the proper way, but, the, uh—I think the conglomerates have taken a bum rap.

There was little in Shultz's defense of conglomerates that McLaren would contest. McLaren certainly did not feel that the conglomerates ran their acquired businesses any better than independent owners (so much for synergism). And McLaren had said, on a number of occasions, that he did not object to "foothold" diversification acquisitions—one by which a "relatively small firm," in the market context, is infused with new capital and management which would enable it to expand to become a viable competitor to the leading industry firms. But McLaren did not consider that his conglomerate merger enforcement policy, as expressed in the ITT and related cases, was attacking foothold acquisitions.

In response to Shultz's encouragement, Nixon delivered his views of product balance and conglomerate efficiency:

I mean the point is that on this antitrust they had deliberately gone into a number of areas which have no relationship with each other, to—whether it's a question of operating more, more efficiently than the rest. There's simply a question of tactically, they've gone off on a kick, that'll make them big God damn trust busters. That was all right fifty years ago. Fifty years ago maybe it was a good thing for the country. It's not a good thing for the country today. That's my views about it, and I am not—We've been, been through this crap.

But Nixon's real grievance was discipline and bureaucratic responsiveness:

This is, this is the problem. The problem is McLaren's a nice little fellow who's a good little antitrust lawyer out in Chicago. Now he comes in and all these bright little bastards that worked for the Antitrust Department for years and years and years and who hate business with a passion—any business—have taken him over. They haven't taken him over. Then of course McLaren is the man. They go into—Kleindienst is busy appointing judges; Mitchell is busy doing other things, so they're afraid to overrule him. By God they're not going to do it.

* * *

They've done several of them already about—They have raised holy hell with the people that we, uh, uh—Well, Geneen, hell, he's no contributor. He's nothing to us. I don't care about him. So you can—I've only met him once, twice—uh, we've, I'm just, uh—I can't understand what the trouble is.

Ehrlichman:	Well.
President:	It's McLaren, isn't it?
Ehrlichman:	McLaren has a very strong sense of mission here.
President:	Good—Jesus, he's—Get him out. In one hour.
Ehrlichman:	He's got a—
President:	One hour.
Ehrlichman:	Very strong—
President:	And he's not going to be a judge, either. He is out of the God damn government. . . . Oh, I know what McLaren is, he believes this.
Ehrlichman:	Yeah.
President:	I know. Who the hell—he wasn't elected [unintelligible] —
Ehrlichman:	That's the point—
President:	He is here by sufferance.
Ehrlichman:	That's the point.
President:	And he is not going to stay one, uh, another minute. Not a minute. Because he's going after everybody, you know, just—Why the hell doesn't he go after somebody that, uh—
Ehrlichman:	[Laughs] That's been suggested.
President:	Oh.

Nixon had, as if for the record, obliquely questioned McLaren's economic theories; affirmed that Geneen was not an acquaintance or contributor; and vented his anger over bureaucratic unresponsiveness. Later in the meeting (the intervening time having been filled by gossip on matters which, in the milieu of the president's office, could only be termed trivia), Nixon's attention spontaneously returned to the subject of imposing discipline upon the federal bureaucracy:

President: You've got to do it. That is the trouble with McLaren. McLaren thinks he's going to do everything. To hell with him. I mean, we, we're willing to go along with it but he cannot deliberately just thumb his nose at everything that comes from this office, John. He is not that big, and of course, if John Mitchell won't stand up to him, I will. I don't want to, but I'll have to. We are not going to have it. All that they have to do in this case—I know what the procedure is—is that the Justice Department decides whether or not it's going to continue to fight the case. Isn't that what it is?

Ehrlichman: Right.

President: Then—well, God damn it, they lost the case before. Lose it. Lose it for once. They fought the good fight, and they lost. And, let the little bastards work on something else. Work on the study that you've asked them to send us. That would be very good.

Ehrlichman: That would be done here.

President: I'll say. You've got to get us some discipline, George. You've got to get it, and the only way you get it, is when a bureaucrat deliberately thumbs his nose, we're going to get him.

Presidential control of the mechanisms of government, as indicated by the April 19 discussion, was a subject that was very much on the president's mind during this period. After the 1970 midterm elections, in which the Republicans had fared badly, the White House set about refurbishing Nixon's image. One prong of the offensive was to picture the president as being in full command of the machinery of government, and as having a plan to simplify the governmental structure. Nixon's State of the Union message in January, 1971 sounded this theme in the form of proposals for general revenue sharing (to return to the states and cities functions now being performed by the central government) and his first reorganization plan. His intention, said Nixon, was "to focus and concentrate the responsibility for getting problems solved."

Nixon remained dissatisfied that control over domestic policy had lagged behind the Kissinger initiative in foreign affairs. Ehrlichman and Haldeman shared this feeling, and blamed the situation on bureaucratic inertia. Haldeman complained: "We came in to a government populated by people who had been placed there by previous administrations, most of them Democratic. . . . And we were dealing with a bureaucracy throughout the government peopled with individuals whose political philosophies were alien to ours." Nixon himself vowed: "I'm going to put into effect exactly the way that government should operate. I'm going to structure this government in a way that will work." While some would see Nixon's plan as an effort to use governmental programs to further his 1972 reelection campaign, others saw a genuine concern over questions of government effectiveness. The *New Republic* columnist John Osborne, for example, commented: "The [reorganization plan] reflects Mr. Nixon's familiar fascination with government and its processes, with the problems of making it work as he thinks it should."

It was thus in the context of an intensification of efforts to further centralize government management in the White House that the ITT cases were considered. In that atmosphere perhaps issues of the substance of public policy toward corporate growth melded into pure questions of control. Ehrlichman, the champion of ITT's position, was also the man in charge of Nixon's reorganization plan. Ehrlichman undoubtedly had some feel for the substance of the conglomerate merger issue; at least he had heard ITT's side. But Ehrlichman had no particular background in economic and antitrust matters. Probably his concern for the substantive policy was subordinate to a desire to have his authority vindicated, coupled with his view of the political situation. A "bigness is badness" image in the business community was far from what Ehrlichman felt the president should have, particularly in the parlous times of 1970–71 when there was an open break with labor and the polls showed his public support sinking.

Nixon himself certainly had more than a surface understanding of economic matters and the workings of the free enterprise system. Since his vice presidential days Nixon had taken advantage of his working relationship with Arthur Burns, an economist with a long history of public service, to gain a knowledge of economic concepts. During Nixon's first term George Shultz came to replace Burns as Nixon's economic mentor. Their teaching expectedly would instill in Nixon a permissive attitude toward corporate growth; and it is apparent from the conversation of April 19 that Nixon was aware beforehand of the issues of the ITT merger cases as related to those teachings.

At the Justice Department the president's telephone call of April 19 presented Kleindienst with a dilemma. Dropping the appeal would alienate

McLaren, and maybe also Griswold. While Kleindienst undoubtedly had the power to discontinue the appeal, the others would feel that decisions within their special province and expertise had been overriden peremptorily after weeks of arduous study. They would undoubtedly demand to know why the order was made. Moreover, the Congress and the press well might explore the reason. Where would this leave Kleindienst? Would the president take the responsibility, or would Kleindienst be left on his own?

On the other hand, outright disobedience of the president's order well might end Kleindienst's political career; his expectation of becoming attorney general would vanish.

Kleindienst felt overwhelmed—the president's call had come only one day before the jurisdictional statement was due to be filed. That left a wholly inadequate time for Kleindienst to sort out the alternatives and come up with a solution. Fortunately, Kleindienst had at hand a ready if not wholly satisfactory means of temporizing—Walsh's request to postpone the appeal pending further study. Kleindienst called McLaren back to his office. Almost pleadingly Kleindienst expressed his desire to grant Walsh's request for an extension of time. Kleindienst referred to his smooth working relationship with Walsh in the selection of federal judges. Would a postponement really be such a serious setback to McLaren's program? McLaren repeated his belief that the Walsh memorandum included no · considerations which had not previously been reviewed and rejected by the Antitrust Division, but had to concede that an extension would not be fatal to the department's position in the ITT cases. On the understanding that the extension of time signified only allowing ITT time to talk to other government agencies—and not an acceptance of Walsh's premises—McLaren said he would not hold to his objection.

Having McLaren's reluctant consent, Kleindienst now called in Griswold and explained Walsh's request. Griswold indicated that a last-minute request, such as this would be, was out of the normal pattern. The solicitor general's office is careful to maintain compliance with the rules and procedures of the Supreme Court, which ordinarily require the request be made ten days in advance. But the request could be made, and Griswold thought it would be granted. Kleindienst asked Griswold to go ahead and make the request. The application for extension of time, filed later that same day, stated: "The additional time is needed for further study of the case and to permit consultation among various interested government agencies with regard to whether the government should perfect its appeal." The next day, the Supreme Court granted the requested extension, and the deadline for filing the jurisdictional statement in the ITT-Grinnell case was now May 20, 1971.

The postponement gave Kleindienst breathing room, but did not solve his dilemma; he still must handle the presidential order to drop the appeal. Kleindienst was later to say that, notwithstanding his career aspirations, he would have resigned rather than execute the president's order. This reluctance was hardly apparent from his telephone conversation with the president where he appeared perfectly amenable. But, in fact, Kleindienst—whether out of trepidation or shrewdness—probably handled the matter in the best way possible. Perhaps he sensed from the president's tone that the latter was in no mood to countenance insubordination; disagreement by Kleindienst probably would only have hardened Nixon's position. It would be best if another pitch were made to Nixon after he cooled down, and by the best possible man for the job—Attorney General Mitchell. In the face of Ehrlichman's vigorous opposition to the ITT cases, and the sympathy for ITT's position already expressed by the administration's economic leaders—e.g., Connally of Treasury, Stans of Commerce, Shultz of the Office of Management and Budget, and McCracken of the Council of Economic Advisers—who else indeed was left? There probably was no man but Mitchell who could obtain a reversal of a presidential decision reached on the advice of that group of administration officials.

Sometime between the afternoon of April 19 and the afternoon of April 21 Kleindienst spoke to Mitchell. The extent of Kleindienst's confidence that Mitchell would seek reversal of the presidential order is unknown. But Mitchell agreed that he would speak with the president. In the late afternoon of April 21, 1971, he did so.

Mitchell introduced the subject with the president by saying he wanted to talk "about this antitrust business, because this is political dynamite." Mitchell had obviously decided that it would be better strategy to avoid substantive discussion of conglomerate merger policy or White House policy control. Mitchell continued:

I'm talking about the whole picture of, of, of this ITT, uh, what can develop out of this, Senate investigation and so forth, if you don't need it. You don't need it for these bastards up there to burden us with it. I don't know who's been giving you the information, but it's a bad political mistake. I'm not talking about the merits of it.

Mitchell's introduction had the desired effect of channeling Nixon's thoughts along political lines. Nixon responded:

John, the problem we've got is this, that we've got a, uh, that, uh—I don't give a damn about the merits either, uh, but we have a situation where, uh, and, uh, Connally has spoken to me about it—but, uh, where the business community, for, for—believes that we're a hell of a lot rougher on them in the antitrust than our predecessors were.

The president added: "And they don't think you are, they think McLaren is, because he leads you to believe this."

The implication that McLaren was somehow acting beyond Mitchell's control seemed to pique the attorney general. He became defensive:

It wasn't McLaren, you know, that started all this. It was your Council of Economic Advisers and Arthur Burns, and it was done in order to help cool this economy and the stock market and I could go on to a lot of other things. And, uh, the things that they're accusing McLaren of are just, uh, uh, made out of whole cloth. It's just not true. There are anti-trust cases here, but [Mitchell had regained his composure] what I want to talk about is the political aspects of it. And if, uh, if this thing should be turned off, it, I mean the general concept of it, you've got a review going now—intergovernmental—well, it's time to do it. But you just can't stop this thing up at the Supreme Court, because you will have Griswold quit, you will have a Senate investigation—Hart will just love this—and we don't need it.

As though to offer a face-saving option, Mitchell added, without further explanation, "There are other ways of working this out."

Something in Mitchell's brief explanation was enough to persuade the president: "Well, go ahead, you could—Yeah, I understand that. If that's the problem politically, go ahead."

But, said the president, someone had to talk to Connally and Stans, who had been pressing him on the cases. ("Yeah, I know. I know," said Mitchell.) And Nixon didn't want to be present for that discussion. "You handle it. If you'll just sit down and convince them, I don't want to hear anything more about it."

And, added Nixon, speak to McCracken also. Mitchell reacted to that: "McCracken, for Christ's sakes, he was the one that basically started this."

Undeterred, Nixon continued: McCracken "feels you ought to go to New York and resolve the antitrust." Mitchell replied, "Yeah. Now, well, what we ought to do is change the policy and not—and we can get rid of this ITT thing, I think." Mitchell again mentioned the Domestic Council antitrust policy project:

Mitchell: Now we have an intergovernmental study going on.

President: I know about that.

Mitchell: The antitrust policies, and this, this is fine, but you don't
               just cut this thing off at the top, and then get up before
               that Hart Committee up there and get yourself chewed to
               pieces.

Nixon by now was thoroughly convinced. "All right, fine." He closed, "I don't care about the ITT. I don't even know what it is."

The next morning Mitchell telephoned Kleindienst to report that the president had changed his mind, and that the Grinnell appeal could go forward. Kleindienst was considerably relieved.

Within a week Ehrlichman knew that Mitchell had persuaded the president to rescind his order to abandon the ITT-Grinnell appeal; he was not happy about it. Again Mitchell had thwarted Ehrlichman's efforts to stop the ITT cases. In the summer of 1970 Mitchell had rebuffed Ehrlichman by the simple device of inaction. Now he had come out in direct conflict with Ehrlichman, and, much to Ehrlichman's dismay, the president had listened to Mitchell. That Mitchell had remarkable power in the White House was shown by his ability to gain a presidential reversal in the face of imposing support in the administration for dropping the ITT cases.

Ehrlichman believed, presumably, that it would be inadvisable to make a direct request to the president to reinstate his order. Ehrlichman's position was not yet secure enough to invite a power struggle with Mitchell. Ehrlichman's approach rather would be to keep the pressure on to channel all antitrust policy decisions through his Domestic Council Antitrust Policy Committee. Under Ehrlichman's plan the Domestic Council Committee was supposed to be the vehicle for gaining control of antitrust policy; Mitchell's direct approach to the president had simply sidestepped the committee.

On April 28 Ehrlichman wrote an "action" memorandum to the president. It began:

The ITT cases have surfaced what we have known to be a problem for some time. Your strong views on how the Administration should conduct antitrust enforcement are not being translated into action.

Ehrlichman asked the president to approve three specific proposals. The first was:

McLaren and the Attorney General be requested to provide you, in writing, with a report of the *posture* of the ITT and associated cases. (My hunch is that McLaren may have invented reasons to appeal the ITT case and he should be put on his proof.) Unless we have a clear picture he will be likely to drive these ahead quickly.

Second, Ehrlichman recommended that a concurrent antitrust policy study being conducted by Arthur Burns, Federal Reserve chairman—which Ehrlichman had discovered when he began to get into the ITT matters—be suspended "for now." Ehrlichman thought that this duplicative effort would further splinter White House control.

The third proposal, which followed from the first two, was that "all government-wide antitrust policy work be coordinated through one White House office," namely the Domestic Council Committee directed by Ehrlichman. One reason given for this unitization of responsibility was a fear that Burns's study "seriously threatens to scare McLaren off our Domestic Council project (getting him to set out Administration anti-trust policy, in writing). That may sound silly, but I'm convinced McLaren's belief that Arthur is about to make conservative recommendations will cause McLaren to be less candid in his work to us. We will, thereby, end up with less ammunition."

What Ehrlichman did not spell out—and probably did not need to—was that the ammunition was going to be used against McLaren himself. The president approved Ehrlichman's proposals, explaining later that his approval was designed "to ensure that the President's views on the subject [of government antitrust policy] could be made known to all the operating agencies."

The Domestic Council Committee's antitrust policy study was proceeding, although at a considerably slower pace than Ehrlichman had anticipated. McLaren had already delivered a lengthy policy memorandum to the committee. Although Ehrlichman had had that paper for over a month, it happened that, on April 30, 1971, through Egil Krogh, he communicated his comments to McLaren. One aspect which Ehrlichman wanted clarified was:

You should also include a statement of present policy on informing and/or coordinating antitrust enforcement policy with other federal government agencies, prior to the bringing of litigation. Emphasis should be placed on the new priority enforcement areas such as conglomerate mergers, patents, reciprocity, etc.

The implication was clear that Ehrlichman believed that antitrust policy decisions must take into account broader input than the parochial views of the Antitrust Division.

Ehrlichman discussed the ITT cases again with the president and Mitchell shortly after the president had approved Ehrlichman's April 28 action memorandum. This meeting resulted in a memorandum from Ehrlichman to Mitchell in early May recording the decision reached in their discussion:

Following up our conversation at the Cabinet meeting the other day, I would like to arrange to talk with Dick McLaren about the present status of the ITT cases in order that we can achieve the agreed-upon ends discussed by the President with you.

Would you like me to make this arrangement directly with Dick or would you prefer to have us work through you?

Those "agreed-upon ends" are still known only to Nixon, Mitchell, and Ehrlichman. It is a fair assumption that they did not include dropping the ITT-Grinnell appeal as such, because Mitchell had put himself on the line with Kleindienst on that subject. The ends could have encompassed a number of possibilities; in view of the tone of Ehrlichman's memorandum, it would seem that he was pleased, ergo the agreed ends probably were on the whole favorable to ITT. Aside from dropping the Grinnell appeal, which was unlikely, the ends could have included dropping—or more likely an agreement not to appeal—the Canteen and Hartford cases. Or, the ends might have been simply that McLaren should do his utmost to work out a settlement of all three cases with ITT. The latter certainly would have been the happier solution, since it would achieve Nixon's objective, later expressed, of avoiding a Supreme Court ruling on conglomerate mergers, and would minimize discord both within the administration and from critics outside the government, which seemed to be Mitchell's main concern.

In fact, on April 20, 1971, the day after Nixon's original order to drop the appeal, ITT had initiated settlement discussions, through an approach by Felix Rohatyn to Kleindienst, and on April 29 ITT representatives had met with McLaren and his staff on the subject. Ehrlichman knew about these settlement discussions, from information provided to him by ITT. Since settlement was such an obviously attractive way to conclude the entire ITT imbroglio, it would have been surprising had that option not been discussed at the meeting between Nixon, Mitchell, and Ehrlichman.

ITT was pleased with the thirty-day delay in the Grinnell appeal; it also "came as a surprise," according to Merriam, "because we understood that on Monday morning Dick Kleindienst had been negative about a delay."

After delivering the Walsh memorandum ITT took no steps of its own to attempt to generate decision making input to the Justice Department from other government agencies. McLaren had assumed that Walsh's presentation was somehow related to the Domestic Council antitrust policy review, but McLaren was puzzled by the implication "that he [Walsh] knew something that I did not . . . about these other agencies—that we were going to get representation from them." In fact, McLaren later said, he received no input during the thirty-day delay from any other government agency. Indeed, after Rohatyn's meeting with Kleindienst, Aibel had instructed Walsh to suspend his efforts on the Justice Department presentation because the initial settlement discussion had gone so well. Still Merriam assumed that the White House was going to continue its efforts on ITT's behalf. In a letter to Peterson on April 30 Merriam voiced the hope that "during the next twenty days Paul and the two Johns can convince the Department that the merger policy as now practiced will be suicidal for the economy of the country." Merriam added that the "work you and your associates have done has been highly effective—so much so that the Antitrust Division seems to show some evidence of concern. This is a step in the right direction."

Merriam sent a similar laudatory letter to Secretary of the Treasury Connally. In that letter, despite the absence in Walsh's memorandum of any discussion of settlement, Merriam reported that the thirty-day delay "of course, was great plus and will give us time to work out a settlement."

14

SETTLEMENT

*While reasonable men may differ over what the goals
and policies of the Department [of Justice] should
be with respect to conglomerate mergers in view
of the existing antitrust laws, . . . the Justice Department has wide discretion to settle government
antitrust actions through the negotiation of consent
decrees.*

Judge Joseph Blumenfeld
in United States v. ITT, 1972

Settlement, of course, is one of the best-accepted methods for concluding an antitrust suit. Indeed, more than half of all government merger
suits end in this fashion, the advantage of the bargain varying from one
side to the other depending upon the nature of the case and the relative
bargaining strengths of the parties. The impetus for settlement normally
begins with the defendant, and of course it usually starts low, intending
possibly to "sweeten the pot" later if necessary.

It is not difficult to pinpoint when ITT first considered settlement,
at least in a general way: as soon as the merger suits against it had been
filed. A defendant *always* considers settlement, from the very beginning,
since there is nothing to be lost—and perhaps much to be gained—from
analyzing the situation with a view to proposing settlement at a propi-
tious time.

The first record of ITT's broaching settlement to McLaren comes in
the early part of 1970—less than a year after the suits all had been filed,
and before any trial—when Gerrity, upon his own initiative, met with
McLaren (strangely enough, without ITT's lawyers being present). Gerrity
sought to feel out McLaren on his minimum deal. When McLaren said
that his minimum included divestiture of Hartford and Grinnell (ITT
could keep Canteen), Gerrity thanked him and left. This was not down
ITT's alley, and Geneen determined to go the political route rather than to
expend effort toward settlement at that point.

During its 1970 campaign to have the merger suits withdrawn in toto, ITT put aside thoughts of settlement, as merely a second-best alternative. There would be, of course, no reason to compromise if ITT could obtain complete victory through the White House. Only after that 1970 effort had seemingly failed, and the Grinnell and Canteen suits had gone to trial, did ITT reopen the possibility of settlement.

This time, as the district court decisions (still unknown, of course) approached, ITT made its first full-blown settlement offer. ITT brought in a new attorney, Ephraim Jacobs, formerly with the Antitrust Division, to present the proposal to McLaren. Near the end of November, 1970 Jacobs told McLaren what ITT was willing to do. To settle all three of the pending merger suits, ITT would divest the Grinnell pipe division (but not the fire protection division which made sprinkler systems); the Canteen in-plant feeding business (but not the vending machine business); ITT's three existing insurance subsidiaries (already owned before the Hartford acquisition); and, to make the offer more appealing, Levitt & Sons's domestic operations (exclusive of the Florida Palm Coast development started after the Levitt acquisition). ITT would also agree to a formal prohibition against reciprocity or intercorporate loans or investments using Hartford's assets.

ITT's interest in settlement was now cast and made known. It expected that it might have to give some more to make a settlement, but there was one precondition: it must keep Hartford. To Geneen, that was indispensable.

McLaren, however, was not in a mood to move from the message that he had given Gerrity earlier in 1970. Any settlement package, he told Jacobs, must include divestiture of Hartford. If ITT was not willing to begin there, then there would be nothing to negotiate. This demand stopped ITT's settlement effort in its tracks, as McLaren presumably knew that it would. In November, 1970 McLaren simply was not interested in settlement much short of capitulation by ITT. McLaren did take some comfort from ITT's settlement approach as a tacit admission of the strength of McLaren's cases against ITT.

By the time ITT came back to McLaren to discuss settlement again, much had happened. The principal development, of course, was Judge Timbers's resounding decision in December, 1970 in favor of ITT in the Grinnell case. Despite McLaren's optimism over the chances of gaining a reversal from the Supreme Court, still that decision must in some degree strengthen ITT's bargaining position. Added to this was Griswold's failure to share McLaren's optimism; although unknown to ITT, this undoubtedly had a psychological effect upon McLaren's view of settlement.

A second major development would be the broad consensus developing within the administration to reverse McLaren's conglomerate merger policy, which culminated in the thirty-day delay which Merriam claimed "will give us time to work out a settlement." Since the president's position in the case was not made known, however, either to ITT or to McLaren, so the latter has maintained, it presumably could have had no direct impact upon bargaining for settlement (although there are those who still find this hard to credit).

Geneen had geared up for a new settlement initiative even before the April 20, 1971 deadline for perfecting the Grinnell appeal had come (and been postponed). ITT now devised a new strategy for the selling of its settlement offer. Its first offer in November, 1970 had taken the direct approach, without avail. Since the only real obstacle to settlement was McLaren's insistence that ITT could not keep Hartford, ITT would begin by convincing McLaren that it *must* keep Hartford. If McLaren could be persuaded to accept the proposition that divestiture of Hartford would be impossible (in an economic sense), then the pieces of a settlement should fall readily into place.

To implement this strategy, Geneen called upon Felix Rohatyn of Lazard Frères & Company, ITT's merger adviser. Rohatyn had been instrumental in implementing Geneen's merger program, and his success had gained him a position on ITT's board of directors. Rohatyn had also achieved a degree of recognition in the financial community. He had been elected a governor of the New York Stock Exchange and was chairman of a special committee which was seeking to solve the severe financial difficulties being faced by the brokerage community in 1971 (a position which fortuitously entailed numerous contacts with the administration).

Geneen's hope that his new plan might work gained some support from the precedent set by McLaren's action in the case involving LTV's acquisition of Jones & Laughlin Steel Company. LTV had persuaded McLaren that a forced divestiture of J & L would drive LTV to the brink of bankruptcy. LTV indeed had experienced serious economic problems, including an extremely unsatisfactory cash flow position, brought about to a large extent because of LTV's debt financing of its numerous acquisitions. (LTV had a consolidated 1969 loss of $40.8 million, equal to $10.15 per share, and 1970 was looking even worse.) In June, 1970 a consent judgment was entered permitting LTV to keep J & L, but exacting alternative divestiture of Braniff Airline and Okonite (copper wire and cable producer). This fit Geneen's concept: he was willing to give up some of ITT's other less-important subsidiaries in order to retain Hartford.

Geneen and Rohatyn discussed the project in early April, 1971. They agreed that ITT should present a case based not upon legal and economic principles of antitrust, but rather upon the adverse financial consequences that would ensue if ITT were required to divest Hartford. Rohatyn set about documenting those adverse consequences. For assistance, and to lend authoritative weight to his presentation, Rohatyn retained two prominent economists as special consultants: Dr. Raymond Saulnier of Columbia University, who had been chairman of the Council of Economic Advisers under President Eisenhower, and Dean Willis J. Winn of the University of Pennsylvania Wharton School of Business. While it must be perfectly clear that ITT's ultimate goal was a settlement matrix, Rohatyn has always insisted that his function was not settlement but rather simply informing the Justice Department of the consequences of a possible divestiture of Hartford.

Normally Rohatyn's next step would be to request a meeting with McLaren to make the presentation. But, said Rohatyn, ITT's management and attorneys told him to go first to Kleindienst, as the man having ultimate responsibility for the cases, who would be expecting him. The groundwork had been laid in mid-April, 1971 when an ITT lobbyist, John Ryan, attending a social party with Kleindienst, asked if he would be willing to meet with an ITT representative to discuss "a matter of importance." Ryan reported back to ITT management that Kleindienst was agreeable to such a meeting. ITT later explained enigmatically that it was decided to bypass McLaren because "the policy considerations to be raised ranged beyond antitrust enforcement policy." Also, certainly, it would not hurt if a sympathetic attitude could be evoked in the top man.

Rohatyn's initial telephone call to Kleindienst came, coincidentally, on Friday, April 16, 1971—the same day that Geneen was meeting with Peterson in the White House, and Walsh was delivering to Kleindienst ITT's conglomerate policy paper. Rohatyn asked Kleindienst for a meeting to discuss the "economic consequences" if ITT were forced to divest Hartford. Kleindienst agreed to meet on the following Tuesday, April 20— the day after the Grinnell appeal was postponed. That meeting, attended only by Kleindienst and Rohatyn, opened on a seemingly strange note; Rohatyn stated that he disclaimed political credentials and in fact was working in Senator Edmund Muskie's presidential campaign. Rohatyn asked Kleindienst to assume, for the purposes of discussion, government success in all three ITT merger suits. What would happen then? The answer, Rohatyn said, was that a forced divestiture of Hartford would have "drastic economic consequences" for the companies involved, their stockholders, the general stock market, and the United States balance of payments. Kleindienst pointed out that the cases fell within McLaren's area in the Justice Department, and that any decision would have to be made in the first instance by McLaren. Rohatyn asked: would Kleindienst "direct Mr. McLaren" to give ITT an audience to hear the full details of these adverse consequences? Kleindienst responded that he would not "direct" McLaren, but he would ask him. (Rohatyn apparently missed this distinction because he continued to think that "Kleindienst directed that a full presentation be made to Mr. McLaren.")

After the meeting Kleindienst relayed Rohatyn's request to McLaren, who has summarized his response as follows:

I said that I would be perfectly willing to meet with the ITT people and to hear their presentation. . . . I told him that it would have to be a very persuasive presentation because I had made what I regarded as a "hardship" kind of settlement with Ling-Temco-Vought, and I felt that any such settlement should be made only under very exceptional circumstances.

Nevertheless, a meeting between McLaren and Rohatyn was scheduled for April 29.

At this point Merriam, following up ITT's previous contacts, reported to Peterson in the White House and to Treasury Secretary Connally that the April 20 meeting between Kleindienst and Rohatyn had been "very productive." Merriam noted that "delicate negotiations" would begin with McLaren on April 29 and that Kleindienst would "monitor" that meeting. Merriam's report was designed to keep open the channels of communication in the event ITT's settlement effort fell through; also, it would not hurt if some of the administration figures were to voice support for ITT's hardship position.

The April 29 meeting took place in McLaren's office in the Justice Department Building. McLaren was accompanied by four of his assistants who had been involved in the ITT merger cases (Walker B. Comegys, Robert Hummell, Charles Mahaffie, and Raymond M. Carlson). ITT was represented by Rohatyn, Dr. Saulnier, and Dean Winn, accompanied by ITT general counsel Howard Aibel and Henry Sailer of Covington & Burling. At McLaren's request the Treasury Department also sent a representative, Deputy Under Secretary Bruce MacLaury. Kleindienst was there to monitor the meeting as promised.

ITT's representatives said that Hartford might be divested in either of two ways: a sale of the stock, or a spinoff to ITT stockholders (either without consideration or in exchange for ITT shares). A sale would probably not be feasible; because of the large size of Hartford, acceptable purchasers would be unavailable. Moreover, ITT could not hope to recoup the "premium" it gave for Hartford, yet would still have to pay a substantial capital gains tax of the magnitude of $250 million on a sale, and the projected proceeds of sale would fall short by some $440 million of the amount needed to redeem the preferred stock. A spinoff would be no better; it would result in an aggregate $1.2 billion decline in the market value of ITT and Hartford as separate entities (a reduction from ITT's $64 per share to an equivalent $52 for the separate stocks). Moreover, a spinoff would leave ITT with an annual preferred stock dividend requirement of $50 million at the same time it would lose its income ($88.7 million in 1970) from Hartford. This requirement probably would cause a reduction in ITT's common stock dividends.

Much of ITT's presentation revolved around its multinational character, and its need for a strong domestic earnings base to support the risks of its foreign operations, which it said are important to the national balance of payments. Diminution of ITT's stable domestic earnings base (Hartford accounted for one-third of its domestic earnings) and its balance sheet deterioration would restrict its foreign expansion and reduce its overseas capacity (since foreign lenders look to ITT's credit rating in the United States). ITT's paper concluded: "The long term consequences of [divestiture of Hartford] in terms of ITT's ability to continue as a major international enterprise would be drastic in nature." Divestiture by ITT of Hartford would also jolt the stock market generally, said Rohatyn. "As Chairman of the New York Stock Exchange Surveillance Committee during that period of financial crisis, I was concerned that so massive a divestiture might unsettle our securities markets, and with possible impact on some financial organizations."

McLaren should not have been, and presumably was not, surprised at the thrust of ITT's presentation. It could not have been unexpected even though, in opposing the government's motion for a preliminary injunction, ITT had assured Judge Timbers that, were the acquisitions held unlawful after trial, complete and adequate relief (i.e., divestiture) would be possible without the necessity of an injunction preventing the merger from going forward. Antitrust defendants always contend that a "hold-separate" order, if anything, is all that is required before trial; later, however, it is not unusual to hear a claim that, for various reasons, divestiture is completely out of the question. Inconsistent perhaps, but not unexpected; this so frequently happens it is almost considered part of the game. Former Antitrust Division official Gordon B. Spivack has explained it this way: "You know on the day of the restraining order, defense counsel always says, 'We will hold it separate.' ... And when it came to divestiture, they said, 'We can't take it apart.' They always say that. They mean it in good faith, but that is the way it goes. It always works that way."

McLaren knew this, but, he said, ITT had presented a claim that at least deserved to be checked out. Not only had Rohatyn made his presentation in a most persuasive manner, but there was also the fact that it was supported by Dr. Saulnier and Dean Winn, both highly reputable economists. Hence, according to Kleindienst, McLaren concluded that

based upon the information given to him by ITT at that meeting, and the written data that they had provided, he thought that a very serious question in terms of the economic impact of the divestiture of Hartford had been raised and he felt that he had a duty in the discharge of his obligations to have the advice and counsel of an independent consultant to furnish an opinion as to whether or not the information supplied by ITT was accurate, and whether or not the projected consequences would ensue.

Under the circumstances, McLaren could hardly be faulted for seeking objective and competent advice. He has been faulted rather severely, however, for the strange way in which he went about it and for the rather narrow scope of the advice that he received.

McLaren turned to only one individual outside the government for advice. This individual, Richard Ramsden, was a Wall Street investment adviser who had spent a short term previously in government service, working part of that time for White House special assistant Peter Flanigan (himself a former vice president of Dillon Read & Company, investment bankers in New York). While Ramsden was in government service, McLaren had utilized Ramsden (who was steered to McLaren by Flanigan) to analyze LTV's hardship claims respecting its acquisition of Jones & Laughlin Steel Company.

McLaren said that Ramsden's prior services had been most satisfactory, and he decided to go to him again, which he did. But, peculiarly, McLaren never met with or talked to Ramsden about the ITT hardship claim. McLaren communicated what he wanted to Flanigan, who communicated with Ramsden. Ramsden's response came back to McLaren via the same route. That McLaren would let the matter filter through Flanigan seems to prove either that McLaren was unaware of the views of the White House on the ITT cases, or that he was and used this as a method to convey his acquiescence to the White House.

In the meantime, on May 10, Rohatyn, apparently impatient, returned to Kleindienst's office to "reiterate our broad policy concerns over so large a divestment." Kleindienst responded that McLaren was studying the matter, and that ITT would be advised when a decision was reached.

Ramsden completed his study in two weeks, and delivered his written report to Flanigan on May 18, 1971; Flanigan in turn delivered it to McLaren and Kleindienst. At least three-quarters of Ramsden's report was devoted to proving the proposition that ITT shares would lose market value if ITT and Hartford were returned to the status of separate, independent corporations. Ramsden agreed with ITT's position that some 16 percent of the ITT stock value would be lost by spinoff. The reason was that there would be a diminution in investor confidence, which was premised upon ITT's "diversification and broad business mix" that furnished a predictability of earnings increases.

Ramsden assumed that a spinoff would be the only practical method of divestiture; he noted that a sale "would be unattractive from ITT's point of view." Ramsden further agreed with ITT that divestiture of Hartford might cause ITT to suffer cash flow problems (without earnings from Hartford to service the preferred stock dividend requirement), and that the debt-equity ratio on ITT's balance sheet would revert to the less favorable position it held before the addition of $500 million in Hartford equity. "The result," he concluded, "would be a reduction in ITT's incremental parent company debt capacity and possibly credit rating," which might cause the subsidiaries' ability to finance to be "somewhat affected." And, to the extent that the cash flow reduction and balance sheet reversal affected ITT's consolidated credit picture, "there could be some indirect negative effect upon ITT's balance of payments contributions."

Certainly Ramsden's conclusions support part of the claims made by ITT in favor of its hardship argument. But Ramsden has later said that his report (which he says was confined to financial analysis and not economic evaluation) probably was construed more broadly than it deserved. He really gave only modest support to ITT's balance of payments argument, and did not mention at all a possibility of affecting stock values generally. Indeed, said Ramsden later, "I would question very seriously whether there would be any significant ripple effect." Nor did Ramsden feel that, as contrasted to the LTV case, ITT would be "in dire financial shape without Hartford."

Perhaps McLaren would have better understood the scope of Ramsden's analysis had he met with him to review it. But McLaren proceeded on his own, relying upon the ITT presentation, Ramsden's written report, and an informal oral report from McLaury of the Treasury Department that there was "merit in the ITT position" as to balance of payments and foreign operations. That McLaren, despite his best intentions, did not fully appreciate the limitations inherent in Ramsden's analysis is evident from McLaren's interpretation of the evidence:

If we are successful in obtaining a divestiture order in the ITT–Hartford Fire Insurance Company case, this will cripple ITT financially and seriously injure its 250,000 stockholders. Essentially, this is because ITT paid a $500 million premium for the Hartford stock but took its assets in at book value in a so-called pooling of interests transaction. It cannot now sell its Hartford stock without (a) suffering a serious loss as opposed to what it paid but, at the same time (b) incurring a large capital gain tax. A "spin-off" to its own shareholders would be a—and probably the only—feasible alternative; however, a spin-off would leave ITT with the large preferred dividend commitment it made in acquiring Hartford ($50 million a year), but without the earning power which was counted on to cover that commitment. The result, we are told, would be a loss of well over $1 billion in ITT common stock value, a weakened balance sheet, and reduced borrowing capacity.

We have had a study made by financial experts and they substantially confirm ITT's claims as to the effects of a divestiture order. Such being the case, I gather that we must also anticipate that the impact upon ITT would have a ripple effect—in the stock market and in the economy.

McLaren thus was forced to conclude, albeit "reluctantly" he said, that ITT should be allowed to retain Hartford. In his memorandum so recommending, McLaren sought to record his unhappiness over having to reach this conclusion: "ITT's management consummated the Hartford acquisition knowing it violated our antitrust policy; knowing we intended to sue; and in effect representing to the court that he need not issue a preliminary injunction because ITT would hold Hartford separate and thus minimize any divestiture problem if violation were found." And Judge Timbers was "perhaps equally guilty" for heeding ITT's plea that a preliminary injunction would have deprived Hartford's shareholders of a $500 million premium being offered by ITT for their stock. "Obviously, if such a premium is being paid on an unlawful acquisition, the acquiring company may lose that and more if forced to divest, and will so plead if found guilty."

But, said McLaren, divestiture of Hartford was not "worth enough more than a decree containing only injunctive relief to justify the projected adverse effects on ITT and its stockholders, and the risk of adverse effects on the stock market and the economy."

The date was June 17, 1971—a little more than two years after McLaren had begun his campaign to restrict large conglomerate mergers. It was now virtually inevitable that the campaign would end anticlimactically, not with a Supreme Court decision nor with a confrontation within the administration, but the way most run-of-the-mill antitrust cases end, by settlement. ITT's new plan had worked.

Kleindienst and McLaren jointly telephoned Rohatyn to convey the news. ITT would be permitted to keep Hartford, said McLaren, if it would divest Grinnell, Canteen, Avis, and Levitt. It also must agree to prohibitions against certain acquisitions in the future or the practice of reciprocity.

According to McLaren, as though to establish his command in the situation, "I made clear that if ITT was unwilling to accept the basic outline of the proposal with negotiation as to details, I did not care to discuss the matter further." Surprisingly, Rohatyn, professing an inability to understand why Avis and Levitt (which had not been the subject of the suits) should have to be divested, protested mildly, but said he would convey the proposal to ITT management.

Geneen, who considers very little to be nonnegotiable, decided that ITT must take a bargaining position regardless of McLaren's statement. The principal point—retention of Hartford—had been won, and Geneen considered that McLaren was on the hook on that one. The next step would be to whittle down McLaren's demands as much as possible before agreeing to the compromise.

Henry Sailer of Covington & Burling, after suitable instruction, was dispatched to negotiate with McLaren. The points which Geneen wanted were basically four:

First, McLaren had proposed a flat prohibition for ten years on acquisitions by ITT of any company with assets over $100 million, and a conditional ban (subject to Justice Department or court approval) for fifteen years on any acquisitions of companies with assets over $10 million. To Geneen, this was much too stringent and had to be softened. (Indeed, McLaren's proposal did go considerably beyond any similar order entered in the past.)

Second, Geneen wanted to keep all foreign operations of the subsidiaries to be divested, particularly those of Avis, which were expanding rapidly.

Third, Geneen wanted to keep all of Grinnell except the Fire Protection Division which made the sprinklers which were involved in the suit.

Fourth, Geneen wanted to retain all assets of the subsidiaries to be divested which had been added after their acquisition, principally Levitt's Florida Palm Coast development and Canteen's finance subsidiary.

McLaren received Sailer, and despite his initial posture delegated Joseph Widmar, who had been principal trial attorney in the Grinnell case, and Raymond M. Carlson, who was slated to be principal trial attorney in the Hartford case, to work out the settlement with Sailer. Almost before they could get started, the impatient Rohatyn was back in Kleindienst's office, on June 29 "to complain about the rather rigid attitude that Mr. McLaren was taking with respect to these settlement negotiations, to complain about the punitive nature of the settlement negotiations, and the posture of the Government, and that he felt, in his opinion, they were unreasonable." Kleindienst says he responded that he was not going to inject himself into the settlement negotiations. Rohatyn, as though not content to leave the matter in the hands of McLaren, then went to see Flanigan in the White House to complain that McLaren's initial proposal was so tough as to be unacceptable to ITT. Flanigan conveyed Rohatyn's sentiment to Kleindienst, but the latter has insisted that he never told McLaren of Rohatyn's pressures.

ITT's bargaining position undoubtedly was strengthened by Judge Austin's decision in the suit against ITT's acquisition of Canteen, rendered when negotiations had barely begun. Having determined to compromise, McLaren hoped that a settlement could be reached before Judge Austin rendered a decision in the Canteen case. At their first meeting on June 24 McLaren and Sailer agreed that "it would be appropriate to advise Judge Austin . . . that we were entering into serious negotiations." But they were too late, to the benefit of ITT, to stop the decision.

Judge Austin issued his decision on July 2, 1971. Judging by his detailed opinion, it is obvious that Judge Austin had already made his decision before he received word of the settlement discussions. By this decision McLaren's new conglomerate merger policy suffered another setback. Following closely the Grinnell decision, Judge Austin also ruled in ITT's favor. Like Judge Timbers, he found it unlikely that ITT would practice reciprocity, and correspondingly unlikely that ITT's suppliers would act on the basis of hoped-for reciprocity from ITT. The government's case against the Canteen merger suffered from virtually the same omissions found in Grinnell. And Canteen's industry—industrial plant feeding services—was unsuitable to reciprocity because quality and service factors so differentiated the various competitors as to negate the use of reciprocity (on the theory that reciprocity will work effectively only where the products or services involved are homogeneous). Canteen's past "trade relations" history was found by Judge Austin to have been competitively ineffectual, and in any event, "ITT's own antireciprocity stand and the changed attitude of businessmen generally toward such activities negate any likelihood of their resumption at Canteen."

As to the government's claim that the merger would raise barriers to entry, discourage smaller firms from competition, and trigger other mergers in the food service industry, the court said that, since it had found no competitive advantages to Canteen, there was no basis for finding a reduction in the ability of other firms to compete. The series of mergers which had already occurred in the industry were not the fault of ITT. "It is as reasonable to expect that any future mergers will be triggered by one or more of those mergers as by the ITT-Canteen transaction."

Judge Austin, to the further chagrin of the Antitrust Division career staff, bought the efficiencies shibboleth. He agreed with ITT's claim that it had made Canteen into a more effective competitor in its food service industry. Judge Austin said that the acquisition had procompetitive effects because "ITT has worked closely with Canteen management and field personnel to increase operating efficiency, to reduce customer costs and to improve client services." The court was careful to note, however, that the increased efficiency was due not to ITT's absolute size and financial strength, but rather to the application of "ordinary industrial engineering and management consultation techniques to the food service field."

While ITT management was gratified by Judge Austin's decision, Geneen still had no intention of scuttling the settlement (which still could have been done at that time). Notwithstanding two decisive district court victories, Geneen did not want to risk the possible loss of Hartford Insurance at the hands of the Supreme Court.

The decision was another dagger in McLaren's conglomerate merger theories. It had been rendered and would now stand as precedent. There was nothing in the decision, of course, to change McLaren's mind about settlement; indeed, it well may have served to soften McLaren's negotiating stance.

The settlement negotiations proceeded through the month of July, 1971. At first McLaren seemed determined to hold fast to his initial stance of accepting no substantive changes to his proposal. ITT's first formal counteroffer, which included most of the bargaining points put forth by Geneen, even though acquiesced in by Widmar and Carlson, was rejected by McLaren. ITT, playing a somewhat dangerous game, perhaps buoyed by its victory in the Canteen case, assumed an insistent position and refused to budge for some two weeks.* Since McLaren gave no signs of budging either, and since the Grinnell case was now before the Supreme Court with ITT due to file a responsive paper soon, Sailer ultimately came back with scaled-down demands. This time the combination worked.

McLaren accepted ITT's request to limit divestiture to Grinnell's Fire Protection Division, and to permit ITT to retain the Florida Palm Coast development. The prohibition against future acquisitions was reduced to a conditional ten-year prohibition (subject to Department of Justice or court permission) of acquisitions of companies with assets over $100 million, those with assets over $25 million which were among the leaders

---

*During this period the insistent Rohatyn was back to see Kleindienst again, "upset and complaining about the rather hard, stringent, rather inflexible attitude of McLaren and his staff."

in concentrated markets, and those over $10 million in the insurance or automatic sprinkler businesses. In return ITT agreed to add two life insurance subsidiaries (exclusive, of course, of Hartford) to the list of those to be divested. Geneen had achieved his principal objective of modifying the future acquisition ban; he had given up, however, another main objective, that of keeping Avis's overseas operations.

The news of the agreed-upon settlement was announced publicly on Saturday, July 31. On the following Monday and Tuesday ITT's common stock price dropped an aggregate of $1.25 billion, about the same as had been predicted if ITT were required to divest Hartford (although the stock subsequently recovered about half of its loss within a few months). The formal proposed consent decrees, delayed by the mechanics of preparation and signing, were filed in the courts of Chicago and Hartford on August 23, 1971. The public had thirty days to file comments before the judgments could become final. The only opposition to the settlement came from Ralph Nader and his associate Reuben Robertson, who had been fighting against the Hartford merger since its inception. They complained that the settlement manifestly would not remedy the evil of adding Hartford's massive resources to those of ITT, with the ensuing opportunity to use Hartford's money to expand ITT's other businesses.

The Grinnell and Hartford cases were now before Judge Joseph Blumenfeld (Judge Timbers in the meantime having been elevated to the court of appeals). Judge Blumenfeld brushed aside the objections to the settlement, commenting that the consent judgments "are carefully tailored to eliminate the aspects of the acquisitions which the original complaints alleged to be illegal. Within the limits of existing statutory law and judicial power, the provisions of the proposed decrees constitute a commendable achievement toward safeguarding the public interest." The consent judgments consequently were entered as final on September 24, 1971. McLaren's announced war against the conglomerates was over, and McLaren himself within three months would leave the Antitrust Division to become a federal judge.

Any description of public reaction to the settlement of the ITT merger cases must be divided into two phases. The first phase was that period after disclosure of the compromise but before disclosure of the reasons behind it. Neither the consent judgments themselves nor any documents filed with the courts by the Antitrust Division or ITT gave any explanation of the bases for the settlement. In support of the compromise the Justice Department's press release merely said:

The proposed consent judgments will assist in stemming the trend toward undue concentration by merger which was alleged in these cases. In addition, he [McLaren] pointed out that most of the companies to be divested are industry leaders which the Department contended would be entrenched in their positions under ITT ownership.

Antitrust consent decree negotiations customarily have been conducted free of public scrutiny, and in this regard the ITT decrees were not unusual. The public has never been told how or why the compromise came about, or what factors the Antitrust Division took into account when it agreed to the settlement. (As described in a later chapter, the ITT compromise spurred Congress in 1974 to adopt reforms to the consent decree procedure which make current practice significantly different from that in effect in 1971.)

On September 24, 1971 then, when the ITT consent judgments were formally entered, the public had no knowledge of the underlying events described in this chapter. There was no public knowledge of ITT's economic hardship presentation, of Ramsden's analysis, or of McLaren's reasons for compromise. There was no way for an observer of the antitrust scene to know of the various settlement offers and counteroffers. And, of course, the entire web of ITT's use of the political route in meeting the merger suits remained hidden from public view.

Commentators in the financial press varied in their assessments of the settlement. The *New York Times* writer Gene Smith thought the consent judgments represented a blow to the conglomerates. He wrote that "the day of the giant mergers may have ended. . . ." *Fortune,* on the other hand, believed that "quite clearly Harold Geneen has achieved something of a victory in the negotiations." *Business Week* took a peculiar tack: the "sudden settlement" was "a singularly unsatisfying end to an important episode in government-business relations" because, while "another scalp" for the Justice Department, the cases failed to do "anything to clarify the vague legal rules under which merger-minded companies must operate." The Nixon administration thus, in the eyes of the *Business Week* editors, had acted unfairly *toward business* by abandoning its "attempt to establish a clear judicial definition of the limits on corporate growth in a modern society." The editorial concluded:

If McLaren and his lawyers feel that the mushroom growth of the conglomerate corporations threatens the U.S. economy and infringes the antitrust laws, then it is their duty to push the point with the courts until the law is established beyond question. It is not fair either to the companies involved or to the public to keep on brandishing the antitrust gun without ever proving that it really is loaded.

On the whole, however, the settlement sparked little hue and cry, nor was there any need for the administration to defend it—until Senate Judiciary Committee hearings in March, 1972 opened up to public view ITT's lobbying efforts and the "hardship" basis for the settlement. Those hearings, set off by the Dita Beard-spurred allegations of reciprocal favoritism to ITT in the settlement of the cases, began the second and more vehement phase of public reaction.

When the "hardship" basis of the settlement, in the context of ITT's lobbying efforts, was revealed, the conglomerate critics could challenge not only the illusory nature of ITT's hardship claims, but also whether McLaren should even have agreed to hear those claims in the first place. Harlan M. Blake, a Columbia University Law School professor, writing in *Harper's Magazine,* expressed incredulity that McLaren could have believed ITT. McLaren's statement of reasons for the settlement, said Blake, "was not persuasive. . . . None of these [ITT] reasons, as McLaren presumably knew, could be taken seriously. . . . These are the kinds of arguments that every antitrust lawyer knows by heart and makes in desperation when his arguments 'on the merits' are not strong enough to prevail. They are likely to be effective only with men who lack experience in the ways of the world, or who are looking for an excuse to be persuaded." Blake concluded: "Even if [McLaren were] somehow troubled by one or more of these [ITT] arguments, he could not accept them without violating every tenet of antitrust policy." Another law professor, Harvey J. Goldschmid, also criticized the settlement for taking into account "extraneous matters to the fundamental goals of antitrust." Former Antitrust Division official George D. Reycraft was among those troubled by the ITT political efforts which surrounded the consent judgments: "Those appearances [of "backdoor negotiations"] have permanently tarnished what might otherwise have been a respectable settlement." Senator Philip Hart thought that the financial hardship argument "is not a fact that ought to persuade either the Department or a court to avoid correcting a violation of the antitrust law."

The dissenters in the career staff of the Antitrust Division—of which there were a number—now began to surface. Since the ITT settlement had been kept in the top echelon, there had previously been insufficient knowledge among the staff to support much public dissent (although some disagreement with the settlement had been expressed within the halls of the division). There was a strong view that the preservation of an opportunity for the Supreme Court to extend the rules against conglomerate mergers was sufficient in itself to reject any compromise, all the more one where ITT was permitted to retain the principal acquired firm, Hartford. Charles Mahaffie, who had been privy to the settlement negotiations, was among those who shared this view.

News of the "hardship" basis for the settlement reenforced the dissenters' posture, and left them with a feeling that ITT had pulled one off. ITT well knew, said these critics, at the time it opposed a preliminary injunction, that divestiture of Hartford would be the inevitable outcome if ITT lost. It was wholly inconsistent with those assurances for ITT, in April, 1971, to claim that divestiture of Hartford would be an intolerable burden.

There were also rumblings that the staff had been wholly excluded from evaluating ITT's hardship claim. Kenneth Elzinga, an Antitrust Division special economic assistant at that time, complained that he had never been consulted, and publicly termed the settlement a "sham and whitewash." Willard Mueller, the government's expert economic witness in the Grinnell and Canteen trials, also thought that the settlement represented a "very drastic about face in policy."

Two professors from the Wharton School, Irwin Friend and Randolph Westerfield, expressed public disagreement with ITT's hardship claims, which, it will be recalled, had been supported by Dean Winn of that same school. Friend and Westerfield believed that any predictions of widespread economic shocks from a Hartford divestiture were unfounded. Any effect on the United States balance of payments position was tenuous, and in any event would be of *de minimis* proportions in relation to the entire balance of payments profile. Any decline in ITT stock value would simply reflect the consequences of "a normal business risk associated with investment in a conglomerate," and it would not be likely to have any appreciable "ripple effect" on other stock prices.

McLaren again stood his ground, as he had before when confronted with the outcries of the conglomerates against his new merger policy. McLaren's principal point was that "the settlement is entirely consistent with the antitrust objectives of preventing the anticompetitive dangers of the Hartford-ITT merger which were alleged in the complaint." McLaren continued: "We got everything we could win or we would want to win in Grinnell, and so far as Hartford was concerned, we pared off other companies which, under the control of ITT, might be used with Hartford for anticompetitive ends. And we thought we had achieved really as much as we could by going through the appeals." From an overall policy standpoint McLaren claimed that the massive nature of the divestiture required of ITT, and the far-reaching prohibition against future acquisitions, minimized increases in aggregate concentration, established a precedent for decrees regulating future acquisition activity, and would serve as a deterrent to other corporations which might be contemplating a conglomerate merger program. McLaren indeed was far from timorous in defending his action: "In my professional opinion," said McLaren, "it is an excellent settlement from the government's stand-point not only as a matter of disposition of this litigation but for its overall impact in promoting compliance with the antitrust laws in deter-ring anticompetitive mergers."

Neither did McLaren back away from his acceptance of ITT's hardship claims as the triggering reason for the settlement. McLaren explained:

What we did here in ITT is really very much what we did in LTV, owing to the financial repercussions of this thing, rather than the straight eco-nomics. . . . The real reason for the decision was the devastating financial consequences to the more than a quarter of a million shareholders, and to the ripple effect that might take place in the stock market and in the economy.

Now the administration joined ranks behind McLaren (in contrast to its splintered position on McLaren's conglomerate merger policy). Solicitor General Griswold insisted that it was "a very good settlement," one which was "extremely favorable" to the government. (Since it had been Gris-wold's "best judgment that the Government would lose all three [ITT] cases in the courts ultimately," his position on the settlement is under-standable.)

In an unusual fashion (since the president normally does not become involved in such matters), President Nixon presented the administration's position in a public statement:

Now, as Dean Griswold pointed out, that not only was a good settle-ment; it was a very good settlement. I think under the circumstances that gives the lie to the suggestion that this administration, in the handling of the ITT case, just using one example, was doing a favor for ITT. If we wanted to do a favor for ITT, we could just continue to do what the two previous administrations had done, and that is nothing; let ITT continue to grow. But we moved on it and moved efficiently.

Mr. McLaren is justifiably proud of that record, and Dean Griswold is very proud of that record, and they should be.

Obviously, whether or not the settlement was reasonable can be, and has been, a matter of difference. A *Chicago Sun-Times* survey of ten law professors and attorneys found six—including Phil Neal, chairman of President Johnson's antitrust task force—agreeing that the settlement was a reasonable compromise, given McLaren's tactical position. (Most believed, however, that McLaren should not have turned to hardship claims to justify the settlement.) Archibald Cox, even after his dismissal as special prosecutor, still believed that "the government received a fair settlement in the [ITT] case."

Disclosure of the hardship basis of the ITT settlement brought forth one last-gasp effort in the judicial arena. Ralph Nader and Reuben Robertson went to court to attempt to have the consent decree set aside. Purporting to represent the public interest, they contended that ITT's economic hardship plea was an inappropriate reason for settlement, and that the government's prior failure to disclose that reason to the court vitiated the judgment. While admitting that ITT's hardship claim was a "motivating factor" in the settlement, the government now claimed that its acquiescence also took into account the desire to avoid time-consuming and expensive litigation and the risk of losing the cases.

Judge Blumenfeld, who had originally approved the consent decree, held that the Justice Department was not obliged to disclose its reasons for negotiating and accepting the consent decree, nor was the court bound to inquire into that subject. The court's sole function had been to ensure that the relief provided was adequate when measured against the anticompetitive consequences alleged in the complaint. This he had done, said the judge.

Nader and Robertson argued that prior Supreme Court decisions in the Du Pont–General Motors and El Paso–Northwest acquisition cases precluded the consideration of economic hardship claims to avoid divestiture. Judge Blumenfeld distinguished those decisions, however, as involving the appropriate remedy following a judicial finding of antitrust violation. "The same rules do not apply to a settlement agreed upon between the parties;" since ITT had not been found in violation of the antitrust laws, the Antitrust Division may take into account hardship claims.

Nor was Judge Blumenfeld's view unaffected by the government's losses in the Grinnell and Canteen cases. He thought it "hardly surprising that the Justice Department was prepared to consider settlement," concluding:

It must be remembered that there has long been a serious controversy concerning the applicability of Section 7 to conglomerate mergers. More than one eminent authority has taken the position that it may be difficult to establish that a true conglomerate merger is violative of the Section 7 prohibition against acquisitions which may substantially lessen competition.

The Nader-Robertson effort to carry their fight to the Supreme Court was unsuccessful; without giving any explanation, the Court refused to hear the case. The ITT consent decrees were final; the last hurdle had been passed, and the judicial side of the cases was a closed chapter.

15

THE POLITICAL ARENA

A presidential aide must listen to all who come in the White House, as they do in great numbers on all sides of all cases with regard to conditions they have or causes that they may wish to work for, just as they go to members of the House and Senate and others in that connection.

Richard M. Nixon, March 24, 1972

We stray somewhat from our main theme, public policy toward corporate growth and how that policy is made, in order to complete the ITT story. This involves a look at the "political" aspects of the ITT cases, in the narrower sense of that term—how the hidden side of the ITT matter was uncovered, and what the political consequences were. Not only would it be untidy to overlook the end of the ITT story, but the political events perhaps also contain more than a germ of relevance to the broader question of governmental determination of public policy.

The events which led to uncovering ITT and to the ensuing public furor began in May, 1971, at the time intense activity was taking place within the administration and by ITT to conclude the antitrust suits. ITT's frenetic round of contacts in March and April had led to the presidential order of April 19; its reversal had led to Ehrlichman's renewed effort at control and to the early May "agreed-upon ends."

On May 12, 1971, at the ITT annual shareholders meeting in San Diego, Congressman Bob Wilson approached Geneen for help in bringing the 1972 Republican convention to San Diego. The White House wanted the convention there, but local financing was required, and it was lagging badly. With less than three months to go before decision date, San Diego looked to be out of the running unless some dramatic new development occurred.

In answer to Wilson's request Geneen supplied that development by a financial pledge to support the convention. ITT had a natural interest in San Diego, aside from Geneen's personal friendship with Wilson. In the

1960s ITT's Sheraton subsidiary had acquired two hotels in San Diego and was in the process of completing another; ITT also was building a substantial cable plant there. According to Wilson, Geneen agreed that ITT-Sheraton would guarantee the entire $400,000 shortfall in private funds needed for the Republican convention. In return the new Sheraton hotel would have to be designated as presidential headquarters. Geneen's version was the same except for the amount, which he said was to be left up to Sheraton management. (When submitted in writing on July 21, the actual pledge was a firm $100,000 and an additional $100,000 contingent on matching private pledges.) Geneen later justified the pledge as an extremely favorable advertising opportunity; for a new Sheraton hotel to be presidential campaign headquarters was well worth $200,000 in publicity (equivalent, said Geneen, to the cost of only six minutes of prime-time TV ads.)

With the ITT-Sheraton pledge in hand, Wilson and California Lieutenant Governor Ed Reinecke were able to mobilize local support and complete the needed financing; in July San Diego was duly selected to host the convention.

It would have been hard for Nixon's campaign planners not to know of ITT's support of the convention, which was unusually large in amount (perhaps unprecedented) for this type of support. Reinecke told Mitchell of it within two weeks after it was offered. It was mentioned in a number of internal convention planning documents written by or addressed to Haldeman, Mitchell, Jeb Magruder, William Timmons, and Herbert Klein. The final convention report prepared for Republican National Chairman Robert Dole disclosed ITT's support; this report was the basis for a planning discussion on July 19 between Nixon, Dole, Haldeman, and Timmons.

Nor could the convention planners have been unaware of the pendency of the ITT antitrust suits. In a memorandum to assistant campaign director Jeb Magruder, Robert C. Odle reported:

Included as part of the understanding in San Diego's bid for the convention was an agreement that the new Sheraton Hotel on Harbor Island, owned by ITT, be the headquarter's hotel. Someone had suggested that the problems which ITT may or may not be having with the Justice Department would pose a problem here but I cannot see any conflict of interest situation at all.

When Magruder approached Mitchell to ask whether the ITT-Sheraton pledge might become controversial, Mitchell responded that there was "no problem."

Public disclosure in August, 1971 of the ITT pledge brought forth questions by columnists and Democratic politicians about the coincidence of the pledge and the settlement. Reuben Robertson, an opponent of the ITT-Hartford merger, wrote Kleindienst about the subject. McLaren responded for Kleindienst: "There is no relationship whatsoever between the settlement of the ITT-Hartford litigation and any financial support which ITT may have offered to the City of San Diego." Democratic National Chairman Lawrence O'Brien later sent a letter to Mitchell requesting an explanation of the settlement. This time Kleindienst responded for Mitchell: "The settlement between the Department of Justice and ITT was handled and negotiated exclusively by Assistant Attorney General Richard W. McLaren."

There the matter lay until columnist Jack Anderson, on February 29, 1972, unleashed a "smoking gun"—a purported memorandum written by ITT lobbyist Dita Beard to her superior William Merriam on June 25, 1971 before the antitrust settlement and before public disclosure of the ITT-Sheraton pledge. The memorandum cautioned Merriam to keep secret ITT's convention pledge, just as the administration had "kept it on the higher level only" (then known, she said, only to Nixon, Mitchell, Haldeman, Wilson, and Reinecke). This document continued:

I am convinced, because of several conversations with Louie [Nunn] re Mitchell, that our noble commitment has gone a long way toward our negotiations on the mergers eventually coming out as Hal wants them. Certainly the President has told Mitchell to see that things are worked out fairly. It is still only McLaren's mickey-mouse we are suffering.

. . . .

If it gets too much publicity, you can believe our negotiations with Justice will wind up shot down. Mitchell is definitely helping us, but cannot let it be known. Please destroy this, huh?

An interview with Mrs. Beard by Anderson's assistant Brit Hume had elicited the further information that, acting under instructions from Gerrity, Mrs. Beard herself had arranged the terms of the antitrust settlement in a conversation with Mitchell at Kentucky Governor Louie Nunn's Kentucky Derby party in early May, 1971. Mitchell had first, said Mrs. Beard, berated her for ITT having gone over his head to the White House. He complained that even the president had said to "lay off ITT"; Mrs. Beard quickly amended that the president, according to Mitchell, had said, "Make a reasonable settlement, would you please?" Mitchell was, he told Mrs. Beard, sympathetic to ITT, but his problem was McLaren. Finally, however, Mitchell got around to asking Mrs. Beard what ITT wanted.

She responded that ITT wanted to keep Hartford and part of Grinnell.

Mitchell initially reacted, "You can't have Grinnell"; after further discussion he apparently relented and assured Mrs. Beard that "it'll be worked out fairly." Hume reported that Mrs. Beard denied discussing the ITT convention pledge with Mitchell, but admitted authorship of the memorandum. Anderson also charged that "Kleindienst told an outright lie" about the settlement in his previous statement that the settlement was handled and negotiated exclusively by McLaren; Anderson had learned of Kleindienst's meetings with Rohatyn.

Unfortunately for the administration, Kleindienst's nomination to succeed Mitchell as attorney general was at that moment pending before the Senate Judiciary Committee. Having already completed his testimony, Kleindienst nevertheless volunteered on his own to return to respond to the Anderson charges. The Democratic Committee majority was happy to accommodate him.

These hearings, stretching over the next two months, became the primary vehicle for uncovering the ITT affair. Needless to say, the hearings extended far beyond Kleindienst's qualifications and his personal role in the ITT cases to the bases and reasons for the settlement and its possible connection with the ITT-Sheraton convention pledge.

The Nixon White House had to decide how to respond to the Anderson allegations. It was a ticklish situation; the main consideration, of course, would be Nixon's reelection (only eight months away). The White House had worked hard to erase Nixon's traditional image of deviousness, with considerable success apparently. In March, 1972 Nixon was untainted by even the hint of scandal; he enjoyed a high public rating (although, by dint of past ups and downs, seemingly a volatile one); and the future looked serene.

The Anderson allegations and the forthcoming hearings (which Kleindienst had precipitously initiated without first checking with the White House) threatened to burst this bubble. The Democrats, led by O'Brien, would play to the hilt this first publicly known apparent breakdown of morality in the Nixon administration. This perhaps would have been sufficient to persuade the administration not to be forthcoming about the ITT matter; the White House had a strong distaste for undesirable public turmoil. Nixon also had a high degree of sensitivity to criticism, even on a policy as opposed to personal level.

Moreover, in the ITT matter, those around Nixon could also work up a moral fervor. They considered Anderson's charges and O'Brien's harassment to be politically motivated and wholly unjustified. There had been no deal on the ITT settlement; the ITT affair was a matter of internal government policy making which had been set off only by McLaren's intractability. The Democrats were attempting to present as a national scandal, with overtones of corruption, that which not only was but a policy difference, but one on which prior Democratic administrations had demonstrated agreement with the Nixonian view.

But explanation obviously would not satisfy the Democrats, nor did Nixon expect that it would be reported with understanding by a national press which he viewed as basically unsympathetic. Public explanation also had the disadvantage of requiring revelation of the White House conflict with McLaren, which probably would only make matters worse. It was then perhaps inevitable that the administration would seek to cover up the ITT matter and simultaneously to strike back at the enemies who had wrought this injustice.

Nixon commissioned a White House task force whose purpose would be to sever any connection between the pledge and the settlement and insulate the White House. The task force, loosely composed of John Ehrlichman, Charles Colson, John Dean, Clark MacGregor, Richard Moore, Fred Fielding, Wallace Johnson, and William Timmons, met almost daily in Ehrlichman's office during March and April, 1972. Members of the task force consulted regularly with Mitchell, Kleindienst, and Robert Mardian from the Justice Department. Nixon was routinely informed of the task force's activities.

Colson contacted ITT's Merriam to ask about the authenticity of the Dita Beard memorandum. When Merriam answered that he had never seen it before Anderson produced it, the task force decided to sound out Mrs. Beard. Perhaps a forgery could be pinned on Jack Anderson, a longstanding entry on the enemies list, particularly when Colson learned that Anderson's secretary and Mrs. Beard's daughter were friends.

The task force sent Howard Hunt of the White House "plumbers" group out after Mrs. Beard. Traveling under alias documents supplied by the CIA, Hunt visited Mrs. Beard on March 15, 1972; he declined to identify himself, saying only that he represented "important friends in high places." Hunt tried to induce Mrs. Beard to sign a prepared statement not only disavowing the authenticity of the memorandum but also carrying the implication that Anderson's secretary had been involved in forging it. Mrs. Beard, who seemed preoccupied with getting the bonus which she claimed ITT was wrongfully withholding, refused to sign this statement, but averred that those portions of the memorandum connecting the pledge to the antitrust settlement must have been added by someone else. Despite this admission, Hunt reported back to Colson that Mrs. Beard was "unwilling or unable to cooperate." Several days later, however, Mrs. Beard did issue a public denial of the authenticity of the memorandum. (Her statement was released, peculiarly, through the office of Senator Hugh Scott.)

The White House faced the problem of what Mitchell and Kleindienst were going to say to the Senate committee. If they testified fully, how could they avoid tying the president and other White House officials into the ITT cases? The obvious solution was not to testify fully.

While Mitchell had to admit meeting Mrs. Beard at the May, 1971 Kentucky Derby party, Mitchell said he had refused to discuss the ITT cases with her, telling her instead that "the proper course would be for the appropriate people reprsenting ITT to take the matter up with the appropriate people in the Justice Department."

Mitchell testified that he had not discussed with Kleindienst or McLaren "the ITT litigation or the negotiations relating thereto." What of the president? he was asked.

The president had never talked to me about any antitrust case that was in the department. The only conversations I have ever had with the president was early in the administration when we did discuss before, not litigation, not pending cases, but policies, and the discussions took place with the Council of Economic Advisers and some of the other cabinet officers as to what our policies should be, and the policies that have developed out of the antitrust decision of this administration came basically from the concepts developed at that meeting. But specifically, with respect to ITT or any other litigation, no, I have never talked to the president about it.

(Mitchell also denied having any knowledge of the ITT convention pledge before late September, 1971.)

Kleindienst professed not to even "recollect why extension [of the Grinnell appeal] was asked," although he later recalled that it had been done as a courtesy to Walsh. Kleindienst insisted that he had never talked to Mitchell "about any aspect of this case." Nor did he discuss "any policy or any aspect of the case" with the president or any of his advisers. "So far as discussing with anybody on the staff of the White House what I was doing, what do you think I ought to do, what do you feel about it, what are your recommendations—no.... I do not discuss antitrust policy there."* When further pressed, Kleindienst responded vigorously: "I was not interfered with by anybody at the White House. I was not importuned; I was not pressured; I was not directed. I did not have conferences with respect to what I should and should not do."

A major function of the White House task force now was to keep the lid on "sensitive documents" which might give the Senate committee

---

*Somewhat inconsistently, however, at one point Kleindienst implied that McLaren's attempt to limit further corporate growth, while opposed by many government officials, was supported by the president, the attorney general, and Kleindienst.

new leads or contradictory information. Ehrlichman assigned White House assistant counsel Fred Fielding to find all "ITT documents" in the executive branch and to put them under lock. Shortly thereafter Colson was able to report to other members of the task force that "we believe we have absolute security on this file." The administration determined to make none of these documents available to the committee, on the claim of executive privilege. But ITT, of course, would also have copies of its correspondence.

The task force could hope that the ITT copies had been destroyed; after being confronted with the purported Beard memorandum, Merriam had turned on the shredding machine in ITT's Washington office to purge the files. It developed, however, that the job was done poorly. This was discovered when the Securities and Exchange Commission (SEC), which was investigating securities law aspects of the ITT-Hartford merger, complained that the Beard memorandum was missing from the materials which ITT had previously produced under subpoena. Stanley Sporkin of the SEC staff strongly suggested to ITT's lawyers that they conduct another file search. ITT's lawyers duly went back through the ITT files; among the additional documents turned up were a dozen of concern to the White House task force.

This discovery caused Merriam to speak to Ehrlichman. On March 6, 1972 Ehrlichman summoned the SEC chairman, William Casey, to his office to ask the SEC to refrain from its document request as beyond the bounds of necessity and showing apparent harassment of ITT. Casey, who later said he considered Ehrlichman's suggestion improper, refused to stop Sporkin's investigation. When ITT's counsel thereafter delivered the additional documents to the SEC, Sporkin suggested that ITT also proffer the documents to the Senate Judiciary Committee.

ITT did not accept Sporkin's suggestion, figuring that was not his territory. But ITT's Gerrity and counsel nevertheless agreed that "it would be wise and proper to apprise counsel for the Government witnesses, including Kleindienst, of the existence of the documents since testimony in the Senate Judiciary hearings related (and could be expected to relate) in part to such contacts." Gerrity telephoned Colson, and made arrangements to have one of ITT's lawyers deliver copies of the documents to Wallace Johnson at a meeting at the Sheraton-Carlton Hotel in Washington. Johnson immediately took the documents back to a night-time gathering of the attorney general, Mardian, and Colson. After their review (Colson found they were mostly duplicates of documents the White House already had), the documents were passed on to Fielding to safeguard.

The White House task force still could not be sure that some sensitive documents would not be uncovered by the Senate Judiciary Committee from some other source, such as Jack Anderson, Ralph Nader, or Reuben Robertson, who were suspected of supplying information to the Democratic Committee members. Review of the documents strengthened the sentiments of a group of task force members (principally Colson, MacGregor, and Johnson) who felt that Kleindienst's nomination should be withdrawn. They believed that the hearings were turning into a protracted sideshow of "rancor and publicity" in which the Democrats were having a field day at the possible expense of Nixon's reelection; Colson told Haldeman: "Kleindienst is not the target; the President is, but Kleindienst is the best available vehicle for the Democrats to get to the President."

The dump-Kleindienst faction argued their case to Nixon and Haldeman at a meeting on March 28, 1972. Colson came away convinced that the president had been persuaded to withdraw the nomination. But two days later Colson learned that Kleindienst, meeting with the president on the afternoon of March 29, had successfully argued against withdrawal. In an effort to persuade the president to reverse that decision, Colson sent to Haldeman a memorandum analyzing the sensitive documents (which, said Colson, had been fully examined only by him, Ehrlichman, and Fielding) and warning of "the possibility of serious additional exposure by the continuation of this controversy." The "documents and/or information that *could* yet come out," said Colson, would:

— show that Mitchell, contrary to his testimony, had "constructive notice" of the ITT convention pledge before the antitrust settlement;
— contradict Mitchell's testimony that he had not discussed the ITT cases with the President, Ehrlichman, or McLaren;
— imply that Mitchell and Ehrlichman had reached an understanding with ITT president Geneen concerning the ITT cases;
— imply that Agnew was pressuring Kleindienst on the ITT cases and that Connally and Peterson had helped in delaying McLaren's planned appeal;
— "lay this case on the President's doorstep" by his instructions to the Justice Department not to pursue a "bigness policy" (as reported by Ehrlichman to Geneen) and by the May, 1971 formulation of "agreed upon ends" for the ITT cases.

Colson carefully noted that Mitchell and Kleindienst should remain ignorant of this information because they might be recalled as witnesses (and Mardian should not be told because he "does not understand the problem").

Colson was fighting a losing battle because *he* did not have all the information—he did not know the details of Nixon's conversations with Kleindienst and Mitchell in April, 1971. So long as Kleindienst kept to himself the presidential order to drop the ITT cases, he was not likely to be abandoned.

ITT's strategy was to try to defuse the situation by going public with its side of the story before its officers appeared before the Senate committee. Gerrity issued public statements justifying ITT's contacts with executive branch officials and legislators as a proper attempt to restore some semblance of rationality to United States antitrust policy. This effort was defended not only as legally permissible but as of a constitutional order: "Mr. Geneen's right to place his views before any and all members of the government involved in national policy is a constitutional right of all American citizens. It is the duty of any businessman or citizen to express his views when he feels he has a wrong that needs redress."

ITT's strategy indeed seemed to put the committee members somewhat on the defensive, particularly since some of their names were on the list of individuals Geneen had visited. The subject of ITT's visits, said Geneen, had been not the specifics of the cases against ITT but rather general "antitrust policy" with emphasis upon McLaren's misguided conglomerate merger policy—a perfectly proper grievance to present to responsible government officials.

The witnesses from ITT (Geneen, Gerrity, and Merriam) did little damage to the administration. All contacts with government officials as described by the ITT witnesses came out as bland and innocuous theoretical discussions of overall antitrust policy and not of specific cases. Some contacts were simply omitted from mention—for example, the key meeting in March, 1971 between Geneen and Ehrlichman. The testimony—vague, broad-brush, and nonspecific—made it difficult for the committee to ferret out much hard information. The White House could hardly have hoped for a better result.

The Senate committee did not gain access to the sensitive documents which most concerned the White House task force. The administration claimed executive privilege. ITT, in responding to the committee's request for all memoranda and reports reflecting lobbying activities in 1969–71 relating to the merger cases or antitrust policy, simply omitted to include the sensitive group that had been supplied to the White House. The committee also asked the SEC to produce its files. Despite his earlier rebuff of Ehrlichman, SEC Chairman Casey now refused to turn over its files on the ground that they included nonpublic investigative materials.

The hearings concluded near the end of April, 1972;* Kleindienst was confirmed in June. A majority of the committee concluded that Kleindienst had truthfully denied participation in the settlement negotiations, and that the "settlement was reached on the merits after arm's-length negotiations." Even some of the majority senators, however, considered ITT's lobbying campaign heavy-handed and unseemly. One of the dissenters, Senator Edward Kennedy, on the other hand, remarked: "I do not blame ITT for trying to get across their views, but I do blame those who are willing to give them the extensive attention they apparently received."

Despite Kleindienst's confirmation, the White House still had to continue its coverup until after the election. Democratic committee chairmen Senator Edward Kennedy and Representative Harley Staggers continued to press for the SEC's files. Chairman Casey continued to refuse, but by September the SEC's investigation of ITT had been completed and it was difficult to base refusal on possible interference with a pending investigation. Casey dispatched Bradford Cook of the SEC staff to present this problem to John Dean. Dean urged that the SEC continue to withhold the documents, this time on the ground of executive privilege. Cook, however, was dubious that executive privilege could be claimed by an independent agency such as the SEC. A few days later Dean went to Casey with a new solution: the SEC files ought to be "consolidated" with a pending Department of Justice investigation into the possibility of perjury at the Kleindienst nomination hearings (an investigation which seemed to be going nowhere). Casey was agreeable if the Justice Department wanted the documents. Dean spoke to Deputy Attorney General Ralph Erickson, who had responsibility for the Justice Department investigation; Erickson agreed to take the documents (even though he later expressed doubt about their relevance to his investigation). The SEC transferred all of its ITT files to the Justice Department. Erickson then refused to release the documents to the congressional committees on the ground that their disclosure might interfere with a law enforcement function.

John Dean later admitted frankly that the White House plan was to hold back the documents until after the November, 1972 election. This plan was successful; not until January, 1973 did a House committee get some of the documents (directly from ITT). The full range of documents collected and safeguarded by the White House task force did not come

---

*In that same month, as a result of the Kleindienst hearings, the Republicans decided to move the convention site from San Diego to Miami Beach. Thus, while ITT received considerable publicity, it was not the kind that Geneen had counted on.

out until they were disgorged by the White House to the special prosecutor in November, 1973.

The coverup worked to protect the president in the 1972 election year. It would be a long time before the cover was blown; but for Watergate and the resultant appointment of a special prosecutor, the ITT matter might have been permanently covered. The White House had practiced coverup with success, and the Democrats were deprived of some potentially explosive facts which could have weighed heavily in the 1972 election.

The Nixon administration's frenetic efforts to strike out at its enemies ultimately brought its downfall. Its enmity over ITT focused upon Anderson and O'Brien, neither of them theretofore regarded with fondness anyway. Both became targets of renewed efforts to discredit them.

For all the mysticism which has grown up around it, the Watergate break-in was simply an effort to "get" O'Brien by (hopefully) uncovering embarrassing information. Nixon's aides viewed the Senate hearings as politically inspired and orchestrated in tune with O'Brien's constant public statements. In the eyes of the Nixon forces, there was good cause to destroy O'Brien's credibility. Ehrlichman had the Internal Revenue Service audit O'Brien's tax returns. Said Ehrlichman: "I wanted them to turn up something and send him to jail before the election, and unfortunately it didn't materialize."

Jeb Magruder, deputy director of the Committee to Re-Elect the President, sent his general counsel Gordon Liddy off to investigate a rumor that O'Brien might be soliciting kickbacks from concessionaires for the 1972 Democratic Convention. Said Magruder: "O'Brien was continuing to give us a hard time, particularly on the ITT affair, and if we could implicate him in a kickback scheme it would do much to discredit him." Liddy came up empty-handed.

John Dean has observed that the White House was becoming obsessed with gathering "politically embarrassing information" about O'Brien. Haldeman was anxious to "get something" on O'Brien. Their best bet seemed to be Gordon Liddy's proposed "Gemstone" operation. Colson finally telephoned Magruder with instructions to "get off the stick and get the budget approved for Mr. Liddy's plans, that we needed information, particularly on Mr. O'Brien."

Near the end of March Magruder took the Gemstone proposal back to Mitchell, who had rejected an earlier version of the plan. This time Mitchell approved the plan; as Magruder explained: "The fact that O'Brien was a prime target of the Liddy plan was added incentive for Mitchell to approve it—he must have hoped that *something* could be found to silence his chief Democratic tormentor." In a sense, then, the Watergate chain which culminated in the resignation of the president of the United States began at the time that Richard McLaren took office in February, 1969.

The immediate casualties of the ITT cases were Nixon and Kleindienst, both charged for their roles in the ITT coverup. Kleindienst fell to the Watergate special prosecutor, who had no problem concluding that there had been a coverup: "It was clear that the Judiciary Committee did not receive the complete 'story' during its hearings and did not obtain substantial numbers of pertinent ITT and Government (White House and Justice Department) documents."

Kleindienst tried hard to convince Special Prosecutor Leon Jaworski not to prosecute. In addition to claiming, on some curious rationale, that his testimony was not technically false, Kleindienst claimed that "but for my threat to resign, the Grinnell case would never have been appealed and we would never have been able to obtain what even Professor Cox has characterized as a settlement highly advantageous to the United States." Over the strong protest of his ITT investigative staff, Jaworski decided to accept Kleindienst's plea of guilty to the misdemeanor of refusing to answer questions before a congressional committee (rather than pressing for a felony perjury charge). Jaworski appeared reluctant to do even this much against Kleindienst, believing that Kleindienst had "successfully opposed a direct Presidential order to abandon an appeal and leave the Government without any relief."* Jaworski also refused to prosecute any of the other major figures in the ITT coverup, even Mitchell, whose role was similar to Kleindienst's. Jaworski's leniency finally caused Joseph Connally, the attorney in charge of the ITT investigation, and two of his top assistants, to resign in protest.

Nixon's role in the ITT coverup figured in the articles of impeachment adopted by the House Judiciary Committee. The committee majority accepted the theory of presidential responsibility for the criminal acts of his subordinates of which he had fair notice. Despite, and in part because of, Nixon's refusal to release tapes of conversations during the coverup period, the committee concluded that he knew about the coverup: "Kleindienst and former attorney General John Mitchell gave false testimony regarding the President's involvement in the ITT antitrust cases. Clearly Kleindienst and Mitchell were protecting the President. The President followed Kleindienst's confirmation hearings closely, but took

---

*Kleindienst's self-credit for Nixon's reversal on the ITT-Grinnell appeal, while apparently otherwise unestablished, also got him a nominal sentence on the misdemeanor conviction, and probably saved his license to practice law.

no steps to correct the false testimony and continued to endorse Kleindienst's appointment." Under these circumstances, Nixon's failure to act to prevent the coverup was deemed to constitute an impeachable offense.

These then were the reasons for and means of exposure of the hidden parts of the ITT cases. Rarely has the process of determining government antitrust policy been so revealed. As former Antitrust Division official George Reycraft commented, the public examination of the government side of the cases was "unusual and virtually unique."

16

THE DYNAMICS OF POLICY MAKING

The [Antitrust] Division does not operate in a vacuum. The perennial ties between Washington and big business constantly threaten vigorous antitrust enforcement. We must bend our efforts to isolate these pressures, to challenge their inevitability, and to minimize their impact—whether conscious or subliminal—on the decision making process. They undoubtedly were part of the context for this major litigation, as they have been for every other.... Would Judge McLaren have weighed these complex factors with exactly the same result if he had been analyzing the policy choice in the groves of Academe, far from Washington? Probably none of us, including him, can say.

Senator Philip Hart, April, 1972

The ITT episode has been condemned as a glaring example of the power of big business to bring to bear political pressure on government officials. The giant corporations, it is said, have pipelines into government through which their special interests can be voiced with far greater facility than that of the average citizen. And the government officials at the other end of the pipeline, to curry political support and the funds needed for election campaigns, are eager to listen and to appease the special interests put forth by big business. Bribery is unnecessary, the critics complain; there need be no express agreement, for the speaker and the listener will naturally act in parallel, each motivated by the unspoken assumption that the favor will be reciprocated.

In *Washington Journal* Elizabeth Drew commented:

Many contributors can say, in all honesty, that they gave because they believed in the politician. And many politicians can say, in all honesty, that they took an action that happened to be in the contributor's interest because they believed the action was right. It is usually fruitless to search for the specific *quid pro quo* between a campaign gift and a political decision by the recipient. The parties to these acts usually do not talk to each other about them. It is rare that the *quid* and the *quo* are discussed.

The conclusion reached by many, then, is that the pattern expressed in the ITT cases is sufficient in itself to prove the need to restrict further corporate growth. The ITT episode, however, falls short of proving this point—but not by much. There are in that episode footholds for the mutual interest theory. Certainly ITT was ill-advised to give substance to this theory by its convention pledge. ITT's officers could not help but appreciate that the pledge would cast ITT as a friend of the administration. Nevertheless, the ITT cases do not present a good example of Nixon administration excesses; they portray better the weaknesses in the White House effort to control the business of the federal government.

The ITT merger suits served as a rare example affording both conservatives and liberals room to criticize. The business community faulted McLaren for heading off on his own to formulate and implement an expanded conglomerate merger policy. The hard-line antitrusters thought that McLaren had abandoned principle by agreeing to a settlement having tenuous support and thus withdrawing the cases from the Supreme Court. Both lines of criticism have the common thread that McLaren was acting in a fashion with which the critics did not agree. Probably this is inevitable in the case of any policy toward corporate growth and size. But the more fundamental question is the dynamics by which the ultimate policy position is reached. Who should make these decisions, how should they be made, and what consultation should be sought by the decision makers? A last look at the actors in the ITT drama may shed some light on these questions.

ITT's communications to government officials can be viewed as input into the policy process. The merger suits were not mere law enforcement; they were a policy making mechanism. The "law" to be applied had not yet been made; McLaren's legal theories could not be found in the language of Section 7 of the Clayton Act itself nor in any directly apposite legal precedents. As Lawrence E. Walsh put it in his April, 1971 presentation on behalf of ITT, "To us this is not a question of the conduct of litigation in the narrow sense"; rather ITT was contesting the thrust of an entirely new policy toward corporate growth.

Our system of government favors public input from all sources on important policy issues. The growth of central government functions from 1932 onward has inevitably carried with it a perceived public need to influence the policies of that government. Organized groups—labor unions, agricultural cooperatives, manufacturers, grocers, and so on—all compete to have their interests heard, considered, and acted on. Self-interest, though often scorned, motivates these lobbyists, from the aggrieved individual citizen to the largest organization, just as self-interest in the form of profit motivation spurs competition in making and selling goods and services.

The ITT suits happened to represent an instance where antitrust policy making was under attack by business, as an extreme interpretation by McLaren of antitrust principles. More usual probably have been complaints by critics who have decried the asserted inadequacy of antitrust enforcement. The right to petition for enforcement action, of course, must recognize the correlative right to petition against what the enforcement targets consider to be over-zealous prosecution. Needless to say, our system supposes that those who govern will have the integrity and discrimination to sift out, from the self-interested pleas of lobbyists, those ideas which are in the public interest.

One can, however, defend ITT's right of petition without agreeing with the content of its statements or the tone of the presentation. An appeal based upon an antibusiness image which the administration was said to be gaining from the merger suits could hardly be called an appeal to economic reason.

If the basic thrust of ITT's communications to the executive branch to influence merger policy was an appropriate exercise of its right of petition, does this necessarily mean that McLaren was in the wrong? Did McLaren, as ITT claimed, act to excess in attempting on his own to enforce a theory which lacked legal precedent or general acceptance among knowledgeable persons? The aggregate concentration theory, after all, not only had been disavowed by Nixon's Stigler commission but also had been seriously questioned even by Johnson's Neal commission. Its support in economic literature was thin; there was no real indication of congressional approval. McLaren's other main theory—reciprocity effect—would extend a theory which itself was the subject of genuine dispute. The Antitrust Division's expert witness at the Canteen trial had to concede that acceptance of the reciprocity effect theory would tightly circumscribe the permissible category of diversification mergers by large corporations.

Manifestly, the authority of an enforcement official is bounded by the confines of the legislation under which he acts. But the Clayton Act's generality leaves enormous enforcement discretion; on a technical plane, McLaren clearly acted within the scope of his authority. (It would be hard to imagine, however, any merger case of which this would not be true.) It is equally clear that McLaren acted in good faith in the genuine and firm belief that the escalation of conglomerate mergers portends a serious long-run threat to the functioning of our economic system.

Whether McLaren ought to have taken it upon himself, without stronger guidance from elected officials, to move as far as he did is a more difficult question. McLaren took an autonomous view of his position, and considered that the Antitrust Division should have a free hand in antitrust policy making. But he did not seek merely a gradual expansion of the frontiers of antitrust law; McLaren wanted a quantum leap. There is much to be said for the proposition—and ITT said it—that a government official holding nonelective office should eschew translating his personal beliefs into radical policy change.

What about those above McLaren in the chain of command, extending up to the president himself? As to them, the handling of McLaren's conglomerate merger policy as exemplified by the ITT cases had almost comic aspects. The Nixon commitment to centralized control and taut management seemed shattered; the White House appeared almost paralyzed.

Mitchell undoubtedly could have sidetracked McLaren's policy early on, simply by refusing to authorize the complaints. (As to the ITT cases, in which Mitchell had disqualified himself, the same result might have been reached by a definition of conglomerate merger policy.) But Mitchell repeatedly refused to take steps to curtail McLaren on either the ITT cases or conglomerate merger policy in general. He ignored the blandishments of ITT and the near-directives of Ehrlichman. Indeed, by speaking out publicly in favor of McLaren's conglomerate merger policy, Mitchell slowed considerably the conglomerates' efforts to use the political route to overrule McLaren.

Kleindienst demonstrated a general lack of enthusiasm for getting involved in antitrust; it was not his area. He was the unwilling subject of a tug-of-war between McLaren and the White House; unfortunately, he lacked Mitchell's clout and knack for smoothing out tough situations.

Ehrlichman, it must be said, showed remarkable persistence and ingenuity as the principal champion within the administration of ITT's cause. His plan to use the Domestic Council to sidestep Mitchell and to channel McLaren in the direction desired by the White House was, in end result, successful. The Domestic Council committee, it is true, never reached the point of writing the final policy recommendations which Ehrlichman wanted. But the committee's existence nonetheless served as a vehicle for gaining tighter White House control over antitrust policy, the objective Ehrlichman sought. In fact, the resolution of the ITT cases—for which Ehrlichman probably thought he was responsible—together with McLaren's departure from the Antitrust Division—Ehrlichman probably would take credit for that also—seemed to satisfy Ehrlichman's desire for control. The Domestic Council committee, then, had served its purpose; it had been a means for mobilizing and systematizing opposition to McLaren's conglomerate merger policy. It had enabled Ehrlichman to take the subject into the Oval Office as a policy matter rather than a litigation matter, and it had helped (as undoubtedly Ehrlichman thought) to bring Mitchell back into the fold.

It probably is not farfetched to say that Nixon's failure to take control of McLaren's conglomerate merger policy from the beginning was an inadvertent omission, rather than a studied deference to McLaren's expertise. McLaren simply moved faster than the White House could get organized in the domestic policy making area, and no one in the White House knew, really, what McLaren was up to. All that went on later was an attempt to correct this original failure of managerial control. Nixon's plaintive protest of his own personal innocence, offered as the Watergate coverup closed in around him, might apply equally to the ITT cases; said Nixon, "I simply was not tending the store on the domestic side."

Some fault the president's later intervention in the ITT cases as somehow an abnegation of the executive's responsibility to pursue enforcement of the laws enacted by Congress. Here again, however, the inherent policy flexibility of Section 7 of the Clayton Act makes that observation overly simplistic. The president's action, while unusual, was not inappropriate as such. Archibald Cox, the first Watergate special prosecutor, has said: "It was proper for the President to have an interest in such a major case. There was nothing improper in voicing his own opinion."

The theory earlier voiced by the conglomerates—and which seemed plausible at the time—that McLaren's conglomerate merger policy was designed to protect established businesses, did not prove out. The White House certainly had no such intention, since White House officials almost universally opposed McLaren's campaign. Thus, the ITT cases do not provide an example of the use of antitrust in an offensive way, that is, to inhibit those disfavored by the administration. On the whole, the Nixon administration was not demonstrably imaginative in attempting to use antitrust as a weapon, and perhaps this was because of McLaren's known independent bent.*

We are ending the factual side of the ITT story as it happened, to move in the remaining chapters to a more general plane of public policy implications. But, the perplexed reader well may protest, why *really* were the ITT cases settled?

---

*McLaren did, for example, refuse John Dean's request to file a suit against the Times Mirror Company, publisher of the *Los Angeles Times* and *Newsday,* which had published a series of articles that angered the White House.

Sad to say, he will find here no definitive answer. The missing link in the chain-communication to McLaren of the Nixon-Ehrlichman instructions to achieve the "agreed-upon ends"—presumably compromise—is still missing. If those instructions were transmitted, via Mitchell, Ehrlichman, or Kleindienst, then the ensuing events make all the sense in the world, again *assuming* without any proof that McLaren (from a desire perhaps to be appointed a federal judge) agreed to follow those instructions. McLaren naturally then would have sought some pretext for settlement, and would find fortuitously that ITT had already supplied it, in the form of "economic hardship." Hence from presidential instruction to completion of settlement.

Similarly, one can only speculate whether the ITT convention pledge played any part in the White House attitude. The timing looks wrong— the pledge was made apparently after the presidential action (as Nixon later pointed out in his own defense). But timing can be deceptive—one ex-ITT employee, for example, has insisted that an understanding about the convention pledge existed well before its formal deliverance on May 12, 1971. (On the other hand, there is evidence that Nixon campaign officials at least did *not* know about it before May 12.) The report of the senators dissenting to the Kleindienst nomination reasoned: "The principal reason why the suggestion of a connection between the gift and the antitrust settlement has so much logic is the lack of any other convincing explanation for the sudden shift in the Department of Justice' approach to an ITT settlement."

But the handling of the ITT cases by the Nixon administration was investigated and cleared by the Watergate special prosecutor. While "the evidence showed that ITT had gained access, directly or indirectly, to important Administration officials who in some instances took some action relating to these cases," nevertheless Jaworski found nothing to suggest that ITT had engaged in anything other than "an intensive though legal lobbying effort." There was no proof that the convention pledge (the only possible quid pro quo) was the incentive for the antitrust settlement. Even if ITT management had contributed the money with the hope in their minds of improving ITT's posture with the government, that was not a crime. (Inasmuch as ITT had pledged no funds to any political party or candidate, but rather to a local agency, under uniform past interpretations it had not even violated the law prohibiting corporate political contributions.)

Similarly, the House impeachment inquiry weeded out the ITT cases after initial study, noting the absence of a demonstrable "direct *quid pro quo* on ITT." As one committee member commented, the president was entitled to his own policy on conglomerates and business size, regardless of whether the committee members agreed with that policy.

McLaren consistently denied that he was acting under instructions—which would mean that Mitchell, as he had before, still refused to carry out White House "suggestions" about the ITT cases. There are some, of course, who choose not to believe McLaren; how else, they ask, can one explain McLaren's abandonment of his goal of Supreme Court review and his acceptance without effective investigation of ITT's flimsy hardship claims? One can only speculate: perhaps McLaren sensed the White House opposition (indeed he hardly could have avoided knowing Ehrlichman's feelings on the subject); perhaps he felt that without the support of the administration he should not go further with his conglomerate merger campaign.

What would have happened had McLaren rejected settlement can now be only a matter of conjecture. It is doubtful that McLaren could have counted any longer on the protection of Mitchell. While the Grinnell appeal evidently would have been allowed to proceed, the president's views on conglomerate merger policy certainly would influence future policy decisions by the Antitrust Division. Those policy decisions undoubtedly would include whether or not the ITT-Canteen and the ITT-Hartford merger cases would be appealed. Since McLaren's favorable assessment of his Supreme Court chances depended to a large degree upon having all three cases considered by the Supreme Court, a refusal to permit him to appeal those cases would have been a considerable setback to his efforts. And, of course, the refusal to authorize appeal probably would have effectively permitted ITT's acquisitions of Hartford and Canteen to survive intact. On this hypothesis, ITT itself might have been in a better position, at least in the short run, had it *not* agreed to a settlement of the merger suits against it. Had it not settled, ITT at most would have lost Grinnell (if the Supreme Court decided against it) and would have avoided the restrictions on future acquisitions to which it agreed.

But the answer to the perplexing question initially posed above really makes little difference now. The fact is that the Nixon White House's objective was accomplished, Ehrlichman was vindicated, the ITT cases were ended, and Supreme Court action was averted. It becomes relatively immaterial whether this happened by presidential direction or by McLaren's own decision; the stance of government toward corporate growth ends up in the same place.

17

ANTITRUST POLICY
IN SUCCESSION

> *Unfortunately, all antitrust law enforcement under any plan depends on the public attitude. It does not make much difference what your instrument for carrying out antitrust policy is, it will not be effective unless there is a strong demand.*
>
> Thurman Arnold, June, 1949

For the first two years of his three-year term of office, McLaren enjoyed if not public demand for his merger enforcement policy, at least the support that immediately counted, that of Attorney General Mitchell. The latter was, it seemed, honoring the commitment which McLaren felt had been made to nonpolitical and independent antitrust enforcement. But, toward the end of 1970, perhaps coincidentally in the wake of ITT's intense lobbying of late summer 1970 and the beginning of Ehrlichman's effort to control antitrust policies, McLaren's actions began to be circumscribed.

In November, 1970 Kleindienst (again acting because of Mitchell's self-disqualification because of a past client relationship) refused to permit McLaren to file a complaint against the merger of two drug companies, Warner-Lambert Company and Parke-Davis Company. According to Kleindienst, he reached this decision on his own after meeting (without McLaren present) with officers and attorneys of the merging companies. While Kleindienst complained that McLaren's request, only several days before the scheduled closing of the merger, came too late for fairness to the companies, he justified his rejection of the suit principally on the grounds that the merger did not fit the criteria for illegality specified in the Turner merger guidelines, and the Parke-Davis representatives had said that without the merger that company could not continue drug research (Parke-Davis later denied the last statement.) At McLaren's urging, Kleindienst compromised by referring the file to the FTC, which did file a complaint six months later.*

---

*This case took on political overtones because Warner-Lambert's honorary chairman, Elmer Bobst, was a personal friend and supporter of President Nixon. Bobst was quoted in the press as having talked to persons in the White House about the merger, with the implication that this had something to do with the Justice Department's decision not to sue.

McLaren had not intended to be bound by the Turner merger guidelines, and had so publicly announced. The rule applied by Kleindienst, therefore, ran counter to McLaren's policy direction. In the latter part of 1971 Mitchell also relied upon the Turner guidelines in turning down two of McLaren's requests to file merger complaints. In the first case, the merger between National Steel and Granite City Steel, Mitchell, having in mind perhaps the Domestic Council study and Ehrlichman's feeling that the Justice Department should not go it alone in important antitrust cases, solicited the views of the Council of Economic Advisers and other government agencies. Mitchell reacted as follows to this input:

It was not absolutely clear that it was in the guidelines because of different market areas. . . . This particular merger provided a matching of facilities between the companies which would have improved their production capacity and, of course, their marketing capacity and, third, we had the problem of the substantial imports of steel which were having a harsh effect upon our domestic producers.

In the second instance Mitchell refused to approve McLaren's proposed complaints charging monopolization and unlawful mergers (all dating back to the Kennedy and Johnson administrations) on the part of Firestone Tire & Rubber Company and Goodyear Tire & Rubber Company. (In July, 1973 Attorney General Elliott Richardson on reconsideration authorized those complaints, but they were later dropped, perhaps proving that Mitchell was right in the first place.)

When the ITT cases ended in September, 1971—closing all of McLaren's conglomerate merger test cases—McLaren had served more than two and one-half years, about average for an antitrust assistant. His tenure, however, had been unusually turbulent, and by this time he had all he wanted. He asked Mitchell for appointment to a federal judgeship that was opening up in Chicago. Mitchell agreed, and McLaren changed positions at the end of 1971.

When he left, McLaren felt that his conglomerate merger campaign had been his most important accomplishment in the Antitrust Division. McLaren's battle against large conglomerate mergers could hardly be called fruitless. Of the six large conglomerate mergers that he attacked under his new theories, only two survived intact. He directly stopped the White Consolidated–White Motors merger. He obtained divestiture by ITT of Canteen and of Grinnell in part. The Northwest-Goodrich merger went nowhere (though this was principally because of Goodrich's defense rather than McLaren's suit). Of the six, only LTV–Jones & Laughlin and ITT-Hartford survived. And in both cases McLaren exacted alternative divestiture (of Braniff and Okonite by LTV, and Avis, Levitt, and the insurance companies by ITT). The decrees against LTV and ITT were sufficient to assure against any formal reciprocity system, if either firm were inclined to initiate that practice. And the ten-year acquisition bans were essentially the equivalent, as to those firms, of the conglomerate merger legislation recommended by the Neal commission.

What McLaren failed to achieve, of course, was any final judicial ruling—by the Supreme Court or even a federal district court—accepting his conglomerate merger theories. An interviewer reported McLaren's feeling upon leaving the Antitrust Division that "his only regret" was "that he had not obtained Supreme Court ratification of his controversial policy against huge conglomerate mergers." But there can be little question that McLaren's expanded conglomerate merger theories set a tone of antitrust policy. One cannot be sure, of course, how many conglomerate mergers were deterred and never undertaken because of the apprehension of an antitrust suit. An antimerger suit can be costly, time-consuming, and generally disruptive of perhaps more productive managerial efforts. Even if an acquiring firm feels that the government's enforcement policy is wrong, and that it might ultimately be vindicated in the courts, it will nevertheless think long and hard before it decides to subject itself to the litigation ordeal. As the Harvard University professor Edward S. Mason has observed, "The consideration of whether a particular course of business action may or may not be in violation of the antitrust acts is a persistent factor affecting business judgment, at least in large firms."

The *Wall Street Journal* acknowledged that McLaren's suits against conglomerate mergers had "helped slow down" the merger trend; "There's no doubt," it reported, "that Mr. McLaren's five lawsuits scared off a number of other merger planners." *Newsweek* quoted Wall Street sources as saying that, in the first week following the formal initiation of McLaren's campaign, "at least three major merger proposals" were canceled for fear of suit. The House Antitrust Subcommittee staff credited McLaren's "vigorous antitrust attack against acquisitions by conglomerate corporations" for contributing to the decline in merger activity in the early 1970s.

McLaren certainly believed that his conglomerate merger suits had achieved a deterrent effect; in 1970 he noted: "The strong stand taken by the Department of Justice contributed in some measure at least to eliminating the biggest and most anticompetitive kinds of mergers which so concerned us a year ago." As an illustration, he pointed out that the proposed merger of First National City Bank with Chubb Corporation, an insurance company, "as well as certain other conglomerate mergers planned for 1969, was abandoned when the parties were informed that we regarded the merger as a violation of law and that we would prosecute it if consummated." By early 1971, even though he had not yet won a single preliminary or final judicial victory, McLaren was proclaiming a "major success with our antimerger policy."

One side effect of McLaren's conglomerate campaign was to draw along, to some extent, the theretofore staid and unaggressive Federal Trade Commission (FTC). Under the leadership of the Nixon-appointed chairman Miles Kirkpatrick, an antitrust lawyer from Philadelphia (like McLaren, a past chairman of the American Bar Association Antitrust Section), the FTC helped stop, by threat of suit, two different takeovers of Allis-Chalmers, the first by White Consolidated and the second by Gulf & Western. It filed a half-dozen complaints against lesser diversification mergers (e.g., Beatrice Foods diversification into dry goods wholesaling and into paint brushes and rollers; General Mills's acquisition of Gorton Seafood Company; the merger of Sterling Drug Company and Lehn & Fink, a cosmetics maker; and United Brands's expansion by acquisition into the lettuce growing business), and it ruled against the legality of the merger of Kennecott Copper Corporation and Peabody Coal Company in an opinion carrying earmarks of McLaren's new theories. In the latter case the FTC, for the first time, applied the potential competition theory to companies whose products were unrelated in production methods, promotion, and distribution. In language reminiscent of McLaren's pronouncements, the FTC went on to express concern that "in the present case one of the nation's 200 largest firms acquired the leading producer in an industry that is well on its way to becoming tightly oligopolistic." Kennecott's "deep pocket of funds and other resources," asserted the FTC, would unduly strengthen Peabody in acquiring coal reserves and financing mining development and competing for long-term supply contracts.

The White House, however, began to get uneasy over the FTC's increasing activism, for which Kirkpatrick drew most of the blame. When the FTC in 1971 brought suit against Warner-Lambert's merger with Parke-Davis (which, said the White House business adviser Peter Flanigan, came "like a bolt from the blue"), the administration began to press for Kirkpatrick's resignation. Rather than suffer possible demotion from his position as chairman, Kirkpatrick did resign from the FTC in January, 1973. By that time Nixon was able to fill three other vacancies in the FTC so that four of the five commissioners were Nixon appointees. These changes in the FTC's composition, together with policy communications from Flanigan (who believed that the White House should indicate to the FTC commissioners the administration's desired policy in the areas of industrial concentration and conglomerate mergers), seemed to take care of the FTC problem. The reconstituted FTC dropped its interest in conglomerate mergers and disposed of all the diversification merger cases filed during the Kirkpatrick period by deciding them in favor of the respondents.

To replace McLaren in the Antitrust Division, after an unusually long search time of some six months, the White House selected a Michigan University law professor, Thomas Kauper. It is improbable that Kauper did not have Ehrlichman's personal approval.

Ehrlichman's effort to centralize domestic policy making in the White House was picking up steam in 1972. He was supervising a task force working to devise means of effectuating the reorganization plan. As Patrick Buchanan noted, "The immediate thrust is to get control over the bureaucracy, and we've got to use the President's mandate in the next six months to get things going." Perhaps because of the embarrassment of the ITT matter, Ehrlichman leaned hard on the Justice Department. Mitchell's departure as attorney general considerably broadened Ehrlichman's power in this area. In a postelection meeting with Kleindienst (Mitchell's successor), Ehrlichman and Haldeman directed that anyone not giving assurance of responsiveness to White House control must be dismissed. While Ehrlichman would have preferred to replace Kleindienst also, he did not want to force that issue, and was satisfied when Kleindienst said that he would leave within a year. Given Ehrlichman's personal interest in the Justice Department and his efforts in the ITT cases, it is fairly certain that Kauper could not have remained had he not met Ehrlichman's standards.

Kauper's philosophy turned out to be closer to the flexible, political approach of Turner, President Johnson's Antitrust Division chief, than to the more dogmatic, bureaucratic view of McLaren. For example, in deciding to dismiss voluntarily the monopolization-merger complaints that had previously been filed against Goodyear and Firestone, Kauper observed that "we cannot now establish the key elements of these cases under any theory *we can or should legitimately advance.*"

Kauper thus was willing to accept, in name as well as in practice, a policy making role. He denied, however, that there was any change from McLaren's time in the Antitrust Division's merger enforcement policy. Nevertheless, fewer merger complaints, by a wide margin, were filed by Kauper. And in his tenure, which continued to midsummer 1976, only three conglomerate—or diversification—mergers were attacked by the Antitrust Division. All were premised upon the traditional theories of potential competition and close product relationships. None sought expansion of the horizons of conglomerate merger law.

Kauper suggested that the decline in merger activity after 1969 made merger enforcement less pressing. This "does not," he said, "signify that our stance on mergers of any type has changed." Among the reasons for the merger decline, according to Kauper, was that "businessmen have gotten the antitrust message. . . . Antitrust suits attacking conglomerate mergers under this Administration have had a substantial deterrent effect." Kauper thus credited McLaren's policy with inhibiting the merger movement and as justification for his own inactivity in this area. As discussed later, the slowdown in mergers in the early 1970s does not mean a total absence of large diversification mergers of the very kind that caused concern to McLaren.

In fact, Kauper did change the government's merger enforcement policy, or acceded to the policy direction set down by the White House. The McLaren view of conglomerate mergers was abandoned, and the Antitrust Division reverted to the pre-McLaren policy.

18

THE SUPREME COURT
OF THE 1970s
The "New Antitrust Majority"

*What we obtained was substantial assured relief.
What we gave up was the chance to have our theories
tested in the Supreme Court.*

Richard McLaren, March, 1972

The judicial side of the ITT merger case battle was focused at a single ultimate point: the Supreme Court. That is where McLaren wanted to go; that is where ITT wanted to prevent him from going. That venerable institution came in for some harsh verbal knocks by ITT and its allies in industry; some even offered a definition of the Court as a body of men devoid of economic knowledge.

Those who believed ITT's lobbying efforts to be improper claimed that, even if McLaren were pursuing a misguided antimerger policy, the necessary checks and balances would be provided by the courts. This is the essential nature of the judicial system; while an overzealous antitrust prosecutor can initiate action, he must prove to the courts the probable anticompetitive effects he claims. Without the concurrence of the courts, the prosecutor's excesses may be viewed merely as nuisances (although the expense and duration of an antitrust trial would be more than just a nuisance to most companies).

But, said ITT, the Supreme Court had nullified this system of checks and balances by its undiscerning constancy in accepting the prosecutor's theories. ITT felt that it must assume, therefore, that McLaren's conglomerate merger theories could well be accepted by the Supreme Court, and that its efforts toward persuasion must be focused principally upon the prosecutorial decision. (ITT's view of the Supreme Court, together with the importance that it placed upon retaining Hartford Insurance, explained its willingness to compromise when it seemed at the time to be in a position of superior strength.)

The role of the Supreme Court in *making* law, as contrasted to applying *given* law to a particular set of facts, of course has generated considerable controversy far beyond the antitrust area. In applying the generally stated principles of the Constitution to our complex and evolving society, the Court has made no secret of its role as a policy maker. As Justice Byron White has admitted, the Court's constitutional decisions "make new law and new public policy." The antitrust laws, of course, are not constitutional principles but rather statutory law given by Congress for enforcement by the courts. But, for good or bad, the antitrust laws lack the usual statutory detail. Indeed, as Chief Justice Charles Evans Hughes remarked in a 1933 decision, the antitrust laws have "a generality and adaptability comparable to that found to be desirable in constitutional provisions."

Nevertheless, it was not right, ITT complained, that the Supreme Court should have what amounted to the final say in the controversial area of corporate growth. The Court looks at a self-contained record in a particular case; it cannot, theoretically, weigh all the implications and ramifications of its decision. Could it—or would it—consider the smoothing and economically beneficial effects of corporate diversification? Would it consider the importance of preservation of a capital assets market and its relationship to new business startups? What about the need for a strong domestic base to offset increasing foreign competition? The United States balance of payments? The answer, ITT assumed, in each case would be no, it would not be considered. The Supreme Court had no mechanism really for receiving or evaluating full information input. And *this* Supreme Court had already said that it did not intend to examine efficiencies or similar economic factors as countervailing forces in merger cases. Why, then, should five men (a majority of the Supreme Court), relying on their own personal beliefs and unexposed to all essential decision making factors, have the power to forge national economic policy?

ITT was not a lone voice in the wilderness. Others before it had questioned the role of the courts in antitrust policy. The law professor Richard A. Posner (a member of the Nixon-appointed Stigler commission) had observed: "The extravagant prohibitory sweep of the antitrust laws, the product of the Supreme Court's unwillingness or inability to formulate antitrust standards, goes far to explain the current assault by the Department of Justice on the conglomerate movement." And Milton Handler has commented: "Policy-making requires mastery over the relevant facts as well as wisdom. The nine Justices, able though they may be, are not omniscient. . . . There are those like me who feel that courts, unlike the executive or legislative branches of government, are unequipped to resolve these imponderables."

And of course, the president also agreed with ITT. Once Kleindienst had disclosed Nixon's efforts to derail the Grinnell appeal, the White House explained this action: "The President originally acted in the case because he wanted to avoid a Supreme Court ruling that would permit antitrust suits to be brought against large American companies simply on the basis of their size."

The underlying premise of ITT's efforts to thwart Supreme Court review was, of course, that the result of litigation in the Supreme Court was virtually predictable, that it was possible to tell, even before the record of proceedings reached it, that the Court would crack down on the conglomerates. (Had ITT predicted otherwise, say its critics, it would not then have attempted to avoid Supreme Court review.) This prediction, of course, was based upon the history of merger cases before the Supreme Court from 1960 to 1968, a period of relatively stable composition. The decisions of the Court's majority, and the explanations given in the opinions, furnished a basis for predicting the outcome of future cases. Hence, during the 1960s, Chief Justice Warren and Justices Douglas, Black, Brennan, and Clark predictably would be disposed in favor of the government's case. They had shown a willingness to mold and stretch the statutory language to its outermost limit.

The business leaders were hopeful that the Supreme Court's activist view of merger policy would soon be changed, simply by changing the justices. Before his election in 1968 Nixon indicated that he favored a more "conservative" Court, and that he would appoint "strict constructionists" to the bench. It was anticipated that Nixon would have the opportunity to replace at least three of the antitrust hard-line justices (Warren, Douglas, and Black, who were all of advancing years).

What McLaren gave up in the ITT settlement, as he said, was the chance of Supreme Court review of the ITT merger cases. To many critics of the conglomerate merger wave, this was giving up too much. To those critics, the settlement, as good in its own right as it might be, was not worth losing the opportunity to put on the books a strong anticonglomerate decision by the antitrust enforcement–oriented Supreme Court of the 1960s. *Strike!* they would say, before Nixon had a chance to place his own brand upon the Supreme Court.

By the summer of 1971, when the ITT settlement was forged, Nixon had not yet had that chance. He had made two appointments to the Supreme Court—Burger for Warren as Chief Justice, and Blackmun for Fortas (who had resigned unexpectedly). From 1969 through 1971 the government continued its unbroken record of no losses in merger cases before the Supreme Court. During that time the Court decided only three cases—none involving a conglomerate merger or any precedent-shattering principles—and the government still carried a clear majority.

By January, 1972 the Supreme Court's antitrust majority had lost another of its stalwarts, Justice Black, who was replaced by Powell.

(In that same month Justice Harlan, who was a vigorous dissenter from the Court's merger policies of the 1960s, was succeeded by Rehnquist.) Still the government's skein of victories continued into 1972, when only one case was decided. This brought the government's record in merger cases in the Supreme Court from 1950 to 1972 to 31 wins, 0 losses, and 1 tie vote. This string of government victories ended in 1973, but with a whimper rather than a bang. (The bang would come in 1974.) The Supreme Court disposed of three merger cases in 1973: one decision for the government; one decision for the defendant; and one tie vote having the effect of affirming a decision for the defendant. The defendant's victory was a summary affirmance of a district court decision holding lawful a bank geographic expansion merger; since there was no opinion and no disclosure of the individual justices' votes, the case, while welcomed by corporate antitrust advisers, was not enlightening. (So also the tie vote, in another bank expansion case, was unaccompanied by explanation or disclosure of votes.) The decision for the government, where the Court did issue an opinion (in fact, there were four separate sets of opinions by different justices), involved the geographic expansion acquisition by Falstaff Brewing Company of Narragansett Brewing Company. With the Nixon appointee Powell not participating, the Court could muster a scant 4–3 vote favoring the government in what appeared to be a fairly straightforward case of potential competition under existing antitrust doctrine. The publication of four sets of opinions opened up to view the cross currents at work in the Court. All three 1973 decisions seemed to presage spreading cracks in the Court's past solidarity.

Beginning in 1974, according to the present-day critics of the Supreme Court (these are the same persons who were its avid supporters in the 1960s), the floodgates opened. In the two years 1974 and 1975, the Court decided five merger cases—four decisions were for the defendant, only one for the government. The tables had turned; the government was now the underdog.

Justices Douglas, Brennan, White, and Marshall, in dissenting from the majority's 1974 ruling in favor of the legality of the General Dynamics–United Electric horizontal merger in the coal industry, noted: "On the basis of a record so devoid of findings based on correct legal standards, the judgment may not be affirmed except on a deep-seated judicial bias against Sec. 7 of the Clayton Act." Later that year, in the Marine Bancorporation bank expansion merger case, those dissenters again complained: "For the second time this Term, the Court's new antitrust majority has chipped away at the policies of Sec. 7 of the Clayton Act."

The "new antitrust majority" which is accused of having "a deep-seated judicial bias against Sec. 7 of the Clayton Act" consists of the four Nixon appointees—Chief Justice Burger and Justices Blackmun, Powell, and Rehnquist—together with Justice Stewart, an Eisenhower-appointed holdover. Although the consistent majority of the 1960s had lost only two of its members, Warren and Black (in Fortas it had lost one who seemed on balance to favor the government), this was enough to destroy the 1960s solidarity. Toward the end of 1975 the 1960s majority lost probably its most effective member with the resignation of Justice Douglas.

As discussed in a previous chapter, from 1950 through 1968 the Supreme Court had decided only two cases involving conglomerate mergers—the Procter & Gamble–Clorox merger and the Consolidated Foods–Gentry merger. From 1969 through 1975 the Court decided no more conglomerate merger cases, unless one counts the Ford Motor Company acquisition of Electric Autolite's spark plug plant and trade name. This acquisition would have brought to Ford the capability to supply its own spark plugs for cars manufactured by it, and to produce spark plugs for the more profitable replacement "aftermarket." Even the newly composed Supreme Court, in 1972, had little trouble in unanimously striking down this merger. The acquisition was held unlawful because Ford, as "a prime candidate to manufacture" as well as a substantial spark plug customer, had a moderating effect upon this oligopolistic market. (The newest Nixon appointees, Powell and Rehnquist, had not been on the Court long enough to participate in this case.)

The Ford-Autolite decision was no great leap forward in the law of diversification mergers. McLaren's conglomerate merger test cases were not premised merely on the potential competition theory; he had wanted to foster a doctrine which would sweep up mergers between companies making unrelated products. His pitch was two-pronged: reciprocity effect, and aggregate concentration. The latter was the more far-reaching and portended more drastic consequences for conglomerate mergers. It was not premised upon high industrial concentration in particular economic markets, but rather upon the coverage of a number of different markets by large firms, i.e., the general concentration of production assets in the hands of a relatively small number of corporations. This was a concept of power, as Geneen complained, of "bigness," attended by hypothetical consequences of forbearance of the large firms from intrusion into each other's markets and of fear engendered in small firms.

The ITT settlement eliminated the opportunity of Supreme Court review, by the 1960s Court or by the "new antitrust majority," of McLaren's conglomerate merger theories as such. But the results of another McLaren merger program—his attack upon bank geographic expansion mergers—sheds considerable light upon the views of a present Supreme Court majority regarding the aggregate concentration theory put forward by McLaren in the ITT merger cases. The commercial banking industry has drawn far more merger complaints than any other single industry. Even the Kennedy-Johnson antitrust assistants were very active in bank merger enforcement (some 25 percent of all their Section 7 complaints involved commercial banking mergers), but they tended to focus on horizontal mergers between competing banks. Many observers of the banking industry, however, saw equally grave dangers in geographic expansion mergers by which statewide bank holding companies were being created. These mergers eliminated the bank holding company as a potential competitor by internal expansion into the territory of the acquired banks, and increased the concentration of banking assets among the large holding companies. Before 1969, however, only a single complaint had been filed by the Department of Justice against a geographic expansion bank merger.

After McLaren took office, to the surprise and consternation of many bankers, he changed the direction of bank merger enforcement policy. He determined that the major problem now lay in the gobbling-up of independent, but noncompeting, banks by the large holding companies. He agreed with critics that regulation of entry in the banking industry and the prohibitions against interstate branching made it extremely difficult for new banks to spring up to replace those eliminated by the merger process. To support his change of enforcement emphasis in the banking industry, McLaren already had available the accepted theory of elimination of the potential competition of the acquiring firm in the territory of the acquired bank, which had been expressed by the Supreme Court in Procter & Gamble–Clorox and a number of other cases. But, as with his conglomerate merger campaign, McLaren wanted more; he wanted an extension of the bases for attack upon these banking mergers. As the Antitrust Division, speaking through Donald I. Baker, McLaren's policy planning director and chief spokesman on bank merger issues, pointed out:

The practical problem is that potential competition makes great sense from the standpoint of economic theory and yet is very hard to prove in reality. One can look back and see the banking business in whole states gradually become dominated by a very few institutions which simply go out and buy bank after bank in markets across the state, and yet each individual acquisition is a relatively small bite in the whole process, and the problem of proving that the particular acquiror was a potential entrant into the local business is extremely difficult.

Thus, said Baker, the Antitrust Division "ought to be able to show the illegality of the mergers on a broader basis than has generally been done." Henceforth the Antitrust Division "shall increasingly stress the importance of broad changes in statewide structure. In the long run, what is needed is a rule of law that in effect says that the largest banking organizations in a state cannot combine with other large banking organizations within those states."

McLaren set about filing complaints against bank geographic expansion mergers. In the first Nixon term twenty of these complaints were filed (which was, of course, twenty times as many as had ever been filed before). During that same period of time the district courts rendered decisions in eight of those cases—all in favor of the defendant. McLaren's record on bank expansion mergers hence was even worse than his record on conglomerate mergers (he had at least obtained one preliminary injunction against the White Consolidated–White Motors conglomerate merger).

As with his conglomerate merger policy, however, McLaren's avowed purpose was to push a bank expansion merger case up to the Supreme Court. He expected to receive better treatment there than he had at the district court level. When McLaren left the Antitrust Division, he had not yet succeeded in gaining Supreme Court review of a bank expansion merger case. But he had filed the suits which set the stage for Supreme Court review in 1974.

The main Supreme Court decision issued in 1974 involved the complaint filed by the Justice Department against the acquisition by Marine Bancorporation, a large bank holding company in the State of Washington, of Washington Trust Bank, which operated only in Spokane (a territory not yet served by Marine Bancorporation). In addition to the theory of elimination of potential competition in Spokane, the complaint included McLaren's statewide structure theory, akin to the aggregate concentration theory in the ITT cases, i.e., that the growth of large bank holding companies by acquisition threatened to lead to statewide oligopolies which would dominate banking, would avoid aggressive competition with each other in local markets, and by virtue of their size and interdependent behavior would deter the entry and growth of smaller banks. Hence, the government argued, competition would be lessened in the state as a whole as well as in the local market immediately impacted by the merger. Since Section 7 prohibits a competitive lessening in any "section of the country," argued the government, it was permissible to consider these statewide effects.

The Supreme Court dealt a setback to the Antitrust Division. In addition to holding that the merger could not be held unlawful under the potential competition theory, the Court rejected McLaren's broader statewide structure theory. Since banking is a local business, said the Court, the competitive effects to be examined are limited to those occurring in the area in which the acquired bank operates. There was thus no way to fit McLaren's theory within Section 7 of the Clayton Act. Justice Powell, speaking for the five-member "new antitrust majority" in this case, explained this holding in language reminiscent of Judge Timbers's opinion in the ITT-Grinnell case:

> The Government's proposed reading of the "any section of the country" phrase of Sec. 7 is at variance with this Court's Sec. 7 cases, and we reject it. Without exception the Court has treated "section of the country" and "relevant geographic market" as identical, and it has defined the latter concept as the area in which the goods or services at issue are marketed to a significant degree by the acquired firm.
>
> . . . .
>
> To assume, on the basis of essentially no evidence, that the challenged merger will tend to produce a statewide linkage of oligopolies is to espouse a *per se* rule against geographic market extension mergers like the one at issue here. No Sec. 7 case from this Court has gone that far, and we do not do so today. . . .

McLaren's aggregate concentration theory had the same ring both in the Marine Bancorporation complaint and in the ITT complaints. It may be stated with some assurance, therefore, that the aggregate concentration "half" of McLaren's conglomerate merger complaints would be rejected by a majority of the present Supreme Court.

Some observers find worrisome the thought that important national economic policy can be changed merely by a switch of several votes on the Supreme Court. Ideally, one might hope that an important antitrust decision, whatever its outcome, would be essentially the same no matter the composition of the Supreme Court. Milton Handler wondered about this subject:

I often ask myself—what is law? Is it nothing more than the idiosyncratic personal conceptions of a few judges commanding a majority at any particular point of time? Or is it a consensus predicated upon history, logic, sociology, experience, and above all, common sense?

Theodore Roosevelt, speaking in 1905, had his own answer to this question:

The decisions of the courts on economic and social questions depend upon their economic and social philosophy.

Richard Arnold, an antitrust practitioner, has put it more bluntly:

Our government ought to be, and is to a large extent, a government of laws and not of men. Theoretically, therefore, it is not supposed to make any difference who the judges are. We all know, of course, that it does make a difference. Sometimes, in fact, it makes *the* difference.

No one should be surprised, of course, that business decisions may be influenced by judicial attitudes. Where the question of legal consequences embodies the exercise of reasoned judgment influenced by socioeconomic philosophy, it is hard for the business manager to refrain from asking where, as a practical matter, he will come out. The legality of corporate growth fits precisely this mold.

19

THE ROLE OF CONGRESS

It is kind of like saying, we have met the enemy and it is us. It is Congress that wrote Section 7 of the Clayton Act, and it is Congress, if it wants to do something about it, which should do it.

Senator Marlowe Cook, March, 1972

Senator Cook's statement, made in response to the plaintive query of Senator Philip Hart why the conglomerates were not being stopped, struck a broad responsive chord. Donald F. Turner, Antitrust Division chief under President Johnson, had been saying the same thing for years. The Neal commission appointed by President Johnson, even with its anticonglomerate bias, had to reach the reluctant conclusion that Congress had not yet spoken clearly enough; it ought to enact new legislation.

In this regard the conglomerates were with the Neal commission—not that the conglomerates favored new legislation, but they felt that the conglomerate issue, if it were to be considered anywhere, ought to be in Congress. Their reason was simple enough: they would rather face the Congress of the 1960s than the Supreme Court of the 1960s. The conglomerates figured, probably correctly, that the chances of the Congress enacting new legislation to curb the conglomerates were near zero. The conglomerates could handle Congress much more easily than they could the Supreme Court. Even Senator Hart agreed with this assessment; he said: "I wouldn't make book on how soon Congress is going to do much about the basic antitrust laws. It is more likely that the courts will." As long, therefore, as the conglomerates could shift the merger emphasis from an antitrust enforcement matter to a legislative matter, they would be free—as they were during Turner's tenure—to continue growing.

New antitrust legislation has always come slowly. The fundamental antitrust statutes—the Sherman Act of 1890, and the Clayton and FTC acts, both adopted in 1914—have seen little change in the past sixty years. Not until 1936 did Congress, after years of study, finally pass the Robinson-Patman Act (an amendment to the Clayton Act) to curb price discrimination said to result in competitive advantages to the newly emerging chain grocery and drug stores. It took until 1950 to secure the Celler-Kefauver amendment to cure the emasculating defects of the original antimerger law, Section 7 of the Clayton Act, even though the FTC had been waging a compaign for revision since the 1920s.

Antitrust reform has long encountered bottlenecks in the congressional judiciary committees, which have jursidiction over antitrust legislation, and in the rules committees which, sometimes at least, can effectively prevent consideration in the chambers. Those committees, functioning under the congressional seniority system, have been of such importance and prestige as to sustain little attrition; hence, they have developed a majority composition of conservative members, in the antitrust area at least. Somewhat incongruously, the antitrust subcommittees of both judiciary committees have been chaired for more than two decades by antitrust progressives. The Senate Antitrust Subcommittee has been in the charge of Estes Kefauver and his successor Philip Hart up to 1976. Its House counterpart was led by a single man, Emmanuel Celler, during this entire twenty-five years until, in the early 1970s, he was succeeded by Peter Rodino. But the zeal for antitrust reform shown by these subcommittee chairmen has been counterbalanced by a considerably more conservative committee membership.

In short, having enacted Section 7 of the Clayton Act in its generality, Congress thereafter has stood aside. Policy making has been left to the executive branch and the Supreme Court. There have been an abundance of investigative hearings on the conglomerate merger phenomenon, principally by the Senate and House Antitrust subcommittees. Senator Hart had a parade of hearings throughout the 1960s on the subject of economic concentration generally, and in 1969 he zeroed in on conglomerate mergers. In the same year Congressman Celler began his own widely publicized hearings which sputtered along to mid-1970. But when the crisis passed, for the time being at least, the subject was abruptly dropped.

Indeed, the legislation to specify unlawful conglomerate mergers recommended by the Neal commission appointed by President Johnson has never even been introduced in Congress. In 1971 Congressman Celler threatened to introduce this bill, following his subcommittee's conglomerate merger hearings, but later dropped his plan without explanation.

On the whole, then, Congress in the 1950s and 1960s demonstrated little proclivity for strengthened antitrust laws. In *The American Corporation* Richard J. Barber commented: "Hardly a member of House or Senate can today [in 1970] be found who is seriously concerned on more than a fleeting basis with issues of antitrust. Such support as does exist is tinged with cynicism and an aura of futility."

There probably was more pressure in the other direction, toward antitrust relaxation. During the 1960s one of the pet projects of the business world was (and still is) to obtain appointment of a legislative commission to study "modernization" of the antitrust laws, to update the country's notions of the concepts of competition. While one purpose of this project probably is to maintain an educational campaign to head off possible efforts to strengthen antitrust, there are areas in which realistic relief would be genuinely welcomed by business, such as in the application of antitrust to foreign operations and to environmental protection programs. In the 1969-71 period ITT backed this legislative project and sought to include reversal of McLaren's campaign against conglomerate mergers (which, said ITT, threatened to reduce United States companies' ability to compete abroad). In introducing one of the annual versions of the legislative study commission proposal, Congressman Price of Texas, in support of the need to restudy antitrust, complained: "We have the spectacle of Richard McLaren, Assistant Attorney General in charge of the Antitrust Division, futilely spearheading suit after suit against some of the giants of American free enterprise." While the conglomerates were unable to obtain relief from Congress, neither were they subjected to additional legislative restrictions.

The legislative scene may be different in the future; prospects for antitrust reform no longer look so bleak. Changes in the composition of Congress and of the important committees, liberalized congressional rules, and the Watergate-related changes in the political atmosphere all have contributed to a perceptible difference in the congressional outlook. The experience of the ITT cases also has been an important factor; these cases have led directly to at least two important legislative proposals.

One ITT-related legislative change already in effect relates to the workings of the consent judgment procedure. After the economic hardship reasons ostensibly underlying the settlement came to light, the critics pounced. Not only were McLaren's reasons insufficient, but the whole process of antitrust settlement, shrouded in secrecy and leaving the public ignorant of the rationale and probable effects of the compromise, needed to be changed; the process must be opened up to public scrutiny. Ralph Nader, a persistent critic of the ITT mergers, remarked: "At least let us give ITT its due, for it has exposed for all to see the weaknesses and failings inherent in the antitrust consent decree process."

Let it be said that the ITT settlement was not the first antitrust consent judgment to attract criticism. Ironically, the most notorious example before ITT of claimed abuse of the consent judgment process involved American Telephone & Telegraph Corporation (AT & T), the domestic telecommunications giant after which ITT had been patterned. AT & T not only controlled the lion's share of the United States telephone communication business but also, through its subsidiary Western Electric (which AT & T had acquired in the 1880s) manufactured virtually all the telephone equipment used by its operating systems. For all practical purposes, the market for telephone equipment represented by AT & T's operating companies was closed to Western Electric's competitors. An antitrust suit to dissolve the AT & T-Western Electric relationship was initiated in 1949 during the Truman administration when Tom Clark was attorney general. The complaint, charging AT & T and Western Electric with monopolizing the market for telephone equipment, sought to separate AT & T from Western Electric and to divide the latter into three competing manufacturing companies. AT & T then would be required to follow competitive policies in procuring telephone equipment. The case dragged on into the Eisenhower administration. Finally, in 1956, the Justice Department anticlimactically settled the case by a consent decree in which, a Senate subcommittee later charged, the government had abandoned "the heart of its case, namely, the AT & T-Western Electric relationship and the effort to sever Western Electric from the Bell System or otherwise limit its role as a virtually exclusive supplier to the system."

The Senate investigating committee learned that, as in the later ITT matter, the AT & T settlement had been preceded by intense lobbying of government officials by AT & T personnel. AT & T's pitch was that divestiture of Western Electric not only would interfere with the efficiency of the telephone system (resulting in higher telephone user charges) but also would somehow weaken our national defense posture. (AT & T succeeded in persuading the Defense Department to back it on this point.) After several personal meetings with AT & T officials, Attorney General Herbert Brownell, disregarding the inclination of the responsible Antitrust Division staff members Walter Murphy and Victor Kramer (who believed that the government would win in the Supreme Court if not at the trial court level), ordered that the case be settled along the lines of a proposal drafted by AT & T's attorneys. The decree thereafter agreed upon merely restricted Western Electric to the manufacture of telephone equipment, and imposed certain patent licensing requirements. The Senate committee called the decree "devoid of merit, . . . a blot on the enforcement history of the antitrust laws." Even *Business Week* considered the decree to be "hardly more than a slap on the wrist" for AT & T. An AT & T official conceded that the decree would do "no real injury to our business." The innocuousness of the decree was considered to be evident from the fact that AT & T's counsel *preferred* the consent decree to outright dismissal of the case by the government. The reason for this preference was the thought, expressed by Western Electric president Frederick R. Kappel, that the settlement lent the stamp of legality to the fundamental AT & T-Western Electric relationship.*

The existence of a high degree of vertical integration in the United States telecommunications industries, permitted to continue after the AT & T-Western Electric consent decree, turned out to be a prime factor in shaping ITT's diversification efforts in the 1960s. Telecommunications equipment manufacture and systems operation were ITT's forte abroad; but Geneen saw that transfer of this expertise to the United States on any significant scale was foreclosed by the captive nature of the United States markets. Hence, lenient antitrust policy in the Eisenhower administration helped to beget (at least so far as ITT was concerned) the circumstances for tough antitrust policy in the Nixon administration.

But the AT & T-Western Electric disclosures produced no congressional action. After President Kennedy assumed office in 1961, the Justice Department did adopt a procedure, drafted by Antitrust Assistant Attorney General Lee Loevinger, whereby proposed consent decrees were spread on the public record for a period of thirty days prior to their entry in court; this waiting period enabled the public in theory (in practice, usually competitors, suppliers, or customers of the merging firms) to provide input on the desirability and adequacy of the consent judgment. Although there was no guarantee that the Antitrust Division would give any effect to the comments received, nor was there any requirement that it explain why it was settling the cases, the existence of this procedure was enough to stave off congressional action. Only Congressmen Celler continued to press for further reforms. It remained, ironically, for the ITT furor to accomplish the changes in consent decree procedures that the AT & T incident had not been able to bring about.

In June, 1972 Senator John Tunney suggested to newly confirmed Attorney General Kleindienst that the Department of Justice voluntarily make a full public explanation of the reasons behind and the adequacy of every antitrust consent decree. This disclosure should be accompanied by a list and description of all ex parte contacts by the defendant with government officials relating to the case. Tunney explained: "The ITT situation presents to the general public a posture of governmental decision

---

*In November, 1974, however, the Justice Department inexplicably filed another suit against AT & T, making charges similar to those of the 1949 complaint. Observers find this action by a Republican administration only somewhat less puzzling than was McLaren's conglomerate merger policy (although AT & T's special circumstances makes the attack less far-reaching in potential effect).

making which gives the appearance, whether legitimate or not, of compromise arrived at and bargains struck through special and perhaps improper influence. Such appearances do nothing to confirm the public's faith in our governmental system." Tunney believed it would be proper to adopt this special policy for antitrust cases alone because "antitrust cases usually involve large economic stakes and they usually involve business defendants most able and prone to attempt massive lobbying or influence."

Kleindienst resisted this suggestion; he fairly bristled over the implication that government enforcement officials could be swayed by political pressure:

Your proposal seems to assume that antitrust officials, and other government officers when dealing with antitrust matters, are so suspect that their every coming and going should be recorded by them and made public. I cannot in good conscience subscribe to this premise. In general, I think that those who over the years have served the Federal Government have done so honestly and forthrightly and have discharged their responsibilities in the public interest.

Kleindienst's rebuff caused Tunney in late 1972 to introduce a bill embodying the changes that he had suggested. As might have been expected from Kleindienst's prior reaction, the Justice Department opposed Tunney's bill. Antitrust Assistant Attorney General Thomas Kauper (McLaren's successor) complained that "the bill will seriously disrupt settlement proceedings in the courts, and would seriously weaken our ability to obtain consent decree settlements from defendants." Any marked reduction in the number of settlements would tax the resources of the Antitrust Division, fewer investigations would be initiated, and fewer new suits would be filed. (Maybe this explains in part why the business lobby kept its silence during the congressional progress of the Tunney bill.)

Furthermore, said Kauper, the policy making function of the Antitrust Division would be seriously diluted, and it would lose some degree of control over its own planning and budgeting. The division's agreement to settle may reflect a decision to shift its policy emphases, to divert resources to another direction. To justify the compromise of a less important case, the division should not be forced prematurely to publicly air and explain its internal policy formulations. Some, such as Congressman Hutchinson, agreed that the bill would seriously dilute the exercise of prosecutorial discretion to the detriment of overall antitrust policy making.

The objections were lost on the bill's proponents. They responded that the opponents of "sunshine in government" always complain that the governmental policy function will be impaired by exposure to the light of day. This time, in contrast to the aftermath of the AT & T–Western Electric consent decree, the Congress was in no mood to sit still. The House Judiciary Committee report sounded the theme upon which the congressional action was premised:

Given the high rate of settlement in public antitrust cases, it is imperative that the integrity of and public confidence in procedures relating to settlements via consent decree procedures be assured. "The consent decree practice has established an orbit in the twilight zone between established rules of administrative law and judicial procedures." [Quoting from the 1959 AT & T investigation report.] The bill, in this respect, is designed to substitute "sunlight" for "twilight."

Congress passed the Tunney proposal in December, 1974. It was vetoproofed by joinder with two other antitrust changes which the administration supported, i.e., an increase in penalties for criminal antitrust violations such as price fixing (which President Ford avowed would help curb inflation), and an amendment to the Expediting Act to eliminate direct appeals of antitrust cases to the Supreme Court (the same proposal which ITT had unsuccessfully lobbied for in 1970).

Under the new consent decree law the Justice Department must file with the court and publicize a "competitive impact statement" explaining the proposed settlement, its purpose, and its anticipated effects on competition. The statement must include a description and evaluation of any other alternatives to the settlement which were considered by the government. The Justice Department then is required to "receive and consider" any written comments relating to the proposed decree. The defendant must file with the court a description of all communications with any officer or employee of the United States "concerning or relevant to the proposal" (excepting only discussions solely between counsel of record for the defendant and the government). The law requires the court to determine that the proposed judgment operates in the "public interest," defined to include the competitive impact and the public benefit of the judgment.

The consent decree law marks an opening-up of the process by which the Government and antitrust defendants negotiate compromise settlements. The law undoubtedly does reduce the flexibility of the Government to stop an antitrust case once started (but the law does not, of course, touch upon the Government's decision whether to bring a case in the first place). While the law will bring forth considerably more information for those interested in examining a proposed consent settlement, nevertheless its ultimate impact will depend (as with the substantive antitrust laws) upon the force which the courts choose to give it.

Had the consent decree law applied to the ITT merger case settlement, one may ask which of ITT's numerous contacts with Nixon administration officials must be disclosed as falling within the standard of communications "concerning or relevant to the proposal." The great bulk of the ITT-Nixon administration communications concerned not a proposed settlement of the cases, but rather a frontal attack upon McLaren's conglomerate merger policy with an attendant request that the suits against ITT be abandoned in toto. Would these contacts be considered "relevant" to the proposed settlement?

It is probable, even without answering that difficult question, that the new law, if then applicable, would have derailed the ITT settlement. Surely, somewhere in the broad statutory language there may be found a requirement to disclose the economic hardship claims upon which ITT's settlement presentation rested and which McLaren says he accepted. (If we do not make that assumption, then the sponsors of the new law would have significantly failed of their purpose.) It is probable that exposure of the economic hardship workup to public scrutiny would have been enough to scuttle the settlement, at least in the terms in which it was cast.

Another proposed ITT-related change in antitrust procedure probably would have done even more; it could have stopped the ITT mergers at their inception. This proposal—to delay the consummation of proposed mergers challenged by the Justice Department pending judicial decision—had been voiced earlier but, in the wake of the ITT cases, was first advanced in Congress with any real hope for success in 1974. Its proponents say that the burden that the government must carry to obtain a preliminary injunction from a court to halt consummation of a merger is unrealistic. The government rarely has been able to obtain a preliminary injunction, and almost never in a case where the merging companies are not in competition as in a conglomerate merger.

The critics of the status quo point to the ITT cases as a prime example of the present inadequacies. ITT was able to fend off preliminary injunctions against the Hartford and Grinnell acquisitions, and to persuade the district court instead merely to impose hold-separate orders. These orders were premised on their according complete protection to the Justice Department to enable it to obtain relief if it ultimately prevailed in the suits; indeed, ITT represented to the court that this would be so. Later, however, ITT turned around and claimed that it must be permitted to keep Hartford because there would be severe economic repercussions from undoing the Hartford merger. ITT's later arguments, say its critics, prove the ineffectiveness of the hold-separate procedure. Had the ITT-Hartford merger been made to wait until final adjudication of its legality, it would not have been consummated; hence, there could have been no economic dislocations from reversing it, and therefore there would have been no basis for the settlement.

In the overwhelming number of cases, delay of a merger for the duration of the litigation is tantamount to its defeat. Thus, delay killed ITT's proposed acquisition of American Broadcasting Corporation even though ITT had won every legal round at the time it abandoned the merger. Similarly, preliminary injunctions against White Consolidated's attempts to acquire Allis-Chalmers and White Motors completely stopped those transactions. And the proposed rule likely would have nullified also ITT's acquisition agreements with Hartford and Grinnell—ITT's counsel told the district court that the managements of all three companies were in agreement that the transactions would be abandoned if preliminary injunctions were granted. McLaren himself later commented that had the government obtained preliminary injunctions against the ITT acquisitions, "I think we would have won the case at that stage, without all of the long, expensive proceedings, without all of the uncertainty that followed on them."

Because of the high probability that a merger delayed is a merger defeated, the new proposal, while procedural in form, is regulatory in substance. A *Wall Street Journal* editorial complained that the sponsors of the proposal, realizing that the Justice Department "can no longer automatically win suits before the Supreme Court and no longer has a coherent economic rationale for the suits it brings . . . has decided to pursue its mission the easy way, strangling mergers with red tape before they've left the womb." The sponsors of the new proposal of course fully appreciate this effect, and see their proposal as a way to extend the merger prohibitions without having to attempt the riskier course of tampering with the substantive coverage of the statute. Adoption of this proposal, given the prosecutorial flexibility inherent in Section 7 of the Clayton Act, would greatly magnify the government's already impressive policy making role.

Faced with the opposition of the Ford Administration,* the merger delay proposal failed of passage in 1976. As a compromise Congress adopted instead a thirty-day prior notice requirement intended to afford the enforcement agencies greater opportunity to study a merger before

---

*Through an apparent mix-up in signals, Antitrust Assistant Kauper, in May, 1975, voiced support for the proposal. The business community and investment banking industry (including Felix Rohatyn, who had played such a prominent part in the ITT merger cases) went to work on White House and cabinet officers and, in February, 1976, the Justice Department announced a reversal of this position.

it can be consummated. The antitrust liberals in Congress, however, have announced that they will continue to press for the proposal to delay mergers pending judicial decision.

Whether the Congress will sustain its brief burst of antitrust activism remains to be seen. The Congress of the 1970s has enacted several other consumer-oriented, antitrust-related measures besides those discussed above. None so far enacted, however, gets to the heart of the issues of concentration and corporate growth which have been of overriding concern to antitrust liberals, such as the Johnson-appointed Neal commission.

20

THE FUTURE OF
CORPORATE GROWTH

The issue is clear in antitrust policy; namely, how to preserve and gain the potential benefits of growth by extension into multiple product markets, and of diversification in general, and of inter-industry competition, without the development of excessive economic and market power.

E. T. Grether
Antitrust Law Journal, 1963

It would be ironic in the extreme if, in the very process of trying to create an economic environment in which the free enterprise system can accelerate economic growth, we unleashed forces which encouraged an unfortunate consolidation and transformation of the system. Since there are not any natural economic forces likely to slow the merger pace, this means that its future depends in large part on public policy.

Willard Mueller
Antitrust Law Journal, 1964

After the spurt of the 1960s, is the history of corporate growth now at an end? Hardly. The blazing conglomerate phenomenon of the last decade has abated, to be sure. For this probably various reasons can be assigned, and undoubtedly McLaren's activism was one of those reasons. But only a temporary one.

Conglomerate growth in the broad sense of that term, i.e., corporate expansion by diversification merger, will continue so long as the laws allow and aggressive corporate managers exist. The pattern will ebb and flow, as it always has, according to economic conditions. But the question of the effects of continuing corporate growth cannot be wished away.

Even in the first half of the 1970s—a period usually described as quiescent in terms of corporate growth by merger—there have been a considerable number of significant mergers. Indeed, since 1970 there have been over forty acquisitions of corporations having assets over $100 million, the category which the FTC staff separates as superlarge. These mergers have included such giant conglomerate transactions as Colgate-Palmolive's acquisitions of Kendall and Riviana Foods; Rockwell International's acquisitions of Collins Radio and Admiral Corporation; United Technology's acquisitions of Essex International and Otis Elevator; Norton Simon's merger with Max Factor & Company; and International Nickel's acquisition of ESB, Incorporated.

Also included is the controversial acquisition by Mobil Oil Corporation of Marcor (the latter a product of the 1968 merger between Montgomery Ward & Company and Container Corporation). Mobil blamed increasing governmental interference in oil and gas activities for the need to adopt "a policy of seeking out diversification opportunities." Although Antitrust Division Chief Kauper made threatening statements about this acquisition, and one of his subordinates even resurrected the McLaren-inspired Mitchell statement of 1969 warning against mergers within the nation's two hundred largest firms (in which category both Mobil and Marcor fell), Mobil went ahead with the acquisition anyway; it was not sued.* In 1976 another candidate for the largest merger in history—General Electric's diversification acquisition of Utah International—received the blessing of the Justice Department after the vertical relationship between the firms was cured by an arrangement to insulate GE from Utah's uranium supplies.

Even McLaren's lone judicial victory in his conglomerate merger campaign—the 1971 preliminary injunction against the proposed merger of White Consolidated and White Motors—did not stand the test of time. McLaren's successor, Kauper, gave those companies permission to merge in 1976 because White Motors's business reverses in the intervening years had brought it to the point of being a "failing company."

On an overall basis, corporate growth by merger in the first half of the 1970s has approximated the level of the late 1950s and early 1960s, which itself was considerably higher than in prior periods. Thus, even in a period considered to be economically inhospitable for significant corporate growth, the picture has been far from static. The problems which McLaren, and other who think like him, perceive in unrestrained corporate growth may have subsided temporarily, but they have not disappeared.

---

*In October, 1976 the FTC, in an apparent throwback to its earlier move against the Kennecott Copper-Peabody Coal merger, did bring suit against Atlantic Richfield's planned acquisition of Anaconda Company, a large copper and uranium producer. Like the Kennecott precedent, this complaint purports to be based upon the accepted potential competition theory but appears at first look to stretch that theory. If this litigation continues, it may someday present an opportunity for broader Supreme Court review of policy toward corporate growth.

One difficulty in making a judgment on the effects of corporate expansion has been the dearth of information about what actually happens in the market following a conglomerate merger. The FTC's economic staff has noted:

> The effects of "pure" conglomerate mergers where there are no production or marketing relationships between acquiring or acquired companies cannot be deduced easily from economic theory. Nor is there a body of empirical evidence as to the actual consequences of such mergers. At best, there are a few broadly-stated hypotheses as to what might happen as a result of pure conglomerate mergers.

Even McLaren, in considering what he should do, had found the conflict of theory puzzling in the absence of some proof to back up one theory or another.

In the early 1970s the staffs of the House Antitrust Subcommittee and the FTC set about to remedy this evidentiary deficiency with studies seeking to determine after the fact whether conglomerate mergers had diminished competition in any of the industries in which the conglomerates operated. Both study groups chose for examination a selected group of the more active conglomerates (both samples included ITT). While the business world questioned the objectivity of the two study groups—assuming that a damning report from each was a foregone conclusion—they were to be pleasantly surprised by the mildness of the conclusions.

The House Antitrust staff, in June, 1971, did issue a damning report, but it added little in the way of concrete evidence on conglomerate impact. While weighty in volume (some seven hundred pages) and universal in its attempted coverage, the report virtually stopped with description of the conflicting theories and selection of those antagonistic to the conglomerates. The conglomerates were bad, the report said, because they increased aggregate concentration, developed reciprocity opportunities, offered cross-subsidization possibilities, and the remainder of the established litany. The House Antitrust staff did come up with some embarrassing examples of attempts to couple products or services for sales promotion purposes, and it labeled "synergism" as nothing more than a code word to justify these undesirable efforts to "team" products. But these relatively minor slaps, coming merely from a subcommittee staff, did not unduly bother the conglomerates.

The FTC economic staff study, while considerably less voluminous, was more to the point. And the conglomerates were actually pleased by this report. The FTC study concluded that, really, nothing much happened to competition after conglomerate mergers. The acquired firms continued on pretty much the way they had before the merger: there were no dramatic increases in their profits; the market shares did not change much; and there was no showing, on the available evidence, of "reciprocity as a generalized, pernicious consequence of conglomerate mergers." The report concluded that "there appears to be no evidence of either improvements or deteriorations in the efficiency of acquired units after they were taken over by the conglomerates." Hence, on the whole, "conglomerate mergers appear to have neither synergistic advantages nor obvious competitive disadvantages.... From a competitive standpoint, the effects of conglomerate diversification ... appear to be largely *neutral.*" (The worst thing the FTC staff could find to say was that conglomeration causes an undesirable information loss which ought to be remedied by compulsory product-line reporting.)

While neither the House Antitrust staff nor the FTC staff agreed with the conglomerates that the latter practice economically beneficial synergism nor that they infuse much new competitive vitality into tired industries, still neither provided much support for the prevailing theories of conglomerate villainy. Since the conglomerates had already abandoned any serious hope of promoting synergism as a viable concept, the reports' refusal to support the affirmative benefits of conglomerate expansion did not bother the conglomerates much. And the FTC staff report could serve as a convenient shield to forestall additional efforts like that of McLaren to bring the antitrust laws to bear upon corporate growth.

Where, then, does the nation now stand on the issue of corporate growth? Was McLaren's thrust fruitless, or have the events of the late 1960s and early 1970s done anything for our understanding of or perspective toward the issue?

McLaren, it must be remembered, began with a clean slate—the prior Democratic administrations had done little to interfere with the new and burgeoning pattern of corporate growth. Even Democratic Senator Philip Hart, while distressed that the conglomerate issue never reached the Supreme Court of the 1960s, noted in 1972 the anomaly of criticizing McLaren for this failure: "The Antitrust Division for the last three years has, by and large, aggressively enforced our antitrust law—particularly in extending its application to conglomerate mergers. For this effort, it deserves our commendation, not condemnation."

The controversy over corporate growth is far from over; indeed, it may still be in its nascent stage. The ITT spokesmen, perhaps unwittingly, pinpointed the issue when they complained that McLaren was equating "bigness" with "badness." The critics of conglomerates indeed do contend that corporate bigness is bad—at least, the more discerning would say, when it passes the point of economies of scale and efficiencies. And they would further contend generally that conglomerate mergers do not bring about any economies worthy of recognition. For many students of our society, that is enough to warrant condemnation; they see corporate power and size as distorting the free enterprise system. According to Joel B. Dirlam, "The large single-product firm can outlast the small single-product firm, but the large conglomerate is in an even better position." Or, as colorfully put by Walter Adams, "In a poker game with unlimited stakes, the player who commands disproportionately large funds is likely to emerge victorious." Mr. Adams further explains:

Conglomerate power does make a difference. It derives not from monopoly or oligopoly control of a particular market, but from diversification over a whole range of markets. It enables a firm, endowed with absolute size and the deep purse, to "outbid, outspend, and outlose" its smaller rivals, and thus to insure its survival almost irrespective of its performance. Finally, as recent events have demonstrated, it conveys a unique access to political power and the opportunity to transform the state into an instrument of privilege creation and protection.

The Columbia economics professor Donald J. Dewey also believes that a distrust of raw power, rather than any genuine concern over market distortions, is and ought to be our major concern: "We are made uneasy and suspicious by great corporate size in the private sector of the economy. . . . We react in this way because we believe that great corporate size concentrates discretionary authority in the hands of too few people."

The main deleterious effects ascribed to the growth of the conglomerates are of the radiation variety, said to spread insidiously throughout our economic system. Indeed, the new outcry against big firms focuses upon their multinational characteristics with attendant power, it is said, to influence even international policies and to shift their resources from nation to nation as economic and political factors dictate. The effects of unlimited corporate growth are measurable only in the long run, and by then it will be too late, say the critics.

If one begins with the premise that bigness is bad in American business, then it follows that stringent controls should be placed upon mergers. Severe restrictions on mergers would, at the least, seriously hamper the further growth of the already large conglomerates and prevent new ones from springing up. But the question of the desirability of large business firms in the absolute sense is one for which the traditional theories of economics and antitrust probably are ill-adapted. The latter treat mainly of the vigor of competition in a defined market, and they handle this pretty well. Even those who show little affection for untrammeled corporate growth have come to admit that a different perspective probably is needed. The Harvard University professor Edward S. Mason, addressing the issue of increasing aggregate concentration in United States business, has noted: "It is certainly true that it is changing the character of American democracy and it may be true that it threatens the continued existence of democratic institutions. But it has no necessary or even obvious connection with competition in the market sense of that term."

Former FTC Commissioner Philip Elman, the author of the FTC's opinion holding unlawful the Procter & Gamble–Clorox merger, has also expressed skepticism over the ability of the antitrust laws to deal with diversified corporate growth. "Much of the concern about conglomerate mergers is derived from political and social consequences which go beyond the antitrust laws," says Elman.

Frederic Sherer, former chief economist of the FTC, while concerned about the direction of corporate growth "from a broad social perspective," is not "sanguine about the availability of appropriate corrective forces": "Antitrust in particular is largely ineffective against conglomerate mergers unless a likelihood of independent potential entry by the merging companies into each others' markets or the exercise of reciprocal dealing leverage can be shown, and the burden of proof is heavy. If then the public is sufficiently concerned about conglomerate mergers to desire their discouragement, new laws are needed. . . ."

Not everyone agrees, of course, that the antitrust laws *should not* reach concentration of economic power on a general plane, above and beyond the technical "market" concept of the economist. A sizeable body applauds what McLaren started out to do, and believes that a judicial thrust against corporate growth is still indicated. The law professor Victor Kramer, for example, urges that the government make more use of the antitrust laws to curb corporate size; he notes: "The antitrust division is too judicious. They're trying to find some divine answer instead of letting the courts do that."

The Columbia law professor Harlan M. Blake, a harsh critic of the ITT settlement, also is dismayed that a theory that would be "effective in controlling corporate mergers [has] not been tested in the Supreme Court more than twenty years after the enactment of the Celler-Kefauver amendment." Professor Blake is confident that the Supreme Court of the 1960s "would have empowered the Antitrust Division to bring an orderly end to conglomerate empire-building." Notwithstanding the falloff in the merger pace in the 1970s, Blake insists that "rapid growth by acquisition is sufficiently attractive to entrepreneurs to require that the public policy issues it raises be finally resolved." Resort to Congress, Blake believes, ought to be unnecessary: "The law is there, waiting to be imaginatively used," he says.

McLaren started from the viewpoint, which seemed sensible to him, that corporate growth by conglomerate merger probably does little good for our economic and social system, and well might do considerable harm. By his willingness to act and to accept the reflex rancor which he knew must follow, McLaren brought the conglomerate issue into vivid profile. This issue, as is the case of many important national questions, proceeds in fits and starts. The ITT cases well may prove important in shaping the public attitude which, as Thurman Arnold noted, must be the foundation of national policy. However made, the corporate growth policy to be adopted must take into account the fabric of our society and the viability of our political system. This requires a searching analysis of the potential consequences upon the free enterprise system. If there is any substantial question of a deleterious effect upon the way we govern and are governed, employ and are employed, or upon our free play to follow our individual ambitions and incentives, then surely no one would dispute the absolute necessity to curb corporate growth. This was McLaren's conclusion; his problem was that he had neither the consensus nor the tools needed to follow through.

REFERENCE NOTES

Page

11 Merger data are compiled in the FTC Bureau of Economics annual Statistical Report on Mergers and Acquisitions.

24 The FTC reports preceding the 1950 amendment of the Clayton Act were: Report on the Merger Movement (1948); The Present Trend of Corporate Mergers and Acquisitions (1947).

27 Citation to the Continental Can decision: 378 U.S. 441 (1964).

27 Citation to the Aluminum Co. of America decision: 377 U.S. 271 (1964).

28 Citation to the Von's Grocery decision: 384 U.S. 270 (1966).

32 Citation to the Procter & Gamble decision: 386 U.S. 568 (1967).

33 Citation to the Consolidated Foods decision: 380 U.S. 592 (1965).

34 Citation to the Brown Shoe decision: 370 U.S. 294 (1962).

34 Citation to the Philadelphia National Bank decision: 374 U.S. 321 (1963).

35 Citation to the FTC's Kennecott Copper decision: 73 F.T.C. 913 (1971), aff., 467 F.2d 67 (10th Cir. 1972), cert. den., 416 U.S. 909 (1974).

37 Citation to the Ling-Temco Electronics decision: 1961 CCH Trade Cases para. 70, 160 (N.D. Tex. 1961).

38 Citation to the FMC Corporation decision: 218 F. Supp. 817 (N.D. Cal. 1963), appeal denied, 321 F.2d 534 (9th Cir. 1963), application den., 84 S. Ct. 4 (1963).

41 Reference to Donald F. Turner's law review article: "Conglomerate Mergers and Section 7 of the Clayton Act," 78 Harv. L. Rev. 1313 (1965).

44 The FCC's first decision in the ITT–ABC case, 7 F.C.C. 2d 245 (1966); the decision after rehearing, 9 F.C.C. 2d 546 (1967).

46 The Justice Department merger guidelines are published in 1 CCH Trade Reg. Rep. para. 4510.

49 The Neal Commission report is published in 115 Cong. Rec. 5642 (daily ed. May 27, 1969).

50 The Stigler commission report is published in 115 Cong. Rec. 6472 (daily ed. June 17, 1969).

62 Citation to the Reynolds case: 242 F. Supp. 518 (D.N.J. 1965).

62 Citation to the Ingersoll-Rand case, 218 F. Supp. 530 (W.D. Pa. 1963), aff., 320 F.2d 509 (3d Cir. 1963).

Page

68 Citation to the Northwest Industries preliminary injunction ruling: 301 F. Supp. 1066 (N.D. Ill. 1969).

73 Citation to Judge Timbers's preliminary injunction ruling: 306 F. Supp. 366 (D. Conn. 1969).

97 Citation to Judge Timbers's final decision: 324 F. Supp. 19 (D. Conn. 1970), appeal dismissed by agreement, 404 U.S. 801 (1971).

106 Citation to the White Consolidated preliminary injunction ruling: 323 F. Supp. 1397 (N.D Ohio 1971).

143 Citation to Judge Austin's decision in ITT-Canteen: 1971 CCH Trade Cases para. 73, 619 (N.D. Ill. 1971).

150 Citation to Judge Blumenfeld's decision denying the Nader-Robertson petition: 349 F. Supp. 22 (D. Conn. 1972), aff. mem., 410 U.S. 919 (1973).

154 Reference to the Kleindienst nomination hearings: Hearings before the S. Jud. Comm. on the nomination of Richard Kleindienst to be attorney general, 92d Cong., 2d Sess. (1972).

162 Reference to the impeachment report: House Jud. Comm., H.R. Rep. No. 93-1305, 93d Cong., 2d Sess. (Aug. 1974).

174 For Kennecott Copper citation, see reference at p. 35.

181 Citation to the Ford Motor decision: 405 U.S. 562 (1972).

183 Citation to the Marine Bancorporation decision: 418 U.S. 602 (1974).

192 Reference to the new consent decree law, an amendment to the Clayton Act: 88 Stat. 1706, 15 U.S.C. Sec. 16 (1975 Supp.).

198 Reference to the House Antitrust Subcommittee staff report: Investigation of Conglomerate Corporations, 92d Cong., 1st Sess. (1971).

198 Reference to the FTC Bureau of Economics report: Staff Report to the FTC, Conglomerate Merger Performance: An Empirical Analysis of Nine Corporations (Nov. 1972).

BIBLIOGRAPHY

The following provides a fair sampling of the literature of corporate growth, particularly of the diversification variety.

Alberts, William, and Joel Segall. *The Corporate Merger.* University of Chicago Press, 1966.

Berry, Charles H. *Corporate Growth and Diversification.* Princeton University Press, 1975.

Blair, John M. *Economic Concentration: Structure, Behavior and Public Policy.* Harcourt Brace Jovanovich, 1972.

Blake, H. M. "Conglomerate Mergers and the Antitrust Laws." *73 Columbia Law Review,* 555 (1973).

Brandeis, Louis D. *The Curse of Bigness.* Kennikat Press, 1934.

Campbell, James C., and William P. Shepherd. "Leading-Firm Conglomerate Mergers," 13 *Antitrust Bulletin* 1361 (1968).

The Conference Board Antitrust Forum. *Concentration: Issues, Convictions and Facts* (Information Bull. no. 9, 1976).

Davidow, Joel. "Conglomerate Concentration and Section 7: The Limitations of the Anti-Merger Act." 68 *Columbia Law Review* 1231 (1968).

Federal Trade Commission Bureau of Economics. *Economic Report on Corporate Mergers* (1969).

Galbraith, John K. *The New Industrial State.* Houghton Mifflin, 1967.

Goldschmid, Harvey J., H. Michael Mann, and Fred J. Weston, eds. *Industrial Concentration: The New Learning.* Little, Brown & Co., 1974.

Gort, M. *Diversification and Integration in American Industry.* Princeton University Press, 1962.

Jacoby, Neil. *Corporate Power and Social Responsibility.* Macmillan Publishing Co., 1973.

Kaysen, C., and D. Turner. *Antitrust Policy: A Legal and Economic Analysis.* Harvard University Press, 1959.

Mansfield, Edwin, ed. *Monopoly Power and Economic Performance.* W. W. Norton & Co., 3rd ed. 1974.

Martin, D. *Mergers and the Clayton Act.* University of California Press, 1959.

Mueller, Willard. "The Rising Economic Concentration in America." 4 *Antitrust Law and Economics Review* 15 (spring 1971).

Narver, John. *Conglomerate Mergers and Market Competition.* University of California Press, 1967.

National Bureau for Economic Research, ed. *Business Concentration and Price Policy.* Princeton University Press, 1955.

Scherer, F. M. *Industrial Market Structure and Economic Performance.* Rand McNally & Co., 1970.

Symposium, "Conglomerate Mergers and Acquisitions: Opinion and Analysis." *St. John's Law Review* (spring 1970, special ed.).

Turner, D. F. "Conglomerate Mergers and Section 7 of the Clayton Act." 78 *Harvard Law Review* 1313 (1965).

Weston, J. Fred. *The Role of Mergers in the Growth of Large Firms.* University of California Press, 1961.

Weston, J. Fred, and Sam Peltzman, eds. *Public Policy toward Mergers.* Goodyear Publishing Co., 1969.

INDEX